IN SEARCH OF
PINK FLAMINGOS
A Woman's Quest for Forgiveness
& Unconditional Love

Susan E. Greisen

IN SEARCH OF
PINK FLAMINGOS
A Woman's Quest for Forgiveness
& Unconditional Love

Susan E. Greisen

Penchant Press International, LLC
Blaine, Washington
United States of America

This memoir represents the author's recollection of her past. These true stories are faithfully composed based on memory, photographs, home movies, diary entries, and other supporting documents. Some names, places and other identifying details have been changed to protect the privacy of those represented. Conversations between individuals are meant to reflect the essence, meaning and the spirit of the events described.

Penchant Press International, LLC
PO Box 1333
Blaine, WA 98231
penchantpressinternational.com

Susan E. Greisen 1951-

ISBN 978-0-9998048-4-1
LCCN 201 9957791

In Search of Pink Flamingos: A Woman's Quest for Forgiveness & Unconditional Love

Cover design by: spokendesigns.com

Dedicated to the memory of my parents,
Paul and Mary Greisen

CONTENTS

INTRODUCTION

We never had pink flamingos on the farm in Nebraska, but when I was a little girl, a magical print I saw one day began my journey of wonder to places far away.

Once a month, on a Sunday afternoon, my family would leave the farm and drive seventeen miles into the nearest big town of Kanton for lunch. We ate at Louie's Italian Restaurant, a flat-roofed, one-story, window-less building. Once I walked in, I didn't see natural daylight again until I left. Nestled in one corner of the dining room stood a white plastic statue of an Italian goddess. On the opposite side was a latticed arbor, laced with fake greenery under which a fountain bubbled, adorned with floating red fake flowers. The effect, for me, was captivating, like going to a faraway place.

Each time we came to Louie's I purposely chose to sit with my back to the fountain and statue. As soon as my eyes adjusted to the dim light, I marveled at a print of pink flamingos hung high on the back wall. Inside its large mirrored frame was a hand-painted image of four pink flamingos wading in a serene lake surrounded by palm trees, lush green vegetation, and a peaceful blue sky. The four sections of the mirrored frame magically reflected portions of the dining room. From my vantage point, one section reflected the fountain, the other mirrored the white statue. In the bottom portion I could see the light fixture hanging from the ceiling. The upper mirror revealed my own image. I smiled to see myself in that small shard.

Louie's was the fanciest eatery around with white table-cloths and linen napkins. My dad always maintained that napkins were a waste when a hand or sleeve would suffice. My mom was critical about most everything. My older brother was always restless. My infant brother only cared about his baby bottle. The waitress always gave us the same menus, and we always ordered the same thing, spaghetti with meatballs.

We ate our meal while my family talked about the crops, the weather, and who we saw at church. My imagination strayed to the flamingos in their serene lake. I'd seen those crazy looking birds on television but they all seemed to be in captivity, standing around in zoos or theme parks like Disneyland. I wondered if a place like that print really existed. Could the flamingos be wild and free? Were these creatures truly pink?

That print in Louie's enthralled me for years. It was central to the woman I became, and the life I have lived all over the world. At eight years old, those pink flamingos excited my wonder, and stirred my hopes to wander. Surely there were wonderful places far from my Nebraska farm and my one-room schoolhouse. Places, like, maybe... Africa.

PART I

NEBRASKA

The Best Place on Earth

If I had to choose where to live and be raised as a young girl, it would be on our family farm in Nebraska—the best place on earth. From the moment I was born in a sixteen-bed hospital in 1951, farming was in my blood just as it had been in my family for generations. We lived and worked on a 160-acre plot of land in the eastern part of the state. The fertile rolling hills provided us with everything we needed to be subsistence farmers, living off the land. We raised cows, chickens, pigs, steers, a garden, and a patchwork of lush fields filled with corn, wheat, milo, soybeans, and alfalfa for animal feed. We sold milk, cream, eggs, pigs, steers, and crops for income which provided us a good living. We were known in our community for having the best looking farmstead: a white house with blue shutters, a red barn, and eight outbuildings for chickens, pigs, grain, and machinery. Dad pristinely maintained all the buildings and mowed the grass and weeds to keep the place neat and tidy. My dad, mom, and two brothers—Bob, four years older and Randy, eight years younger—and I had our assigned duties and roles contributing to our prosperous farm.

Anything we couldn't raise or make on our homestead required a trip to the nearby towns. We often traveled four miles to the nearest one of Morgan, population 260. One major dirt street ran through the heart of the small town with everything of great importance on one side—a bank, tavern, grocery store, post office, a Lutheran church, and a hardware store. Across the street was a small park and a car dealership, which closed during my grade-school days. Extensive shopping was found seventeen miles away in the major town of Kanton, with about 15,000 people. There we found everything else we needed: clothing stores, doctors, dentists, a hospital, a drive-in theater, and restaurants, including Louie's Italian Restaurant. The farm, Morgan, and Kanton were the extent of my small world until the age of six. Then, one day in 1957, it all changed.

That autumn afternoon, in great anticipation, I pressed my nose against the kitchen window while I watched the plumes of dust rise over the dip in our half-mile driveway. Within minutes Dad and Bob arrived and backed the pickup truck into the garage. Mom and I stood out of harm's way as Dad and Bob squeezed a large bulky object through the door leading into the living room. It was so big it would never have fit in the trunk of our pink DeSoto. It felt like an early Christmas when Bob and I pulled off the big protective olive-green Army blanket to expose a large wooden box. It measured about four feet high, three feet wide by three feet deep supported by four spindly legs with woven fabric at its base and a round-shaped gray glass screen. The top right corner held a round dial surrounded by numbers. I remembered a box like this at our cousin's house and another at the local tavern. Dad said, "I bought it right off the showroom floor." It was our first television set, our TV!

Dad had already rigged up the antenna on the roof and angled it purposefully toward the TV towers in Kanton. When he turned on the television for the first time, the black and white wavy lines rolled and tumbled on the glass tube followed by some Z-shaped images that made my stomach turn. The fuzzy pictures flickered back and forth for a few more minutes, when a person inside the box began to speak. Bob was now on the roof with his hands on the antenna when Dad yelled, "Turn it more to the east." Given detailed instructions from the salesman, Dad manipulated all the moving parts of that box and within thirty minutes, a clear image emerged of a man talking about a newfangled washing machine called a Maytag. Dad yelled at Bob to come down from the roof and the four of us stood motionless for a few moments and smiled as the talking box became alive. One snowy and two clear stations were all the reception we could get, but we never cared. With the long cold winter on our doorstep, we looked forward to this new addition to our household.

Before the arrival of our TV, Mom and I entertained ourselves by listening to Arthur Godfrey on the radio each day. While I ironed the pillowcases and hankies, we enjoyed music, talk shows, and news, with intermittent news reports and Paul Harvey telling us *The Rest of the Story.*

Information came to our home from two other sources. One was the weekly *Morgan Booster,* our local newspaper. The four to six pages consisted mostly of advertisements, photos, and stories about the local boys who joined the service, as well as announcements about engagements, marriages, births, and deaths. To learn about happenings in other parts of the state, once a month Mom bought the *Kanton Telegram,* a daily paper that reported those news events. But the radio and newspapers took a backstage when the television entered our home.

That TV was strategically placed to be viewed from multiple angles, including the kitchen. Watching television became a nightly ritual. At suppertime we sat as a family in our huge country kitchen around the white Formica table with silver curved legs. Mom perfectly timed our evening meals to have a clear sight of our TV's big glass tube every night precisely at 6 p.m. to watch Walter Cronkite and his famous closing, "And that's the way it is...." Mom and Dad seemed to respect him; he was like a President. Whatever he reported was the gospel truth.

We watched shows including *I Love Lucy, The Honeymooners, Kids Say the Darnedest Things, The Ed Sullivan Show,* and *The Carol Burnett Show.* I reserved Saturday mornings for cartoons until 10 a.m. There I met Popeye, who quickly became my idol. Strong and loving to his girlfriend, Olive Oyl, he always helped those in need. The Road Runner, another favorite, was a crazy bird who defied the odds with every obstacle placed in his way. I liked them both for what they stood for. They were my heroes and as real to me as a best friend. So real in fact that I took my idol, Popeye, to a new level one fateful day not long after my seventh birthday.

In the summer of 1958, I sat with my family around the kitchen table finishing supper when I forked that last green glob of spinach into my mouth. I waited, feeling a surge of strength rising through my body, just as I'd witnessed Popeye experience so many times before. I rose defiantly from the table and said to my mom, dad, and brother, "Watch this!" In a trance-like state, my strength became superhuman as I marched into the living room, made a big fat fist with my right hand and punched it straight through the window with only a slight blink of an eye. Shards of glass flew around me as I watched my fist penetrate the window all the way past my elbow. I felt no pain, only pride and power—spinach was my painkiller. My family sat in shock as blood dripped to the floor. Mom ran to get a towel and Dad picked the glass fragments out of my arm then wrapped it tight to stop the bleeding. Despite the bubbling of the peroxide and the stinging of the Mercurochrome, I held my head high. I refused to cry.

So it was, in the beginning—a life of hard knocks on the farm. By age seven, I already understood getting hurt was how lessons were learned. "Only babies cry. Besides, crying is shameful and weak," Dad said. I certainly proved that day how tough I could be and not shed one tear.

The television program, *Tarzan of the Jungle,* left a lasting impression. The mysteriousness of the rainforest and the compassion between the animals and the human captivated me. More so was Tarzan's life, one so entirely different from my own. Glued to the TV every week, I watched Tarzan swing from tree to tree as his new beloved family of apes cared for him. He adapted to their language and way of life while he developed his own special Tarzan yell echoing throughout the rainforest. He gained deep respect from the animals of the jungle while he took me to a faraway place— new, exciting, and exotic. I daydreamed of Africa while I ironed the pillowcases. Tarzan's image of courage, intelligence, and loyalty to his ape family captured my heart. My heroes Popeye, the Road Runner, and Tarzan meant every-

thing to me. They were symbols of courage, strength, determination, and compassion.

TV continued to influence our lives. 1963 proved to be a
challenging year for America as Walter Cronkite unfolded
news events right in our living room. On May 11 we watched
from the kitchen table the TV images of the black riots in
Birmingham, Alabama. Black men, women, and children ran
in the streets. Gunshots, attack dogs, tear gas, firehoses, and
screams rang out as white policemen beat the black people
with clubs.

"Those God damn niggers," my dad blurted.

What did they do, I wondered? I didn't understand their
struggle or Dad's hatred.

Three months later, Martin Luther King prepared to give a
speech on the steps of the Lincoln Memorial in Washington,
D.C. On the day Walter Cronkite was to report the televised
event, Dad turned off our TV and yelled, "Those niggers are
taking over everything."

Insulated from the troubles of black people, our all-white
farming community neither discussed those issues at home nor
at school. TV and my family were my only means of learning
this information. Once I overheard Dad tell a neighbor of his
experience as an Army military policeman in Tampa during
WWII. "Those worthless niggers," was his description of his
search for predominately black AWOL soldiers. The struggles
of black people, the hatred I saw on TV, along with the comments from my dad, made no sense to me.

On November 22, 1963, the TV brought us more tragedy
as we watched coverage of the assassination of President John
F. Kennedy. A hush fell over our household for four days after his death. Through that box in the corner of our living
room we felt the sadness, especially for Caroline and little
John. I remember the braveness of the President's small son
when he saluted his dad's casket that day and never shed one
tear. Grief gripped our home as if the President's death happened in our backyard.

With the television's arrival in the autumn of 1957, my
childhood senses were overwhelmed with everything from hu-
morous shows, movies, cartoons, human tragedy, dramas, and

news from all over the world. We saw marriages, funerals, riots, and a Pope's Coronation right in our living room. It seemed as if God unbolted our front door and the world came in.

The Little Black Boy

My eyes hardly blinked as we drove through the city. Omaha resembled places I saw on TV. At seven years old everything seemed huge, including tall buildings, ten and fifteen stories high. I'd never seen anything bigger than a haystack or a grain elevator. "A million people must live here!" I touted. But Dad assured me there were only about 300,000.

Dad turned the corner and there on the curb stood the first black person I had ever seen in real life—a small boy about my age. As we slowly drove by, I stared at his dark skin. He wore a tattered white shirt with his pants rolled up to his ankles and a cord cinched around his waist. With a stack of newspapers next to his feet, he waved one rolled in his hand, and meekly called out, "Paper, Newspaper!" His face seemed unhappy to me and I wondered why he wasn't home with his family. I never asked my parents because I knew my dad didn't like black people. I did not see another person like him on that trip. Was he the only black person in the city of white people? Ashamed for gawking as long as I did, I couldn't help but wonder if he worked for money to help his family. He seemed so alone. Then I recalled my dad's hateful comments about black people. My heart poured out for him and I wanted to help somehow. His image followed me the remainder of our drive back home and many more times after.

My questions about life and the world at large began to mount. I wondered about the little black boy in Omaha, about my dad's hatred for black people. I wondered if the pink flamingos I saw in a print at Louie's Restaurant were ever wild and free and if I could be as brave, strong, and courageous as Popeye, the Road Runner, and Tarzan.

Country and Catholic to the Core

Remote and isolated from the rest of the world, our all-white community was comprised of mostly Germans and Poles who emigrated to Nebraska years earlier for farming opportunities. My formal education began in a one-room schoolhouse, grades one through eight, called District 20. The schoolhouse, three miles from our farm, measured one-hundred feet by one-hundred-twenty feet upstairs, with a basement of equal size. My class was the largest with five students. A young woman of twenty, Mrs. Bartley, the sole teacher of our entire school of about twenty children, called each grade, one by one, to the front of the classroom to teach while the rest of us did our homework.

I have many fond memories of grade school except for my struggle to count. I wasn't the brightest in my grade. At six years old, when I needed tutoring to count to one hundred, Lea, from the third grade, sat with me while I invariably counted ...58, 59, 100. She corrected me and I started again from 60. ...67, 68, 69, 100. This went on for days and Lea never ran out of patience. One day, I finally got it. I learned a painful lesson—some things cannot be rushed.

With no library in District 20, a bookmobile came to the rural grade schools once every two weeks. I showed little interest in books because being outdoors filled my curiosity. A friend once told me her parents read her children's stories at bedtime. Who needed that? Just go to bed and go to sleep, but not before my bedtime prayer and reading passages from the Bible. We only had two kinds of books on the farm, the Bible and a twenty-four-volume set of Encyclopedia Britannica Dad bought when a vendor came to our front door one day. Both the Bible and the encyclopedias sat side-by-side on a shelf next to my bed and I often browsed the pictures before I fell asleep.

My secondary education was at Morgan High, one of the smaller schools in the region with only sixteen students in my 1969 graduating class, large compared to my grade school experience. Morgan High offered the basic educational requirements of reading, writing, and arithmetic with no emphasis on college preparation. Extracurricular reading was never mentioned. In all my years through high school I never read a single novel or any other books beyond our textbook assignments. Education took a backseat in our farming community. In our pioneering tradition, all that was required to succeed, according to my dad, was how to read the newspaper, write a check, and get the correct change at the cash register. Finally mastering the count to 100 in grade school, I was well on my way to being a successful farmer's daughter.

With education and reading low on the priority list, I spent my extra energy playing outdoors and being athletic. The year I became the softball pitcher on our District 20 team, we beat every school around. When I competed at the annual grade school track tournament at Morgan High, my long skinny arms and legs helped me win every blue ribbon in my grade: high jump, softball throw, broad jump, one-hundred-yard dash, fifty-yard dash, and the three-legged race. The endless teasing about my gangliness wore off when I proudly carted home six blue ribbons each year.

My athletic strength came from my bike riding skills. On the farm I soared like a bird on the wind. I could go as fast and as far as I wanted, as long as I was back by mealtime. I never ventured beyond the sightline of the farm except when riding to our one-room schoolhouse three miles from home. Learning how to ride for the first time at age five on a full-size bike was a monumental feat without training wheels. Those cost too much; besides, they were too sissified for farm kids. Bob balanced me on my bike seat at the top of a small incline at the front of our granary and gave me a push. My long blonde hair blew in the breeze that summer afternoon. He shoved me down the hill maybe a dozen times. I couldn't keep my feet on the pedals and my butt on the seat at the same time, so I abandoned the seat of my precious one-speed blue bike and stood on the pedals learning to push backward to brake and forward for power. A couple of bloody knees later I succeeded. Scars were a small price to pay for that feeling of freedom and pride. And I didn't cry once. "You dare not cry if you fall," Dad often said. Falling was where lessons were learned and crying was a sin in our family—our unwritten rules.

By age ten I easily raced across the dirt-access roads woven throughout our 160-acre farm. Some cornfields were surrounded with electric fences so the cattle could graze on the fallen corn from the fall harvest. I kept the fences on my periphery as I blazed down the hills as fast as I could, to ascend the impending climbs. My goal was to make it up to the corncrib at the crest of the hill without stopping once, something I hadn't yet achieved. Straining my lanky arms and legs, I raised off the seat and pushed the pedals to their capacity, I lowered my head, leaned over the handlebars and sucked air into my lungs and blew it out with all my might.

In my single-minded zeal to get to the summit, I failed to see the single-wire electric fence. In a split second, I lay on the ground entangled in the fence with jolts of electricity pulsating every two seconds through the wires gripping me like a spider's web. Zzz...zzz...zzz.... Electricity traveled freely through the metal of my bike and particularly favored my fleshy body lying on the ground. With every effort to free myself I became more entwined. The relentless shocks of current pulsated through my body. For a moment, I wondered if I might die, right then and there, in the clutches of the spider's jaw. But if I could just get on my feet, maybe I could jump free and save my bike too. I lost track of time as I battled the electric fence. Between the pulses of current, I strategically maneuvered myself and the bike as much as I could. Then, with my bike upright and me standing on my feet, I absorbed one final zap, grasped the handlebars as tightly as I could and jumped out and away. With a puff of dust, I slammed to the ground two feet from the wire fence now mangled in a heap beside me. My bike and I were free from its clutches.

Residual currents still pulsated through my body as I rode home more slowly and cautiously, keeping an eye out for other fences. I never told a soul when I got home. Surely Dad would suspect the cattle ruined the fence.

I learned early to be strong and courageous as a girl on the farm. But the foundation of our family beliefs and values stemmed from our Catholic faith. We attended Sunday Mass weekly in a rural Catholic Church called St. Anthony's, eight miles from our farm. Situated between two small towns, the white wood-framed country church with the belled steeple was our place of worship. In preparation for my First Holy Communion at age seven, we arrived early for service so I could attend a six-week catechism course. Soon after my training I became serious about God, Jesus, and Catholicism. I begged Mom and Dad for us to attend daily Mass, but our farm chores and distance from church didn't accommodate my religious aspirations. My desire to be closer to God culminated at age nine when I decided to become a nun. Some strict Catholic families sent their children to a parochial school where a few followed a religious tradition to encourage at least one family member to seek the ministry. I wanted to be *that* family member. I spent spring and summer reading the Bible cover-to-cover. Except for Moses parting the Red Sea and Noah's Ark, I understood or remembered little of what I read, but surely my effort would bring me sanctity. Only after confessing my white lies and bad behavior to the priest on Sundays did I believe I could be worthy. I probably wasn't the perfect daughter—but damned close. My religious conviction continued through age eleven when I received my Confirmation and my second middle name of Diane. Susan Elizabeth Diane Greisen. I liked how it sounded—very pious. I hoped God would forgive me for not attending daily Mass. I was certainly Catholic to the core.

Paul and Mary

My dad, Paul, was a third generation farmer with his granddad emigrating from Germany in the 1800s. His grandfather moved across the country from the East Coast, homesteading a 160-acre plot of land in rural Nebraska. Like his paternal lineage, including uncles and great-uncles, my dad at six feet, two inches shared the classic Greisen physical characteristics: tall, thin stature, prominent nose, large ears, and an angular face. By his early twenties Dad was marked with a severe receding hairline and by his mid-thirties only a curly band of hair on the sides and back encircled his prominent dome. Adding to his baldness, the sun and wind prematurely wrinkled his face and aged him beyond his years. Whether due to genetics or no fluoride in the well-water, Dad wore a full set of dentures in his twenties. Farming was the core of this rugged German.

Dad was just five years old when in the aftermath of a severe rainstorm in 1924, his father was draining the rainwater from the field with a hoe when he was struck and killed by lightning. With three children too young to work on the farm, his mother moved to Kanton and rented the farm property for income, while the kids all finished the eighth grade. Some children were often not educated beyond that. "Book learning is for teachers, doctors, or kids who want to goof off, not for farmers," my uncle once told me.

My dad served as a military policeman in Tampa, Florida, during WWII. A military sponsored dance provided a chance meeting with Mary, the most beautiful woman he had ever seen. As a high school graduate working as a bank teller, Mary was the most educated sophisticated woman he had known. She was a pure city girl from a middle-class Italian family. Her stunning beauty with jet black hair and dark eyes caught Dad's fancy, and he fell in love with her immediately. Her life, however, was not easy. Her father died when she was a young girl, and her mother passed away when she was eighteen. Mary and her younger sister were sent to live with her maternal grandmother, a domineering, unpleasant woman. After Dad completed his service, he married Mary in Florida in 1944. He plucked his new bride from Tampa, introducing her to the fertile rolling farmland of eastern Nebraska. Dad bought his own 160-acre plot of land to create our Greisen farmstead.

For Mary, the move to the Midwest initially seemed like an adventure, but shortly after, the novelty wore off. She complained about the Nebraska wind, dirt, and dust. And when the gusts blew just right, the wonderful aroma of the chicken, cow, and pig manure wafted into our house. "That's the smell of money," Dad said. Mom could not challenge that comment. "This ain't Florida anymore," Dad snickered as the cold winters and blizzards put an end to her daydreaming.

Everything about Nebraska and the farm was foreign to her. Farming was a lifestyle she never truly embraced. One day as she washed dishes, Mom told me in disgust, "Being a farmer's wife is a thankless job. It's boring and you never get any praise or reward." Nonetheless, she dedicated herself to the farmstead and learned how to grow a garden, preserve fruit and vegetables, milk cows, and use a corncob-burning cook stove, a root cellar, and a crank wall phone.

My dad's mom, my only living grandma, was rather suspicious of Dad's new wife being an outsider: educated, sophisticated, and different from all the rest of the women in our farm community. She asked my mom one day after frowning at her dark Italian skin, "Are you part nigger?" A scalding water bath would hurt less than calling someone a nigger in my family. That comment resurrected several arguments between Mom and Dad and exacerbated the bad feeling between her and Grandma my entire childhood.

Mom was out of her element but Dad was firmly planted in his. He approached farm life with his mastery of intuition. He read the clouds, the animals, the plants, the soil, and the insects. No need for book learning: instinct drove his success. Not only was Dad a farmer but also a mechanic, plumber, electrician, builder, veterinarian, and almost a doctor. We had no health insurance in the 1950s and Dad fixed most minor family injuries and certainly those of our animals. Farming was his life and all my dad ever knew. During the spring, summer, and fall, he often left the house at sunrise and returned at sunset—twelve to fourteen-hour days. The days were even longer when we milked cows as the milking was done by hand before sunrise and before bedtime. Winters were less busy, but the cattle, milk cows, pigs, and chickens all required many hours tending to their care. Dad possessed all the stereotypical German traits: hardworking, committed, determined, and stubborn beyond measure.

When work was put aside, a fun-loving aspect to his personality emerged. Among his male friends and family, he became known for his mastery of jokes and trickery. He built all kinds of contraptions including one where he demonstrated blowing through a tube with gunpowder exiting out the opposite end. When he asked his victim to do the same (who didn't know of the trap), the gunpowder covered their faces. I watched at least ten men fall victim to his antics and Dad never failed to be amused.

Dad and Mom burned up the dance floor with polkas and waltzes. Wearing our finest outfits, our family frequented family dances on Saturday evenings. The live band played the Tennessee Waltz when Dad took my hand, led me to the dance floor, and told me to stand on his toes. At seven years old, my eyes looked directly into his belt buckle. Soon our feet began to move in unison. I looked up to see him gazing across the dance floor like he had the best dance partner at his side. I cherished that moment of closeness and tenderness because I knew sensitivity was neither his role nor his lot in life; toughness and tenacity were more the norm.

What Mom lacked in adaptation to farm life, she made up with her amount of class. No women in Nebraska looked like that dark-haired beauty with her soft, olive-toned skin from her full-blooded Italian background. In the summer sun her skin turned the most beautiful bronze color, unusual because most farm families in our area had a German or Polish pallor. Conscientious about her appearance, Sunday church saw Mom's finest when she wore nylons and high heels most farm women didn't own. Clip-on earrings, necklace, and a fashionable matching purse were the coordinated trimmings she wore when venturing into God's place. She resembled her *Photoplay* icon, Elizabeth Taylor, and carefully applied makeup to mimic the look. Methodically she plucked her eyebrows to make a perfect arch then colored them with a special black pencil. Mom topped it off with rosy-red lipstick. Pink sponge rollers curled her dark hair, and she began to dye it black when discovering a few grey hairs. Maintaining her hourglass figure was a struggle after Bob and I were born. So, weekly, she marked her weight on the inside of the bathroom linen door to monitor her progress to stay under 135 pounds. Little did she know, I watched and made a mental note of all these tricks and traits that I took seriously when I would become a teenager.

Typical farm meals consisted of the northern European classics of beef and potatoes. Mom stood out from the other farmwives with her Italian culinary craft. No one could hold a candle to her specialty of chicken cacciatore or spaghetti with meatballs, recipes I carefully noted to replicate one day. I often took second helpings and would be so full that I buckled with pain. If any of us took extra helpings, we were forced to eat it all. Besides, I didn't want to hear that there were "starving children in Africa." I wondered how she knew about those children so far away.

Dad, however, longed for his German cuisine and tried his best to teach Mom how to fry calf brains with onions for breakfast or rocky mountain oysters for lunch. Mom drew the line and refused to prepare his two German delicacies. The foul odor of fried brains woke me on more than one occasion as Dad cracked the eggs over his steaming skillet of white curdled mush at 6 a.m. I never embraced that strange custom.

Where Mom lacked in farm skills, Dad excelled. Many farmers acquired a variety of skills to survive in the '50s and '60s, but Dad possessed the unique talent of being an inventor. He used his welding skills to make incredible creations including his one-of-a-kind tractor-pull irrigation system, becoming the first in our region to irrigate the rolling farm hills singlehandedly. Normally irrigation pipe is hand-carried by two people over rows and rows of five-foot tall corn. To eliminate this extra work, Dad planted our rolling fields into a patchwork, intermixing the shorter crop of milo in eight rows followed by twenty-four rows of taller corn. Our neighbors scratched their heads as they watched Dad pull the one continuous string of irrigation pipe with his John Deere tractor through the strips of milo, between the rows of corn. It cut the manual labor in half. He was a genius even though he couldn't spell worth a damn. Farm-smart, not book-smart, with only an eighth-grade education.

The Greisens were proud of their German heritage that included not only a strong work ethic but strict discipline. "Behave" was probably etched on my forehead and "children are to be seen and not heard," were words that frequently rang in my ears. Dad was a strict disciplinarian and there was no getting away with anything. His rule over our family left Mom as a mere messenger of his commands. I only witnessed physical violence once when Mom and I helplessly watched

Dad kick Bob across the kitchen floor with his heavy work boots like a feral dog—all because he flunked the sixth grade. I have no memory of what happened afterward—only a residual fear filled my core.

I certainly never wanted to cross him knowingly. I did as I was told and never asked why. We were taught through our Catholic faith about sins—mortal and venial. Honor thy father and thy mother is the fourth commandment. For me that translated into obeying them. And that I did. Not wanting to suffer any consequences, I became the perfect child, not ever grounded like some of my friends. Besides, being good limited my visits in the confessional on Sunday.

I can't recall being hugged as a child. I never heard the words "I love you" from either of my parents toward each other or toward us children. Love and affection were just assumed, no matter how much the lack of it felt empty to me at times. When Dad became affectionate and grabbed Mom from behind to put his arms around her, she pushed him away. As a child, I rarely witnessed other adult relationships outside our own home. I thought that was how all families conducted themselves.

Tough Farm Kids

My older brother, Bob, became my ardent role model and competitor. We not only played for hours in the winter snowbanks or in the farmyard but also worked side-by-side at our assigned duties. As much as I adored Tarzan, Bob loved Superman. He attempted to mimic his hero's flight when he tied a bath towel around his neck like a cape, climbed to the top of the fifteen-foot haystack in the barnyard, ran, jumped, and flew a couple feet with his white towel flopping in the wind. The pillow-like hay at the base softened his landing, and he laughed and did it all over again. I tried my darnedest to do everything he did. I wanted to jump, but was too chicken, and he knew it. So, he won that competition round.

Bob also revered Hercules, his TV idol. To emulate his hero, he lifted hay bales for weights to build his physique. By age sixteen his muscles rippled on his legs, torso, and arms.

Just because he could, and had something to prove, he picked up my twelve-year-old stick-like-frame and twirled me—straight-armed, like a barbell—above his head and threw me on the couch. He did this more than once. He laughed and I snickered. He was Hercules and I believed him. If I ever married, my husband would be someone like Bob. Besides, who wouldn't want to marry Hercules?

During the winter of 1958, I overheard Mom tell someone, "It wasn't planned, but we were glad anyway." I had no idea what "planned" meant. I never had a baby doll to play with like some of my friends so at eight years old, I was thrilled to have a real baby in the home. When Randy was born he took on Mom's traits with his dark curly hair and olive skin tone. Ever so cute and full of personality, my sweet baby brother made us all laugh. As his big sister, I fulfilled an important role by holding, feeding, and amusing him.

My delight became short lived when Randy reached four-months of age and Dad bought a home movie camera. My dad documented everything about our newest family member. "Randy did this, Randy said that." I was *sick* of Randy. Bob being the oldest had his firsts, now the youngest had his firsts in movies. And me? Well, I became invisible. Even my straight As in school brought no praise. Being perfect at home or school made little difference. I now had new competition.

When Randy turned one, I found a way to get noticed—make him cry. Just a little tap or push and he'd be wailing. My sad-dog eyes blew my cover and Mom knew my guilt. Often she chased me with the wire end of the flyswatter as I ran into the only lockable room in the house—the bathroom. One day, I stayed there for two hours until she tired of the whole ordeal and gave up. That wire handle left a welt on my arm lasting for days when I didn't make it in time. Eventually I tired of the teasing, mostly because Randy began to talk and mastered the art of fighting back.

I knew I wouldn't die from Mom's flyswatter assaults, but there were many other ways farm kids and adults brushed with death. A multitude of tragedies happen on the farm: overturned tractors, electrocutions, farm machinery accidents, or falls have left many farmers or their children either maimed or dead. In our small community alone, we knew of more than ten neighbors or relatives who suffered injury or death from farming.

Mom and Dad nearly lost my brother, Bob, at age three. While he played outside in his blue snowsuit, Dad cleared the snowdrifts from the farmyard with the snow blade attached to the back of the John Deere tractor. As Dad maneuvered the tractor, forward and backward, to clear the yard of snow he yelled, "Bob, keep clear of the tractor or I'll run you over!" But right as he shouted his command, Dad put the gear in reverse and Bob moved out of his view, blocked by the rear five-foot tractor wheel. As luck would have it, Bob fell into the snow and Dad backed the gigantic wheel over him. The massive tire treads pushed his three-year-old son into the soft snow. He saw Bob's blue imprint lying motionless in the tire track and rushed down to him. He cradled the limp child in his arms and ran to the farmhouse.

Mom, stunned by her lifeless child in her husband's arms, watched helplessly as he laid Bob on the kitchen table. When Dad unzipped his snowsuit, Bob took a deep breath and his pale color turned pink. The incident never elicited a physician's visit or exam; besides, Dad fancied himself nearly a doctor, anyway. Bob lived with no ill effects and my parents were relieved their firstborn son lived to see another day. The life of hard knocks on the farm and survival of the fittest was certainly not a myth.

Bob tempted death again at age seventeen, while driving his 1956 two-door Chevrolet back from his girlfriend's house. He crested the hill and hit a snowplow head-on. The snow blade, a four-foot edge of curved steel, caught only the front bumper and left Bob uninjured. Mom and Dad were easy on him realizing they could have lost him again.

Farm deaths also came from grain elevators that posed a particular danger in our community. Most every town had this agricultural facility that often consisted a steel and concrete structure up to fifteen stories tall where grain was stored and sold. From time to time the *Morgan Booster* and the *Kanton Telegram* reported grain elevator explosions from the combustible dust particles, and at least two deaths were reported during my years on the farm. Thousands of bushels of corn or wheat stored within the elevators required periodic inspection to examine the interior walls or the grain. However, for an unskilled person walking on top of the grain, the kernels or seeds could pull you down. The harder you tried to get out, the deeper the grain sucked you into the abyss, like quicksand, up to your waist. My brothers and I were advised to steer clear of the smaller grain storage sheds we had near our house. Farm tough and curious, I experimented, to see if this was true. Sure enough, only a few feet in, I experienced the pull of death. The corn kernels sucked me down just below my knees. Within reach of the door entry, I pulled my panic-stricken body out; I lived another day and never told a soul.

Stuck in the Middle

I found myself always a bit different from my family and peers all the way through high school. Even though no one called me the commonly used term, "black sheep of the family," I often felt like one. It began when I came out of the womb different, born with a crooked nose. According to Mom it took days for it to straighten out. She pushed it sideways, but I wished she had pushed it *in* to make it smaller. I got the Greisen schnoz anyway.

I hated popcorn as a child. Each Saturday night Dad cooked a huge batch as we sat in front of the TV to watch our favorite shows. Everyone, except me, scooped a bowl-full from the huge enameled washbasin overflowing with salted buttered kernels of popped corn. Yuk, it tasted like salted Styrofoam pellets and the smell of fried popcorn oil and burnt kernels turned my stomach.

As the only left-handed member in my family or in my school, I felt even more different. Fortunately, Mrs. Bartley, my grade school teacher, was the first person outside my family to have such a profound influence over my life. During my first grade penmanship class, she took note of my left hand cranked nearly upside down over my paper. Never once did she slap my hand or try to make me change, as so many other parents and teachers had done. Mrs. Bartley gently guided my hand downward as she turned my paper to my left so I didn't have to crank my hand over to write. With her guidance and encouragement, my penmanship transformed from an awkward backhand to a lovely print. She accepted my uniqueness and didn't try to change me. I will never forget her.

Tall and gangly for a girl, the Greisen genes ran deep to my bones. I always towered over others in my grade up until high school, including the boys. The older kids teased me incessantly and called me "bean pole" or "rail." Store-bought clothes never had sleeves or pants legs long enough to cover my wrists or ankles. Mom found my left-handedness difficult and threw her hands up in frustration teaching me how to sew. I met that challenge and taught myself to make fashionable pants and tops to fit my awkward body.

If those weren't enough challenges, I found myself firmly stuck in the middle between Bob's first endeavors and Randy's cuteness. Essentially, I was ignored. I constantly sought my parents' approval and attention but even failed on my multiple attempts with my straight As in school. I wondered how to fit in. Being a boy on the farm might be a good way to be appreciated. I noticed how much praise Bob received from helping Dad and I certainly wasn't gaining any praise doing household chores.

So, I approached my preteen years by becoming a tomboy, wanting to do the things boys could do. My proud scars served as my rite of passage to be like one of them: the scar on my leg when I cut it accidently while sawing a high branch in a tree; the wounds from my multiple bicycle falls; and a huge dog bite on my left shoulder from an attack by a neighbor's German shepherd. Over time, I added those to my one-inch badge-of-courage scar when I channeled Popeye and shattered the living room window with my fist. I did most anything to get noticed.

With little impact from those previous attempts, I moved to bigger endeavors by helping Dad with farm duties and engaging in more boy activities. As a girl, I quickly learned I had a different set of rules to follow than my brothers. Additionally, boys were given more privileges, like being able to play high school sports or shoot guns. Shooting and killing animals were a part of life on the farm. Dad shot anything wild that moved:

gophers, jack rabbits, birds, pheasants, squirrels, coyotes, and deer. Not particularly fond of guns, I, however, felt privileged to join in shooting practice with the guys. As I stood between Dad and Bob pointing the gun at the tin can resting on the fence post, I could hear my mom's voice, "Girls and guns just don't mix." I pulled the trigger anyway.

Dad reveled in my willingness to help him. In the summer of 1962, when I was eleven, he taught me how to drive the John Deere tractor. I sat just so my little butt rested on the edge of the tractor seat and my legs stretched for the clutch and brake. My skinny arms barely reached to each side of the steering wheel and it took all my strength to turn those two front wheels in the soft harrowed fields. I never gave up until I became expert at driving the tractor and machinery around the farm. Because of my skill, Dad asked me to harrow the wheat field all by myself at age twelve. Sixteen-feet wide by ten-feet long with five-inch tines evenly spaced, the harrow was an unwieldy piece of machinery pulled behind the tractor. Like a gigantic rake, it broke the hard clods after the plowing and disking, turning the clumps into fine soil. Dad plowed, Bob disked, and now I would harrow. I beamed with the notion that my role in our farming family had increased. Dad gave me a quick lesson before returning to the house and cautioned me about turning the front wheels too tightly.

As I sat in the adult seat riding that tractor alone in the field for the first time, I had my chance to make him proud. Not more than thirty minutes passed when I made my first 180-degree turn in the field. I worked diligently to crank the front wheels of the tractor in the rough field when simultaneously I heard a clashing sound of metal and rubber. The tractor abruptly stopped, and the engine stalled. When I turned my head, I was shocked to find the harrow had crawled up the five-foot back right wheel of the tractor with its sharp tines three feet from my head. I had turned too sharp, just as Dad told me *not* to do.

So, *this* was how people die on the farm. I thought it might be better to die in the field than receive my reprimand when I got home. Maybe I should just jump into the jaws of the electric cattle fence and do myself in. But being a brave, tough farmer's daughter, I needed to be served my punishment.

My legs trembled as I walked the half mile to the farmhouse to report my accident. Dad wasn't mad, thank God, because I had done no permanent damage to the equipment. Mom rolled her eyes possibly indicating a previous conversation they had about sending me out on my own in the first place. Maybe I *was* too young. I was never allowed to harrow again—my privilege rescinded and trust was broken.

However, Dad needed me out in the field and soon put me back on the tractor doing other tasks. He taught me how to unload grain from the tractor wagon and the truck. Maneuvering a vehicle backwards required skills and practice especially when hooking up a wagon or aiming the back end just right to have the truck gate meet the auger. Backing vehicles could not only damage a lot of equipment but possibly knock out a family member.

By the time I turned fourteen, I regained Dad's trust. He bragged with pride to his friends, "Give Sue any vehicle and she could back the damned thing up square!" Those were rare moments of approval. And I treasured them.

Birds and the Bees

Tall, thin, blond, blue-eyed, and athletic, he wound up his arm to throw the pitch from the mound, and I temporarily lost my bearings. An unfamiliar tingling rushed down from my head to my feet as I laid eyes upon the most incredible fourteen-year-old boy named Shane. I wanted to marry him... eventually. In the summer of my eleventh year, my desire to become a nun waned, and my focus on baby Jesus and God diminished, while my interest in boys increased. I abandoned my convent dream when I realized getting married and having children were more in my future.

The reproductive habits of animals on the farm were never discussed or explained. We simply observed the aspects of breeding, birthing, suckling, and neutering. Religion drew a clear line between the animal kingdom and mankind, so I never made the connection. But then one day, the unexplained happened. Mom handed me a twelve-page booklet to read after I discovered dark spotting in my panties. We never spoke about it again. She simply supplied the torn-up tired bed sheets or towels that I folded and pinned to my panties. Being the first girl in my grade school class to get the "curse," as it became known, I suffered many days of cramping for reasons never explained.

With all my religious training and beliefs, I was convinced all pregnancies were from the divine intervention of God, like the Virgin Mary. My older schoolmates begged to differ. Only one person could settle this controversy—Mom. That may have been a mistake because she never answered the question. Changes in my preteen years mounted with my infatuation with Shane, the "curse," and now *my* question of "where did babies come from?" All this happened within months of each other. And it led to the *talk* with my dad.

Later that fateful fall, Dad asked me to accompany him on our new Case combine for the milo harvest. There was no place I'd rather be than riding with him on any kind of machinery. Mom packed a cooler with sandwiches and water as we would be out past lunch. I took my position in the jump seat next to Dad. I couldn't have been more content as we headed out that beautiful morning. Our new upscale combine was fitted with an enclosed cab and even a radio which he immediately turned on blasting a Johnny Cash favorite, "I Walk the Line." Watching the combine roller head gently comb the milo heads into the cutter bar was almost dreamlike. This must be why Dad loved farming—it was such a rewarding profession. A perfect farm and a perfect life.

Normally Dad and I didn't talk much while riding together on the tractor or the combine, but for some reason he seemed a bit nervous that day. Dad turned off Johnny Cash as the combine continued to harvest the milo and then said, "I want to talk to you about the birds and the bees."

I didn't have the foggiest idea what he meant, but from his tone, it was going to be something big.

Dad straightened in his seat and gripped the steering wheel hard, then said, "You will soon be interested in boys and they will be interested in you."

Little did he know I already had two boyfriends in grade school. Or should I say, I had a crush on them. The boys may not have known, but I giggled and flashed my ponytail whenever they'd come near. I wore the pretty white bow in my hair on Sunday to catch the attention of a few special boys. A tingling rush ran through my body when they said "Hi." I was pretty sure I would marry my classmate's older brother, Larry, one day.

"Well," Dad stammered and stuttered, "It...it happens like this. When I met your mom, she was the most beautiful woman I had ever seen and one night I took her out dancing and I held her body close to mine. And, well, I...um...things got out of control, I mean, uh, my lower body got out of control, while we were dancing, that is, and I pulled her closer and your mom pushed me away and kept things safe. And that's it. When it comes to the birds and the bees, it is up to the girl to say 'No' and push the boys away cause...well...the boys have no control over their bodies. You know, you don't want to get pregnant before you're married—ever."

I asked no questions because I didn't even know *what* to ask. What did this have to do with the birds and the bees anyway? Did this mean I carried the huge responsibility and sole burden of becoming a teenager and almost a woman at age eleven? *Push the boys away*, that's all I remembered. I had observed Mom pushing Dad away when he showed his rare affection to her. Whatever he meant, my Catholic religion and Dad had spoken: my virginity must be upheld.

I suppose I nodded in agreement, but I clearly remember welcoming the thrashing sound of the combine harvester that broke the awful silence that now permeated the cab.

After a long pause, Dad made a final declaration. "One more thing—I will never trust you."

I kept silent. I had no idea what he was talking about. Trust must have something to do with me and boys. What could it be? I dared not ask.

On the Road

So much had already happened in my life by the time I was eleven. I never expected that something profound was about to change my life forever. Dad arrived from town with a truckload of supplies from Kanton a few months earlier. He bought items I had never seen before: a load of angle iron, huge sheets of plywood, and rolls of aluminum sheeting. Being an inventor and builder, he told us his plan to make a camper to fit on the back of our red Ford pickup. When completed, our family was going to the World's Fair in Seattle, Washington, the following summer. My eyes lit up with the possibilities. Dad must have learned about the World's Fair on TV because we certainly never read about it in the local papers.

He labored on the camper construction all winter and spring, and I helped hold the aluminum sheeting as he attached it to the plywood. This iron frame sort-of-thing began to look like a home when he added the miniature refrigerator, two-burner stove, table, and mattress. The table to the booth collapsed to convert into a bed for me and my brother. Mom, Dad, and Randy would sleep above the cab on the double mattress. We were going on an epic adventure.

The news of Dad's construction project traveled like a prairie fire in our small community. When the neighbors and friends caught wind of our adventure, they came over to see Dad's contraption.

Our friend, Willie, stared at the camper and wondered what that Greisen was up to now. Scratching his head, he asked, "How long are you going to be gone?"

Dad brushed his hands on his blue bib overalls and said, "Five weeks."

"Wow, Paul. That's a long time to be gone from the farm. What are you going to do with the cattle, pigs, and chickens that whole time?"

"I'm going to hire a neighbor to take care of the animals."

Willie's eyes rolled while he shook his head and asked, "*Why* are you going?"

"I want to see the Pacific Ocean," Dad beamed.

Willie removed his John Deere cap, wiped his forehead with the back of his forearm and snickered in disbelief. "And why in the hell do you want to see the Pacific Ocean?"

"Because, well...I've never seen it before," Dad said with a dream-like look in his eyes that I never forgot.

That summer of 1962 as our camper rolled down the highways of eight western states, I lay on my belly gazing out the window above the truck cab seeing the world—and not just on television. We saw snowcapped mountains reaching to heaven, redwood tree trunks bigger than our entire house, the Grand Canyon so deep I thought I saw the beginning of hell. We even went to the top of the Space Needle in Seattle as it turned and rotated three-hundred-sixty degrees. This was not a TV program about America—this was for real!

Earlier that year Dad bought me the only childhood gift he ever gave me without Mom's input, and it wasn't even Christmas. Because of my interest in his movie camera, he bought me a Kodak Instamatic as a reward for all my hard work helping on the farm. On our family adventure, I used my new camera to capture all the important sites on our trip.

The Adventureland tour in Disneyland topped the chart with my first glimpse of what Africa might really look like. The riverboat Safari trip was breathtaking as I scanned the terrain for Tarzan. I didn't see him, but I heard his famous call. We marveled at some animals while others frightened us. Plastic hippos roared and jumped out of the water, robotic trumpeting elephants peered out of the bush and submerged mechanical crocodiles lunged at our boat. In the distance I saw real pink flamingos. They rested in their picturesque location of a serene lake surrounded by palm trees, lush green vegetation, and a clear blue sky, just like the print at Louie's Restaurant. I wondered if those creatures could live somewhere in the wild, but again they were in captivity. Regardless of this make-believe environment, my heart filled with contentment. I saw so many things I'd never seen before. Click, click, click, my camera captured those unforgettable images— memories I would keep forever.

Back on the road again after Disneyland, we drove for several miles when Dad quickly pulled off the highway into a parking lot and stepped out of the truck. The setting sun lit up Dad's bald scalp like a shiny hood ornament and his full set of dentures nearly left his gaping mouth when he called out, "There it is!" He ran back in the camper and grabbed his single-8 movie camera and its clicking turns documented our epic sighting. Our trip culminated when we saw the Pacific Ocean for the first time. He lowered his camera to gaze at the crashing waves, their retreat and return again. He flashed his dentures ear to ear as his eyes feasted on the rolling waves. "Now I can say I've seen it."

His wish had come true. I stood by Dad's side feeling privileged to explore America through his eyes and dreams.

The Blizzard

On January 15, 1965, the radio announced the blizzard, packing sixty-mile-an-hour winds, had arrived and for everyone to take shelter in their homes. A phone call came from our neighbor, Mark, who told Dad his fifteen-year-old son, Allan, had headed out to fetch the cattle from the field before the blizzard hit. Allan was heading toward our fence line, and his father feared for his life. Against Mom's protests, Dad bundled up and exclaimed, "Allan will probably freeze to death within minutes, not hours, if I don't find him fast."

Within seconds of hanging up the phone, flashlight in hand, a huge overcoat, leather gloves, overshoes, and a kerchief tied around his face, my dad prepared for the storm. We knew there was no stopping him as we became silent with disbelief of what he was about to encounter. Blizzards and tornadoes were probably the two most deadly acts of nature in Nebraska. But to walk into a blizzard willingly was something I, as a fourteen-year-old, could not imagine. Outside the kitchen window, the blinding storm obscured our cast-iron dinner bell on the post just ten feet away.

Farmers often grazed their cattle in the fields on corn that fell to the ground from the fall harvest. Mark's field adjoined our property about twenty-five yards to the north. In his phone call he explained to Dad the cattle were along his eastern fence line closest to our property, making this precisely north-east of our house. Allan and the cattle were heading our way.

By the time Dad opened the door, daylight was gone. Snow blew horizontally across the sky. He stepped outside with a flashlight in hand. Once in the midst of the blizzard, the flash-light only lit up the snow flurries whizzing by and blurring any vision he had. He dropped the useless light into the snow and went on. Walking like a blind man with his arms outstretched he bumped into our eastern fence. He turned left and headed north toward Mark's field. Bracing from the freezing north wind he pulled himself along the barbed wire fence line.

Fences were the checkerboard grids designating property boundaries and contained the cattle. They acted like roadmaps and crossroads. Dad had ours memorized as he walked them many times over the years repairing our fences and could trace them with his eyes closed. In the blinding blizzard the fence line became his Braille.

Minutes later Dad came to the fence junction joining our properties. Climbing over the barbed barrier as the snow pelt-ed his eyes, he staggered north following Mark's fence line. Hand over hand in total darkness he lumbered.

While Dad battled the brutal blizzard outside, our house moaned and the windows rattled; the wind whistled through every small crack. Filled with fear, Mom, my six-year-old brother, and I silently watched the clock and listened to the blizzard reports on the radio, not knowing what to do or what to think. Could Bob, who had moved away for work, have given us comfort? Now I wondered if Dad would even come back alive. Prayers were all I had for my sanity.

Twenty minutes after he left the house, Dad assumed he located the area Mark had designated. His eyes strained and as he looked into the blackness, he yelled Allan's name several times and listened. Only the wind replied. With determination he pulled himself north along the fence line, as the barbed wire pierced his gloves.

Step by step, lifting his knees high over the one-foot snow drifts along the fence line, his legs tired. Then he ran firmly into a snow covered mass—a heifer. Dad discovered about five in the cluster along the fence line. He continued to weave between them when he felt something resembling a person—Allan huddled among the cattle. Dad grabbed and pulled him back toward our house.

As blindly as he began, Dad carefully and methodically retraced the memory of his footsteps pulling Allan who clung to his coat sleeve. If Dad went too far, they would miss our house completely. If he went too slowly, they could both perish. All his previous footprints were drifted over with snow. Dad moved as if in slow motion. The cold and fatigue seemed to consume him as he pushed toward the house with Allan in tow.

Tick, tick, tick...the clock above the kitchen sink marked the time. A half hour passed. Too scared to cry, I listened to the radio report. Mom's face was filled with worry while she wrung her hands, and Randy looked aimlessly out the living room window. The radio reception flickered in and out. Forty-five minutes passed since Dad walked into the storm when our front door opened and two snowman-like figures entered, coated in a fine white powder. Slumped by Dad's side, a bundle of frozen snow collapsed and fell to the kitchen floor. We removed the stiffened clothing to find Allan beneath, pale and nearly motionless. Suddenly his eyes opened. We immediately wrapped him in warm blankets.

Dad went directly to the phone and called Mark to tell him his son was alive. We rejoiced.

Amazing as it may seem, Dad knew all along what the cattle would do. He understood they would walk away from the wind and huddle together for warmth. That meant they would move south toward our property fence line. He assumed Allan would follow the fence from his house to guide himself toward the cattle. Dad's intuition and innate understanding of the animals, the weather, and the human condition found them all together just as he predicted. Later that year the Morgan City Council gave my dad "The Citizen's Award for Bravery and Courage." I had only known what TV heroes looked like. I never saw a *real-life* hero before. That day my dad became one in my eyes.

Teen Angst

By age fifteen my disproportioned body became more womanly as I developed Mom's hourglass figure. Attractive and about an inch taller than Mom, I garnered some of her other traits: cooking, sewing, and looking good with an artistic flair for decorating. Italian drama and emotion poured from my genes. I found it hard to talk without using my hands and often got my feelings hurt. But my paternal DNA was evident with being lanky and thin, and possessing Dad's humor, smarts, athleticism, passion, stubbornness, and determination. I evolved into the perfect blend of my parents.

Throughout my teen years I took careful beauty notes from Mom. Vanity overtook my sanity when I substituted the pink sponge rollers with orange juice cans to straighten my wavy hair. Lying in bed, I looked like the freezer section of the refrigerator, but this was a small price to pay for sleep when looking good was paramount. I felt shame rather than pride at becoming a woman when I was one of the first girls to get boobs in grade school class. Teasing from several boys, including my dad made my breast development a sensitive issue. Some referred to my new buds as fried eggs. Those comments hurt me deeply, especially because my pubescence was out of my control. Maybe, because of that teasing, I slept in my bra until age sixteen.

When I asked to shave my legs and wear nylons, Mom met me with a resounding "No!" Sure, I only had six long hairs on each leg, but they wouldn't look neat under nylons—I'd have to wait. After another year of nagging, I got permission to use Dad's straight-edge razor. No one warned me of the carnage my legs would endure with multiple nicks as the razor showed no mercy for an inexperienced young teen. Wads of blood-soaked Kleenex pasted to my shins stopped the bleeding.

Proudly I wore those grown-up female nylon trappings to church. But the garter belt clips dug into the backs of my legs as I sat on the wooden pews and left deep pink painful indentations. Why was I doing this? Oh yes...I remembered, all for the sake of beauty and to attract the right boy. Maybe, just maybe, Shane would notice me.

Perhaps, as with any teenager, clashes with the parents were inevitable, but questioning or challenging their commands or demands were simply not done in my family. I met with more struggles as I began to stand up for myself and seek autonomy. My sense of injustice intensified especially once I entered high school.

With my athletic abilities, the coach asked me to play sports. My parents forbade it. I asked Dad, "Why can't I play volleyball or join the track team?"

"'Cause we don't want to run around picking you up after school when you can take the bus home," Dad grumbled. "No is no! Stop being sassy. We'll have none of that."

My older brother never met the same resistance and joined the track, football, and basketball teams. Bob drove his own car to team practice and attended all the games. In my junior year, the student body encouraged me to try out for cheerleader. I would have been a shoo-in with my athleticism, outgoing nature, and energy. My parents, of course, said no. "But why," I asked, "why can't I be a cheerleader?"

"Because you'll end up pregnant like two of your classmates did. What a disgrace!" Mom shouted.

In fact, two cheerleaders did become pregnant in my high school class of eighteen students. The girls were forced to drop out of school and shamed, while the well-known boys continued their everyday lives. This inequality seemed so unfair. My girlfriends and I whispered about the misfortune of these pregnant girls, but the decisions about their fate was never challenged. It was then I realized my role as a girl would abide by a different set of rules based on my sex. "Push the boys away,"—Dad's message just a few years earlier now had a vivid meaning with a real consequence.

When my classmates saw my potential and voted me as president of both the junior class and the pep club, my mom met me with another resounding rejection of my skills and talents. "Why do you always have to be the leader?" Mom complained. "Why can't you be like the rest of the girls?"

There were days I hated being a girl. I possessed all the qualities that would be accepted by my parents if I had been a boy: self-directed, determined, stubborn, smart, creative, and above all, a leader. Mom told me I was even bossy as a baby. Why are boys not labeled as bossy? Surely I must have some redeeming qualities that would get approval from my parents, but they never seemed to acknowledge them.

I asked God to give me a sign to ease my struggle with my parents. That day came when I was sixteen, while on a drive to Omaha with Bob's fiancée, Joan, and her sister, Judy, to search for Joan's wedding dress. It was a typical ride on a two-lane Nebraska highway, with some hills, mostly flat. We passed cornfields on one side, grazing cattle on another, hay bales lying in the alfalfa fields. As we rounded a bend in the highway, on our left, a beautiful red brick castle-like building surrounded by a black wrought-iron fence came into view. Two brick pillars with huge lanterns on each side supported the enormous locked iron gate. The place seemed magical and something I saw on TV before. "I want to work there," I told Judy.

She said, "You can't work there."

"Why not?"

"Because you need to be a nurse to work there. It's a Children's Home."

"Well then, that's what I'll be," I exclaimed. It was that simple. That day I decided to be a nurse. My decision wasn't as abrupt as it might seem. Before age sixteen I witnessed plenty of blood, guts, birth, death, and surgery on the farm.

My first obstetrical training occurred at eight years old when my dad asked me to help a sow deliver her pigs. Before Dad left to work in the field, he instructed me on how to pull the birth sacks off the noses of each baby pig as they delivered and get them to suckle. I became the delivery nurse. I sat all afternoon, one foot from the back end of the sow's rump, helping her deliver eleven baby pigs. I saw plenty of blood, mucus, and slime—but it didn't bother me. I grabbed the babies one by one, pulled the sacks off their noses, and guided them on their wobbly legs to nurse at the teat. Until that day, I could never have imagined the wonderful feeling of helping a newborn live.

My birthing experience continued when I witnessed Dad delivering a baby calf and nearly a gallon of amniotic fluid drenched me when the birth sack broke. Informally I learned about anatomy and physiology while watching Dad butcher animals. He separated the organs from the meat and cut off the heads of chickens while I plucked and gutted them. I was introduced to surgery when I restrained the baby pigs while Dad castrated the males with a razor blade and sutured them up. I saw my own blood when Dad bandaged my arm after I punched it through the living room window. My orthopedic courage soared when I tried not to flinch when he sawed off my leg cast with an electric Skil saw and when he stitched up our dog's leg when he nearly cut it off with the tractor mower.

The true test of my nursing instincts and the building of my skills began the day Dad asked me to be the nurse and caretaker to a newborn runt from a litter of pigs. This little guy, much smaller and underweight than his aggressive siblings, would never have survived the competition to nurse at the teat. In the past, Dad terminated any small weakling, especially from a large litter. That time, Dad told me to raise him by hand—a great honor and challenge for an eight-year-old.

The runt was a boy when he was born, but Dad castrated him after a week and so he became a girl. I called her Daisy. A pure white Yorkshire with a little pink nose, big pink ears, dark eyes, and a curly-q tail became the cutest pig on the farm—maybe because she was mine. A heat lamp on the porch at night kept her warm, and I used my old baby bottle to feed her cow's milk several times a day. She slobbered and squealed with excitement whenever she saw that baby bottle. Daisy squirmed with delight when I brushed, talked, and sang to her. I loved her so much.

With all my nurturing, she soon graduated from the bottle to ground oats and corn. When Daisy became too big for the porch she slept outside under the granary; she never seemed to mind being separated from the others, she had free rein of the farmyard. In the mornings I'd head outside to call her. "Daisy, Daisy, where are you?" Down the hill she came, half asleep and ran into my arms. I hugged and may have even kissed her—she was that special. Daisy nuzzled me like a dog while I bathed her with the hose. She followed me everywhere while I played and worked in the farmyard all summer. We were bonded like family.

She grew quickly the summer of 1959 and even though her weight caught up to that of her siblings, about one hundred pounds, Daisy never joined them in their enclosed pen. Monthly, Dad filled truckloads of pigs to sell in town, but he never took Daisy and I was sure he would let me keep her as a pet.

One day Dad asked me to call her, something he never had done before. When Daisy came to me, he put her into the pen with her siblings and proceeded to load them in the truck. To challenge or plead my case to Dad was not permissible in our household, especially as a young child. I said nothing as Daisy walked up the ramp with her siblings. I stood back in disbelief. She looked back at me in confusion, yet her mouth curled with elation to be with her own for the first time since her birth seven months ago. Dad drove the truck away, and I never saw Daisy again.

The day Daisy was taken from me, I cried for a full day, but only in my room. The word sympathy was reserved for only human death—never an animal. I rebelled by not eating pork for a month. I understood about the shame of crying and feeling sad. I had to get over it. But in reality, I have never gotten over Daisy...ever.

Evidently, I was the only one in my family labeled as sensitive. "Oh look, Susan is crying, she got her feelings hurt," Mom mocked my tears and Dad shook his head in disgust. I cried easily until age six when shame stopped my public display of emotions. Shame was a powerful tool in my family. I shed my tears in the privacy of my bedroom after that.

In addition to the nursing skills I'd acquired on the farm, I also learned about caretaking and death—how to nurse a weakling to life, watch her taken away forever, and how to channel my emotions. Just like farming was in Dad's blood, nursing was in mine.

During my junior year of high school, I became ecstatic as I read in the *Kanton Telegram* about the construction of a community college offering a nine-month practical nursing program. I now had a way to become a nurse and escape the thankless job of becoming a farmer's wife, as Mom described it. Even with her dislike of the farm, I was uncertain how she would respond to my nursing aspirations. With reserve and caution, I walked into the kitchen to tell her of the news. "I want to go to the nursing program at the new community college next year."

"Why do you want such a dirty job?" she sneered. "All you'll do is clean people's asses. You need to be a secretary."

"Why?" I asked naïvely.

"Because you're going to get married and end up on the farm. You don't need to waste an education."

My prior experience proved arguing or pleading would be a useless endeavor. So, without much choice in the matter, I took shorthand and typing in high school. I did well in those classes, but I still longed to be a nurse. By the end of my junior year, my parents' vision of my future was clear: I would be a farmer's wife. Yet I struggled with Mom's unfavorable messages about her own role. The TV in the corner of our living room exposed me to options of finding another life. Our trip around the western states opened my imagination to places other than the farm. Even though I loved our home, the animals, and the outdoors, being a farmer's wife was not my vision. My teen angst surged as I wrestled with my desire to please my parents while at the same time wanting to follow my own dreams. My confusion escalated.

Mom and Dad made it clear that nothing less than a good Catholic boy from a respectable family would do. At age sixteen I began to date but found the whole ordeal stressful. Keeping the boys under control, as my dad instructed, was a big task. After a few false starts, I fell in love for the first time with a wonderful classmate, Doug. Tall, handsome, blond, blue eyed, and caring—everything a girl wanted. Not only gentle and kind, he also respected my religious constraints on heavy petting and was willing to wait. By seventeen, dating became fun.

We were a handsome pair—both tall and good looking. By my senior year we were going steady and his yarn-wrapped class ring adorned my finger. Many of my classmates were also going steady by that time, with marriage in their future. Doug supported my desire to become a nurse while he showed little ambition for furthering his own education. He didn't want to be a farmer like his dad. Becoming a truck driver like his uncle seemed to be more appealing and most likely what he planned to do. We talked briefly about our future marriage, but my parents only half-heartedly approved of our steady relationship because he wasn't Catholic; I rejected the other Catholic guy Mom kept suggesting. My courage to resist increased.

In 1969 I graduated as valedictorian from my high school class of sixteen students. Being smart and ambitious only led to more conflict, arguments, and tension with my parents. That same year the junior college in Kanton opened its practical nursing program and, now with more determination and force, I prayed, pleaded, and nagged for my parents to allow me to attend. They finally succumbed to my badgering when I received a $100 scholarship to apply toward tuition. I enrolled in the charter class of Practical Nursing at Kanton Community College.

My parents never wanted me to attend nursing school or be a leader. To deepen their dismay, my leadership skills continued to be recognized by others: I was elected the first president of the charter class of practical nurses. My confidence surged.

My Ticket Out

"The toughest job you'll ever love. Join the Peace Corps." The words of the TV commercial resonated deep within me. An advertisement clip displayed a map of Africa followed by a video of a young female volunteer walking through an African village of thatched houses followed by a group of happy children. As I neared the end of my senior year in high school, that commercial sparked a vision for the possibilities of my future.

That night I went upstairs to my room and pulled volume "A" from the set of encyclopedias to look up "Africa." I ran my finger over each country on the colored map of the vast continent and wondered if I could live in one of those places. A picture of an elephant drew my attention to the country of Kenya. A short paragraph described the theory that Homo sapiens began in the Rift Valley of Kenya, referred to as the "Cradle of Mankind." Only a few years earlier I read in the Bible that Adam and Eve were created by God—the beginning of mankind. These two theories were in direct conflict, but I couldn't deal with it that night. I preferred instead to imagine where would I live and travel in Africa.

That summer all the symbolic images that were important to me converged: my TV idols including Tarzan, the little black boy in Omaha, and the pink flamingo print in Louie's. All my pieces of a complex puzzle finally came together: I was going to be a nurse and help save the people in Africa. I was going to join the Peace Corps.

That night I requested an application by mail. Not wanting my parents to find the correspondence, I walked the half-mile driveway to the mailbox daily, awaiting a response. Within a couple of weeks, a large manila envelope finally arrived, and I ripped open the contents. The Peace Corps booklet described everything I dreamt of: helping people in need, learning about foreign cultures, living with the local people, and being of service to the world and my country. I studied the application and mulled over how to approach my parents. I prayed for guidance those next few days. It took every ounce of courage I could muster to *tell* them of my plans, *not ask* them. Now eighteen, I vowed no more pleading, begging, or whining for what I wanted.

Later that week when my parents were finishing supper, I walked into the kitchen with my brochure and application in hand. I planted my feet firmly on the linoleum floor, faced them and said, "I am joining the Peace Corps and going to Africa."

Mom slapped her hands down by her side, cast her eyes to the floor and shook her head. Dad roared, "Why in the hell do you want to go and help those niggers? Why don't you stay and help people here?"

For a moment that felt like forever, my limbs froze in place. Rejection was familiar to me, but this time his words cut deep. My legs quivered and the papers rattled in my hands as I searched for what to say, hoping God would help me with an answer. Out of nowhere the words left my lips. "Dad, you were in the Army and people like you joined the military and served their country abroad. And well...that's what I'm going to do. I'm going to serve my country, just like you did. JFK said, 'Ask not what your country can do for you. Ask what you can do for your country.'"

My parents' faces turned from anger, to blank stares, and then to sheer disgust. They spoke not another word. Their silence emancipated me. I was over eighteen and they couldn't stop me. With my pamphlet and application in hand, I went upstairs to my room and carefully printed—Name: Susan Elizabeth Diane Greisen. Place of Birth: Nebraska. Age: 18. Occupation/Education. Practical Nurse (to be completed in December 1970). Choice of Continent: Africa.

The following morning, I walked the half-mile driveway to place my application in the mailbox. Mom and Dad never brought up the topic again. I was on my way to Africa.

Nine months later I graduated at the top of my practical nursing class. Standing proudly on the stage with my colleagues, I wore my new white uniform and nurse's cap while our lead instructor placed the nursing pin on my collar. Everyone important to me was there, and I hoped I made them proud: my parents; ten-year-old brother, Randy; brother, Bob and his wife, Joan; and Doug. Everyone except my parents congratulated me. After the ceremony Doug presented me with a silver ring with two entwined pearls professing his intent to marry me at a later date. I had no reason to forego my future to this wonderful man. I shared with Doug my desire to join the Peace Corps and promised to save my virginity for our marriage. I did not, however, fully understand my reserved happiness. Could Doug and my life in Nebraska wait while I fulfilled my dream?

A bigger question remained. Why, exactly, did I want to go to Africa? The best short answer I gave was, "Because I've never seen it before." These were Dad's exact words when he took our family to explore eight western states five years earlier. Perhaps, with that response, he could understand my reason.

Many people thought I was crazy. Maybe I was. That pink flamingo print planted the seed of wonder, the image of the black boy in Omaha gave me a purpose, and the TV in the corner of our living room gave me Popeye, the Road Runner, and Tarzan as my mentors. That Peace Corps commercial gave me my ticket out. My eyes were now open to the world outside our small farm.

By late 1970, the Peace Corps accepted me with an assignment to Liberia, West Africa, in their Health Education Program. My dreams and prayers had been answered. Eight months later I stood on the runway at the Kanton Airport boarding the Frontier Airlines, my first plane ride. Reluctantly, Mom drove me to the airport with a reminder, five times if not ten, to use my rubber boots, rain hat, jacket, and umbrella. She said, "It rains a lot in Africa, you know." I put on a somber face to spare her feelings but I was smiling inside.

I wore my handmade navy-blue polyester bell-bottom jumper with daisy rickrack on the hem. To straighten my wavy hair, I slept with my orange juice can rollers all night and teased it the following morning to create the perfect flip. Eyeliner and perfectly arched eyebrows accentuated my eyes. Clip-on earrings accompanied my fashionable pumps to complete my ensemble. I'd be one of the coolest girls in the Peace Corps training. I turned to wave to Mom from the flight stairs as the lyrics to the Peter, Paul, and Mary song, "Leaving on a Jet Plane", rang loudly in my head. Yes, I was leaving on a jet plane and I didn't know when I'd be back again. A brand-new life outside our remote farm beckoned...and I was going to find it.

PART II

THE VIRGIN ISLANDS

Peace Corps Training

Confident and determined at age nineteen—armed with a suitcase full of farm-smarts and a license to be a practical nurse—I arrived in the Caribbean for six weeks of Peace Corps training. One-thousand miles off the Florida coast, our training site was located in the U.S. Virgin Islands, an archipelago composed of three main islands: St. Thomas, St. John, and St. Croix. The main Peace Corps training facility was full to capacity, so seventeen women and I, destined for the Health Education Program in Liberia, trained separately at the nearby resort of Dorothea Beach on St. Thomas.

After spending a few days in New York City to secure our documents, the first item of business in the Virgin Islands was to vaccinate us for the onslaught of tropical diseases we would encounter. These were serious illnesses that kill people including typhoid, cholera, yellow fever, rabies, tetanus, diphtheria, and malaria. The PPD (purified protein derivative) test ensured we didn't have tuberculosis before we arrived, and gamma globulin, 5cc's administered in the buttock, boosted our immune system for anything we might contract for which there was no vaccine. The gamma globulin injections could have been used for prison torture. The injected serum, as thick as Karo Syrup, sat like a painful golf ball in my buttock for days until absorbed. Had I known more about these maladies, I may have never left Nebraska. But helping people in Africa awaited me.

The trainees ranged in age from nineteen (me, the youngest) to seventy-one, with most in their mid-twenties. Many quickly singled me out as young, green, and naïve. All true. Only later did I realize how isolated I had been on the farm. Some teased me and corrected my grammar when I said "boughten bread" and "we was." That's how we talked on the farm. Pointing to a bowl on the table, a fellow trainee asked me to pass the Brazil nuts. My dad called them "nigger toes." I never knew the proper name. My shameful ignorance only deepened. I made my grammatical and vocabulary changes quickly to fit in. My dining etiquette left something to be desired. A select group frowned when I wiped my mouth with the back of my hand, ate with my elbows on the table, and used toast to sop up my runny egg yolks. I thought eating fried chicken with a fork and knife was silly.

Only a couple of trainees never teased me, including one particular young woman, different from the rest. First, she had a weird name, Rainbow. I later discovered it was not her real name, but her chosen one. Rainbow was a Texan with a bachelor's degree in sociology. I found her feminine boldness foreign to me. As a self-described hippie, Rainbow wore long, loose-fitting clothing, John Lennon-type round eyeglasses, and long brown wavy hair parted in the middle streaming halfway down her back. Some trainees labeled her as a "free spirit."

Rainbow and I didn't fit in with the others and so our bond seemed likely. This puzzled me because of our opposite behaviors and background: she was city- and book-smart; I was farm-smart; Rainbow was a vegetarian, I ate meat three times a day; she practiced yoga, I never heard of it before; Rainbow had no religion, I was a devout Catholic. The more we talked, the more I learned about her life filled with excess and freedom, while I lived with boundaries and control.

But with all our differences, one common thread bonded us from the beginning—we both loved George Harrison. George began to branch out from under the umbrella of the Beatles and wrote and sang his own songs by then. Like Rainbow, George was a full-fledged hippie by the early '70s. Off key and intermingled with giggles, she and I stood arm-in-arm swaying to our favorite tune, "Here Comes the Sun." Unlikely as it seemed, we became kindred spirits and hoped our assignments would be near each other in Liberia. Rainbow was the sister I never had—my soul sister.

She became my meal partner. At our dining table was where I had my first taste of a foreign culture. The sweet tang of fresh pineapple could not compare to that from a tin can Mom served us on the farm. Bananas lit up my taste buds with sweetness rather than a starchy residue on my tongue. The miracle of a ripe buttery avocado and the floral essence of papaya were new fruits my mom only spoke of before. Fresh grilled fish melted in my mouth compared to the dried, frozen, cornmeal-coated fish sticks we ate every Friday during Lent.

On weekends our training group took bus trips to the shopping district of Frenchtown on St. Thomas. The duty free port of the Virgin Islands provided me with an opportunity to leave my Kodak Instamatic at home and purchase a new SLR camera and a movie camera, like my dad's. After several stores and guidance from my peers who owned fancy cameras before, I acquired an Olympus SLR and a Fuji movie camera to document my journey to Africa. Not knowing how remote my assignment would be, I learned about prepaid mailers. Each roll sent in for processing was returned with a new roll of film. That night I studied my camera booklets like a final exam, because I hoped to be proficient by the time I arrived in Liberia.

As a diversion from training, group outings included a trip to Charlotte Amalie for the annual festival called Carnival, an endless parade of calypso dancers, steel drum bands, and masses of adults and children in elaborate beaded, feathered costumes. Their joy and spirit made our subdued parades in Morgan seem like a funeral processional. Somewhat uncomfortable with the uninhibited pelvic gyrations displayed by the dancers and spectators, I restrained myself to a gentle sway. After a few minutes, I closed my eyes and began to spontaneously pulsate with a reserved excitement of the new and different.

Toward the end of the parade, a performance act emerged for only the brave—men in full colorful, feathered costumes walked and danced on five-foot stilts. Skillfully they whirled to the music and threw candy to the children. Their magical image emanated joy and celebration—something like a circus clown.

Once back at the Dorothea Beach training camp, we attended to more serious business. In our open-air classroom with palms swaying in the breeze and the waves lapping on the beach, we reviewed U.S. and Liberian current events. Discussions about Nixon, the Vietnam War, and the struggles in America were topics of which I knew very little. The local papers never covered such things. Walter Cronkite's thirty minute news summaries, five days a week, were all I knew. Even then, I didn't understand those complex topics. Many fellow trainees graduated from four-year universities and talked about protesting the Vietnam War. A few were from big cities like New York and Chicago. Some had toured Europe. Except for the camper trip with my family and a couple of trips to Omaha and Tampa, I never knew city life. My inferiority complex seemed to grow in those training sessions, but if I didn't let their snide remarks bother me, I could hold my own. During our health training, I exhibited more knowledge than my fellow English or history majors.

A popular question by the training staff was, "Why did you join the Peace Corps?" Most of the girls answered, "to travel," "to see the world," or "to learn about another culture." When my turn came, I sat erect, pulled my shoulders back and said with my most confident voice, "I joined the Peace Corps to help save the people in Africa." My pride turned to shame, as giggles and rolling eyes emerged from my colleagues. What was so funny about that, I thought? What I said was true and besides, their answers seemed shallow and self-serving. If I lived in New York, traveled to Europe, or graduated with a four-year degree, my answer might have been like theirs. But I didn't. I was Susan Elizabeth Diane Greisen, a hick from Nebraska. None of them knew how I defied the odds and my parents to be there. I knew what I wanted to do, where I wanted to go and why. Only Rainbow and a few others seemed to respect my answer.

Our Liberian and Peace Corps staff covered topics of health care, health education as well as the history and culture of Liberia. We also practiced Liberian English, a pidgin-English-of-sorts. The staff spiced things up when we engaged in hysterical role-playing skits. My jovial and dramatic personality gradually won over a few skeptics and naysayers.

I found the classes on history and geology of Liberia intriguing. Liberia lies on the Atlantic coast in the western bulge of Africa with its bordering neighbors of Sierra Leone, Guinea, and Ivory Coast. It is comparable in size to Tennessee. Most of the country is covered by dense tropical forests and thrives under an average annual rainfall of about 160 inches. A monsoon climate of alternating wet and dry seasons characterizes the weather. Plateaus and mountain ranges in the northern region are rich in iron ore, gold, and diamonds. The coastline of 353 miles has no natural deep-water harbors and is pounded by heavy surf.

Liberia was founded in 1822, as a result of the efforts of the American Colonization Society to settle freed American slaves in West Africa. The colony became the Free and Independent Republic of Liberia in 1847, becoming Africa's first republic. The new name for the country, Liberia, comes from the English word, liberty. The capital, Monrovia, named for U.S. President James Monroe, is the original landing site of the American settlers.

These descendants of former American slaves became known as the English-speaking Americo-Liberians and make up only 5 percent of the population but have historically dominated the intellectual ruling class. At the time of my arrival, President William Tubman, an Americo-Liberian descendant, had been in power since 1944, twenty-seven years, with William R. Tolbert, Jr. as his Vice President.

Many of the official national symbols were closely related to America, including its official language, English; its currency, the U.S. dollar; and the flag, a replica of the American flag, but with a single large white star on a blue field representing Liberia's long history as the "Lone Star"—the only independent republic in Africa during the colonial period. Even with English as its official language, only about 15 percent of the population could read or write it. The English language bridged communication among Liberia's sixteen ethnic groups: Kpelle, Bassa, Dan (Gio), Ma (Mano), Klao (Kru), Grebo, Mandingo, Krahn, Gola, Gbandi, Loma, Kissi, Vai, Bella (Kuwaa), Dei (Dey), and the Americo-Liberians.

Our Health Education Group was requested by the Liberian government to assist with improvements in rural health education in areas of greatest need. The statistics given to us were sobering and deepened my desire to serve this needy population. The average life expectancy of men and women was around thirty-nine and forty-one years respectively, with the major causes of death coming from malaria, acute respiratory infections, diarrhea, and complications from childbirth. Infant mortality was 40 percent in the first two weeks of life; if the infant survived, there was a 60 percent chance of mortality before the age of five. The postpartum mortality rate of 40 percent was often due to hemorrhage, sepsis, and no access to medical care. Mortality and morbidity were particularly high in the rural areas where villagers had no or little access to Western health care. I reflected on my history of the pioneers in Nebraska during the early 1900s when access to health care and medical treatment was not readily available. The Liberian statistics were not so different.

Our assigned goals were to initiate new programs or replace existing volunteers in the Well-baby and Antenatal (also known as prenatal) clinics in our various sites around the country. Education, vaccinations, and preventative care were the main objectives. With many regions having illiteracy rates as high as 85 percent, even the simplest health principles such as potable water and clean hands were not well known.

The areas of greatest need ranged from small villages to large towns. The staff provided the trainees with a written profile of each site including the size of the village or town, access to services, number of current volunteers, and the predominant tribes in the region. Some sites had existing health programs while others required the volunteer to establish a new program. From these descriptions, we were instructed to choose our top three sites. The staff planned to conduct individual interviews based on our skills and background, review the trainee's wish list, and then select our assignment.

I took the profile handout to bed with me that night and studied it carefully. One location kept rising to the top of the list—Zorgowee. This village of about 100 huts, or roughly 1,000 people, was not only the smallest, but also the most remote, being one of the farthest from the capital of Monrovia, about 170 miles. Although not far by American standards, it could take a person two days by public taxi to travel from Zorgowee to Monrovia on the poorly maintained dirt and paved roads.

Gio was the main indigenous tribe of Zorgowee, with a lesser percent being Mano and Kru, yet their dialects and customs were similar. The fourth tribe present was Mandingo, a migrant tribe from the nearby countries of Ivory Coast and Mali. The Mandingos, present throughout the country, were often the small local merchants, because by law, they are denied land purchase or the ability to farm. The indigenous tribes were predominantly animists, and the Mandingos practiced the Muslim faith.

Peace Corps elementary school teachers were assigned in Zorgowee in the past, but currently there were no volunteers there. In addition, no health volunteer had ever been assigned to the village before. I would be responsible for implementing their first Antenatal clinic and a Well-baby clinic in their existing rural facility that employed one dresser, a type of physician's assistant. With only a few weeks of formal training, like that of an advanced first aid worker, the dresser could make simple diagnoses and provide wound care. Treatments were performed with minimal supplies and medication like bandages, peroxide, aspirin, penicillin injections, and malarial medication.

I jotted notes about Zorgowee on the back of the profile handout. Pros: remote, small, startup Antenatal and Well-baby clinic in an existing facility, no other volunteers in the village, no electricity, no running water. I would be the only white person in the village. This would be like camping for two years and I wanted to be chosen.

Cons: none.

I added a couple of other location assignments, just in case I encountered competition for Zorgowee.

The following morning, anxious and nervous, I handed the staff my top three choices in order of priority. Among our group, none of us discussed our wish list as if guarding a precious territory. By the following evening the staff completed their interviews, chose our assignments, and prepared for the presentations to our Health Education Group.

In preparation, the staff set up a party atmosphere. The Liberian trainer, Mrs. George, pulled a cloth from a flip-chart pedestal unveiling a map of Liberia with our names next to the site assignments. To my astonishment, my misspelled name was next to Zorgowee. I later discovered that no one else picked that village precisely for the reasons I *had*. Maybe my green, farm-girl image from the sticks proved to be a stronger character than my fellow trainees imagined. Or maybe I was naïve.

The map revealed that Rainbow was assigned to Zwedru, Lofa County, a twelve-hour taxi ride from Zorgowee. Saddened by our distance apart, we vowed to visit each other as often as possible and maintain our close connection.

I knew what I could do and what I could accomplish. I delivered and castrated pigs, plucked and gutted chickens, shot a .22 rifle, drove a tractor, punched my fist through a glass window, was chosen president of three groups, and braved my parents' rejections. No stronger woman stood in the room at that moment. And I was only nineteen years old.

"Zorgowee, here I come."

PART III

LIBERIA, THE FIRST MONTHS

The Toughest Job

On May 4, 1971, I arrived in Liberia at Robertsfield International Airport. When the Pan Am Airline door opened, after eighteen hours in the air-conditioned compression chamber, I stepped onto the flight stairs, temporarily blinded by the African sun. The hot jungle air gripped my lungs like a heavy steam blanket. I choked for breath. After a slight hesitation, my respirations became normal again. Jet-lagged and exhausted, I dragged myself down the sweltering stairs to the even hotter tarmac. Gradually I recovered from my first sensory shock, only to be initiated into the world of African smells. Wood-burning fires, damp vegetation, jet and car fumes were smothered under the ceiling of humidity. Then came the wonderful smell of fried dough coated with sugar followed by the stench of a rank sewer as I passed the restrooms. Thank God I'd used the airplane lavatory.

The small international airport terminal, the size of a large one-story house, bustled with friends and families greeting the arrivals. My visual field met a color explosion of Africans dressed in vibrant print shirts, pants, dresses, and head ties. Taxi drivers shouted their fares and grabbed bags. Pandemonium ruled as overly eager taxi drivers bartered and bantered with the awaiting patrons. Fortunately, Peace Corps staff met us with a prearranged bus transport for our group. I felt giddy and euphoric. Was it from a couple of alcoholic drinks onboard, lack of sleep from my overnight flight, the Liberian humidity, airport mayhem, the bumpy ride from Robertsfield, or the adrenaline from months of anticipation? Yes...all those combined.

The airport was only the precursor to the chaos that followed. Forty-five minutes later, we arrived in Monrovia, Liberia's capital. Our bus deposited us with our training staff on Broad Street, the main thoroughfare. The streets were ruled by what appeared to be a racing derby of honking taxi drivers. Amazingly no one crashed. There may have been one or two streetlights and a few stop signs, but no one seemed to bother. Car exhaust fumes filled the air from hordes of four-door Datsun and Toyota taxis jam-packed with people as they jostled in the streets with occasional pickups overloaded with more people, animals, and produce. As we roamed the streets on foot, I had a sudden awareness that my colleagues and I were just a few white flecks in a sea of black Africans. For a fleeting moment, I wanted to be invisible.

I snapped out of my wonder as children loudly hawked their wares. The sidewalks brimmed with young boys and girls selling all sorts of items balanced on their heads. One sold newspapers, like the little black boy I remembered in Omaha. There were many boys like him soliciting vehemently, "Missy Peppa, Peppa." Small girls balanced trays on their heads selling individual cigarettes for a penny each. For 3¢ you could buy roasted peanuts, known as ground pea, rolled in newspaper cone or a whole orange peeled down to the rind, cored in the center, to squeeze and suck the sweet juice. We were unable to walk more than two feet without being solicited to purchase these items.

A single door opened to the storefront of a Liberian tailor sewing all kinds of beautiful fabrics on a treadle machine, an antique back home. Massive garage doors that opened to the streets were entrances to the large stores owned by Lebanese, the common foreign merchants in the country. These stores sold all types of nonperishable items like fabric and canned goods. Suddenly, rhythmic melodies of song, horns, drums, and guitars entered my ears. The infectious syncopated music known as "African highlife" blasted from the boom boxes carried on peoples' heads or emanated from the doorways of the various stores. The people, vehicles, shops, sidewalks, and streets were one frenzied blur. Sensory overload added to my adrenaline high. Rainbow and I stayed in close contact with each other as our training staff led us through the maze. Suddenly, Rainbow grabbed my arm and shouted, "Watch out!" I was one step from falling into an open sewer/storm drain that intermittently separated the streets from the sidewalks. I could have been killed at that moment before any tropical disease could have claimed me.

Before traveling to our assignments, we had one more week of Peace Corps training that revealed a deeper, more complex understanding of Liberia's history. The earliest immigrants to the country had either been slaves freed by their masters under the conditions they would emigrate to Liberia, men and women born free of slavery, or recaptured slaves taken from smugglers—all of whom would settle in Monrovia. By 1870 more than 13,000 immigrants from America had put down roots in Liberia. They were not welcomed with open arms by the indigenous tribes. Brutal battles and animosities developed over the decades toward these foreigners, commonly known as Americo-Liberians, but politically they triumphed. By 1878 they created the most powerful political party known as the True Whig Party (TWP). The TWP remained dominant for over a hundred years, making Liberia essentially a one-party state. Although democratic in structure, the government was not democratic in practice. President William Tubman had been in power for over a quarter of a century. The founding of Liberia, thought by many to be a just and reasonable action for the U.S. to take, turned out to be a type of democratic dictatorship.

During our final training day in Monrovia, we prepared for a week's homestay in our assigned village or town which provided another orientation and indoctrination to the local culture while giving the individual one last chance, before the swearing-in ceremony in two weeks, to weed out any naysayers. Not able to contain my excitement, flashes of the Peace Corps TV commercial and images of *Tarzan of the Jungle*, kept me awake that night. The following day I would see my new home for the next two years—Zorgowee.

On May 10, I headed upcountry, sitting in the front seat of a Datsun taxi with four other locals in the rear, enduring a ten-hour ride with multiple stops and one taxi change. My stomach tightened with excitement and anticipation. The rust-colored dirt road, commonly known as laterite, kicked up dust en route. Taxi windows were wide open to stave off suffocation from the ninety degree heat and humidity.

"We coming to Zorgowee, ya?" our taxi driver said as the road gently curved and we drove over a one-way wooden-plank bridge crossing the Yar River. I glanced to my right to see women and children washing clothes on the rocks below. "I say, look at da Go tree, ya," the driver announced happily pointing toward the sky.

My eyes were drawn straight ahead and upward to a towering monolith. Majestically perched at the crest of the hill stood the Go Tree, Zorgowee's namesake. The Go tree, according to folklore, was sacred, and was given a female designation. Stories have been told of historic cannibalism in a nearby clan where the bones of their victims were buried beneath their sacred tree. The locals in Zorgowee adamantly denied cannibalism as part of their culture. Rising to over 150 feet, she stood taller than any of the surrounding trees. Her white smooth bark and high canopy with arms and green-leaved hands stretched over the main road in a commanding way. "Zor" was the name of the clan, composed of sixteen small walk-in villages with Zorgowee as the governing center. "Wee" meant village. Thus, Zor-Go-Wee.

A lone Lebanese store and a few local Mandingo merchants selling items on small wooden tables lined the right side of the road adjacent to the Go Tree. The taxi turned left off the main road, weaving through the village of predominately thatched huts and only a few tin-roofed homes, one being the house of my homestay host, Jacob.

As I stepped out of my transport a strikingly muscular man came to greet me. In Liberian English he flashed a broad warm smile and said, "Hello ya! You mus' be Miss Sue. I am Jacob."

"Yes, I am. I am so glad to meet you." I brushed the thin film of red laterite dust from my arms to look presentable but found my white t-shirt red-stained as well.

His erect posture and puffed-out chest gave an illusion of a six-foot man, but as I approached, he was only about 5'7", my height. His broad nose, full lips, and a part between the two front tooth were characteristic of the Gio tribe and he wore them proudly. Jacob, an assistant to the village chief, exuded an air of strength that could demand respect from the other villagers.

Within minutes, his three wives and two children came out from the house to greet me. As Jacob began the introductions, the wives lined up behind him in order, giving me the impression that Sawee, the eldest of the three, was the head wife. Thin and muscular, she, too, radiated strength and determination. She spoke to Jacob in her Gio dialect only when spoken to. Second in line stood Glyee. Shy but jovial and easy to smile, her stocky stature revealed a hardworking woman. Younga, the youngest and most recent wife, possessed an infectious smile. Quick to talk, laugh, and ask questions, Younga's playfulness and beauty drew me like a magnet. Her tall, thin stature easily supported her six-month pregnant-looking tummy. She took to me immediately. None of them were formally educated or spoke English, so Jacob translated everything. But Younga giggled and squirmed as she spoke her few choice English words of "Hello" and "Goodbye."

Jacob's two younger children, Matthew and Simon, ages three and four, did not speak and they shyly hid behind their parents. The six of them lived in their small two bedroom mud-and-stick home. With Jacob's permission I took a picture of his family with my new SLR camera. They specially dressed up for my arrival; Jacob in a grey leisure suit, the three wives in colorful traditional outfits and head ties, and the two boys with matching light grey leisure suits, all stood in a row beaming with pride.

Jacob then escorted me to a furnished three-bedroom house next to his home—the one I would be renting from him for $25 per month. Villagers with more wealth could afford corrugated tin roofs, wooden doors, and shutters with hinges and locks. My house had all of these. These luxuries were present in about twenty of the 100 homes in Zorgowee. Supposedly, a lock was required if you owned something of value. My status in the village seemed to be determined at that point. For me, these luxuries had nothing to do with status. Instead, Peace Corps had minimum requirements for safety and comfort. Crafted of mud and stick with cement-like stucco on the exterior, topped off with whitewash, my home was the nicest in all the village of Zorgowee. If you saw my house, you'd never suspect its inner structure to be made of mud and stick, except that wouldn't measure up to a carpenter's level or follow a plumb line. Dad would have said something about that. But it didn't matter, it was beautiful and it was mine.

Jacob guided me through the three bedrooms, a living room, dining room and a good-sized kitchen as well as an indoor bath area and an outdoor latrine. Peace Corps standardized the living experience by providing each volunteer with a bed and mattress, a kerosene refrigerator, a propane gas stove with an oven and required shuttered, screened windows.

I recalled my handout of Zorgowee in the Virgin Islands—no electricity or running water. However, the three volunteer teachers who came before me all lived in my house and made home improvements along the way. It was the only one with a highly coveted Western standard—pseudo-running water. Four years before I arrived, the male volunteers developed a rain-barrel system with two fifty-five-gallon barrels collecting rain from the corrugated-tin roof. Two more barrels erected on stilts had a garden hose attached to the bottom of each. The hoses passed through the wall: one directed to the shower and the other to the kitchen sink. Essentially fed by gravity, I did have running water, but not an unlimited source.

This region of Liberia received about eighty inches of rain annually leaving little worry about water shortage. However, potable water was in rare supply. Other volunteers alerted me to carefully plan the usage of this valuable resource from the barrels and never let the tap run without a good reason. Zorgowee did have a dry season lasting two to three months, therefore I must stretch my 220 gallons of water to last during that period. I learned how to bathe and wash my hair with about one to two quarts of water and clean my dishes with one quart or less.

Right outside the back door Jacob showed me my palaver hut, an outdoor kitchen for cooking on a wood fire. However, the volunteers used it to hang their hammock, and I planned to do the same. Palaver in Liberian English means "discussion or argument." Everyone gathered, talked, debated, and argued by the traditional wood fire in the palaver hut, similar to our kitchen back home. From the hut, at about a half mile distance as the crow flies, sat the highest peak in the region, part of the Nimba mountain range. Along with the Go Tree and the Yar River, stood another iconic landmark—Mount Bele. The view of this mountain from my palaver hut resembled the TV images of Diamond Head in Hawaii. A gradual slope ascended from the northwest then terminated with a steep drop off to the southeast. Mount Bele wore a full headdress of tropical trees and vines. When the weather was just right, dancing ribbons of fog draped over the tallest trees and tucked into the mountain crevices arose to the heavens.

Next to my palaver hut stood a small mud and stick storage shed with an attached latrine. My African latrine, a hand-dug pit, was a luxury and a rarity in Zorgowee. Only two or three other private latrines existed in the whole village because the outdoors or the bush was the natural outhouse for the locals. I should have felt privileged by my primo facility, complete with a wooden box atop the pit and a hole for the seat with a lid—all surrounded by a wooden structure for privacy. My luxury seemed more like a misfortune when the smell, spiders, and cockroaches were impossible to control. This must be why villagers used the bush. I hated this aspect of my new home. Mom needed to stop complaining about barnyard odors; this was far worse than cow and pig manure combined or daddy long-legged spiders. Besides, we never had cockroaches on the farm. While I used this facility during my stay with Jacob, I struggled to conquer my fear of those damned African cockroaches: the size of a small mouse, flat, shiny, and rust-colored. They even flew. Although the round hole in my latrine came with a cover, the critters clung to the bottom of the lid each time I lifted it. When they crawled from the underside of the seat, I jumped when their antennae tickled my butt. To say the least, I went to the latrine as infrequently as possible. Constipation became my frequent unwelcomed companion.

Jacob eagerly showed me another source of income in Zorgowee, besides farming—the diamond mine. About 100 yards behind our houses we came upon a hand-dug pit, about twenty-five yards in diameter. Inside the hole stood five men digging and sifting the dirt for these precious gems. Jacob said northern Liberia was rich in diamonds and the men could help support their families as paid laborers. I hoped to learn more about this industry.

We continued our tour that led us to the elementary school near the main road and on the northern edge of the village. We approached the simple one level, white-washed, tin-roofed building with two doors containing separate class-rooms. Not much different from my one-room grade school back in Nebraska. The teachers greeted us outside as we ap-proached. Jacob introduced me to James and Andrew who taught basic reading, writing, and arithmetic from 8 a.m. to noon, Monday through Friday. Their attire gave them a sense of importance as both were well-dressed with Western shoes, long pressed pants, and white shirts. Andrew, the taller of the two, even wore a tie. School sessions ran from March through November, during rainy season when little farming could be done. Each classroom contained three or four long wooden tables with benches on one side. On a painted blackboard at the front of James' barren classroom were written the words "tree," "taxi," and "town" for their English lesson that day. Two English textbooks sat on his desk, the only books in the school. Public schools were essentially free, although families must pay for uniforms as well as any needed school supplies like paper and pencils. Generally, thirty boys and girls attend-ed up to the sixth grade; however, only fifteen were present that day. Attendance was neither compulsory nor monitored and Jacob explained turnout varies due to illness or farming duties. Many of the girls dropped out before grade six to either work in the fields or get married. Some became pregnant. Too overwhelmed to ask more about his loaded statement. I hoped to learn more during my stay.

On our way back from the school we stopped by the chief's house, just off the main road opposite the Lebanese store. Manuel, selected by the village leaders, not only served as the Chief of Zorgowee for the Gio, Mano, and Kru tribes, but also as the clan chief of the sixteen walk-in villages in the Zor Clan. He greeted me warmly wearing his traditional chief's robe—a long cover made of handwoven indigo country cloth with ornate embroidery at the neck and chest along with a matching cap. He kept local order, served punishment when needed, and followed the Liberian government's requirements. From there Jacob and I walked across the main road to meet the Mandingo chief, Ahmadou. His traditional Muslim embroidered skullcap and his full-length *white* robe indicated he had made the pilgrimage to Mecca. He also served as the clan chief for the Mandingo tribe living within the clan. The two chiefs followed similar rules regarding law and order but were unique when it came to their religious and cultural differences. The Mano, Gio, and Kru were animists honoring witchcraft, medicine men and midwives, while the Mandingos worshiped Allah and practiced their Muslim traditions such as Ramadan.

When we concluded my tour and returned to his home, Jacob said, "The people in Zorgowee are happy and so so strong-o." His voice beamed with pride while I filled with joy, now certain I had made the right decision to come to this remote village. During my first evening in Jacob's home, he escorted me to a table with two bowls and two tablespoons. Customarily, the men ate alone while the women and children ate together. Being a white woman and in a health education position in the village, I did not fit the customary Liberian female role. Because of my elevated status, I ate alone with Jacob. Generally, Liberians eat by hand from one large shared bowl. Any cooked Liberian dish was commonly called *chop*. Be it local greens, ground pea, chicken, or meat often prepared with tomato paste—all would be cooked into a stew and served over rice. We were each given our own white enameled dish with a tablespoon to eat our chop—resembling my mother's chicken cacciatore. However, this was no cacciatore. The moment the food hit my mouth, my tongue and lips lit on fire and the flame traveled down my esophagus, turning on the faucet to my nose and eyes. Jacob laughed. Even though forewarned about the Liberian pepper before I departed Monrovia, no one could have ever prepared me for the burn. My taste buds could be paralyzed for life. Five glasses of water did little to squash the flame. Areas of my lips became swollen where the pepper had touched. Would this be something I could get used to?

Jacob escorted me to my bedroom in his home for the night. I learned he vacated his own room for me, moving instead to another bedroom shared by his three wives and two sons. After our meal, I exited Jacob's house, walked next door, and sat alone on the foundation outside my home-to-be looking up at the stars in the moonless night. Without artificial light of any kind, the Milky Way illuminated the sky like a solid white band of light. My mind, swirling with new information, sounds, smells, sights, and people, suddenly became peacefully still. Without warning, a welling in my chest rose up to my eyes and tears rolled down my cheeks from sheer joy. I said to myself, "I made it to Africa. I am really here." In that moment, a deep gratitude and happiness penetrated deep inside my heart. That must have been how Dad felt when he saw the Pacific Ocean for the first time—a dream come true.

The following morning after breakfast, Jacob gathered his wives to announce a Liberian tradition—to give the Peace Corps volunteer a local name. Jacob decided my Gio name to be Younga Ti. "Ti" translates to small, young, or new and "Younga" means lively as far as I could tell. If it had anything to do with being like his wife, Younga, I was proud to have that name. The wives cheered, especially Younga.

The next day, Jacob continued my village tour of the tin-roofed clinic building next to his home. The sole function of the clinic was for first-aid type care and triage. The Ministry of Health provided few supplies including a blood pressure cuff, a stethoscope, thermometer, bandages, tape, peroxide, a pair of scissors, a gas primus stove, and pots for sterilizing the glass syringes and stainless steel reusable needles. Aspirin, vials of penicillin, and chloroquine tablets to treat malaria were the only medications supplied. The clinic's windows had shutters without screens and contained four main rooms: One large waiting room in the front, a moderate-size exam room with a small storage room on the right, and a large education room in the back.

He introduced me to Peter, the dresser of the clinic, my work partner for the next two years. Peter's proud peacock-like posture made him appear much taller than his 5'5" frame. He took a dignified stance with a stethoscope hung around his neck and his dark black skin accentuated his freshly ironed white nurse's coat. He displayed the familiar part between his two front teeth, like Jacob. Peter's conversation and stories gave me the impression he functioned more like a doctor, although he only attended an eight-week first aid-type training. Even though the clinic was armed with minimal supplies and medications, it provided the best care the village had to offer. He spoke in a commanding tone with an air of confidence, yet I wondered how much he really knew. Education of any type appeared to give villagers power and clout when likened to those who had none.

Peter introduced me to Duo, his assistant, a small dark-skinned young man, about eighteen who had little formal education. He could barely write and had little command of English, but his eagerness outweighed his qualifications.

Peter collected 25¢ for each clinic visit, the money intended for clinic maintenance and purchase of small supplies such as fuel for the primus stove. Early on, I witnessed the contrary. Charges would vary by patient. Non-indigenous tribal people, like the Mandingos, could be charged more, but certain attractive women might not get charged at all. I saw the gamut of fee collection, but supervising Peter wasn't my job. The Medical Director, Dr. Walton, was his boss and he visited infrequently.

Rather than focus on fee collection concerns, I turned my attention to sanitation. Washing hands with soap and water between patients as well as boiling the syringes and stainless steel needles were critical. I walked softly in the beginning, trying to be patient with change as I witnessed many areas for improvement.

Even though nursing was not a part of my educator role, I offered my skills to assist Peter with an intramuscular injection of penicillin during my first week of clinic orientation. Never having treated a black man before made me nervous. My hand trembled as I plunged for the mark in his left upper buttock. The needle bounced back as if trying to penetrate a block of wood. The patient and I both jumped with surprise. My fingertips examined the missed target to discover a strong muscular buttock with his skin exceedingly tough, probably with exposure to harsh living conditions. But those alone couldn't explain my grave error. I looked further for a cause and carefully examined the needle that didn't penetrate his skin. The beveled tip was bent up. When I discussed this with Peter, I found that the reusable needles must be sharpened on a sharpening stone and the burrs removed, a task normally managed by central supply back home. I took great care to assure the needles were sharpened and filed as needed before sterilization. Never did I have a needle bounce back at me again.

While in the clinic that morning, the head midwife, Bendu, came to introduce herself. Standing barely five feet tall, her thin frame, nevertheless, emanated strength and confidence. Speaking only Gio, Peter translated as she explained her role in the community regarding midwifery—she was mentor to all the local indigenous midwives. My educator role was not to be present at births, but to help educate them on safer birthing practices, even down to the basics of hand washing. I needed and wanted to learn more. Bendu agreed with my request to observe her perform a country delivery. I could only hope and wait.

Even though the Zorgowee clinic was merely a Liberian house with minimal first-aid supplies, a few medications, two employees and a community head midwife, I remained hopeful that with my knowledge and gumption I could make a difference and help the people. "The toughest job you'll ever love"—that catchy phrase now had a meaning.

The Fishbowl

Two weeks after my homestay with Jacob and his family, I returned to Monrovia for my swearing-in ceremony with my seventeen other colleagues. I survived all the Peace Corps requirements: the Virgin Islands training, in-country orientation, and my village homestay. On May 30, 1971, I was sworn in as an official Peace Corps Volunteer. A week later, I arrived back in Zorgowee to begin my work. I passed the familiar route to my home: over the Yar River Bridge, by the Go Tree, the Lebanese store, and the Mandingo merchants. As I was dropped off in front of my house, I received an unexpected welcome when about twelve shoeless, shirtless young boys surrounded me. The two older ones immediately grabbed my two oversized green duffle bags weighing about forty-five pounds each. A single bag easily weighed more than each boy and they struggled with their load. After placing them on the living room floor, they scurried back outside to join the masses.

I began to unpack my Western possessions I'd methodically purchased in Nebraska some weeks earlier. I placed the two blank diaries Doug gave me on my bedside stand. On these crisp white pages, I planned to carefully chronicle my life in Africa. My Olympus SLR and Fuji movie cameras that would capture my adventures, went into my chest-of-drawers. I found a special place in the corner of my bedroom for my rubber boots, rain hat, jacket, and umbrella. It rains a lot in Africa, you know.

Whatever room I entered, the children outside my house moved from window to window. Three to five black faces with big eyes were plastered against the screens. I endured the chatter, laughter, giggles, sometimes pushing and shoving so small ones could get a better view of me, the new white woman in town. Did I stare at the first black boy I ever saw in Omaha? Probably not much different, I'm ashamed to say.

When nighttime fell, no one called the children home. Tired and hungry faces vanished and fresh new faces arrived. The chattering in dialect and giggles were constant background noise. In the dark moonless night, my sole Aladdin's lamp reflected off the whites of their eyes and their pearly teeth. Thank God for the shutters I could close at night to sleep. If I wondered about being *alone* in this remote village, I needed to think again. I was *never* alone. My pen and my diary became my best friends as I documented my experiences. That night I lay in bed creating my future dreams while the excitement of my first day as a volunteer in my new home imprinted in my memory, and the sound of distant drums lulled me to sleep.

The following morning, I arose with vigor. But once I opened my shutters, many children still waited outside my windows. That day I found far fewer faces plastered against my screens. Some parents shooed them away, but it took nearly four weeks before my newness wore off.

My house sat directly in the heart of the village, adjacent to the prominent path from which all villagers walked going from the main road to the bush to access small outlying villages and farms. I need not venture far from my house to have an understanding and awareness of my surroundings. I could experience everything right from my windows and doors. To the right of my house were many huts and the main road. To my left was Jacob's house and then the clinic followed by the path to the bush. Daily, groups of several women walked to their farms in the morning, each carrying babies or small children strapped to their backs. A yard of fabric, folded in a special way, secured their human cargo with another secured around the woman's waist as a skirt. Those women without babies were often bare-breasted—a custom more common upcountry. When the women returned in the evening, a load of firewood, a basin of rice, or a bucket of water balanced on their heads. Those loads often weighed up to twenty-five pounds, not to mention a child strapped to her back who could weigh as much. Men ventured to the bush with a machete, or cutlass, and returned with a large bunch of palm nuts balanced on their heads. Their hardworking character reminded me of our Nebraska farm. However, *all* their work was done by hand.

Six young boys were regulars outside my front door and a constant source of amusement. Their ingenuity astonished me as they created something out of what we called "garbage" back home. Their poverty never limited their creativity or impulse to play. Dad would have marveled at their inventiveness as he was a master at "making something out of nothing." "Waste not, want not," Dad often said. He created my playhouse out of a discarded broken pig feeder. He hauled it out to the west edge of the farm with his tractor, turned it upside down, cut out windows and a door. I played in it for years. These children, too, found a purpose for discarded items. An empty tin can, a broken bicycle rim, a stick, a used rubber tire all were made into toys. They used the bicycle spokes attached to tin cans to make all kinds of contraptions like cars and trucks. A discarded rubber tire, powered by a running boy with a stick, rolled through the village followed by a gaggle of laughing, giggling children. Maybe we lived on a different continent separated by the Atlantic Ocean, but in the heart of children, albeit in Nebraska or a village in Africa, we were much alike; only the toys were different.

These boys displayed all sorts of expert engineering skills when they stripped the outside of a weed stalk down to its dried fibrous center leaving a material like a Styrofoam rod about the size of a large pencil. Cut to the proper length, the rod was connected with small stalk splinters to construct the most elaborate miniature trucks and cars one could ever imagine. One vehicle functioned with hinged doors, rotating wheels, and was fully loaded on the inside with seats and a steering wheel. Most likely these African *Tinker Toys* were created way before our U.S. invention. One car, about twelve-by-five-by-six inches secured to a long stick, was proudly steered around the village by a young child. So impressed, I purchased it for 25¢ to bring back home. Those six little boys, all barefooted with shorts and shirts, posed proudly by their wonderful creations as I captured them on film.

Something new and different occurred regularly without notice. On my second day while finishing my breakfast of bread and instant Nescafé, I heard a band of people laughing and jeering outside my house. From my front door I observed a group of about twenty men, women, and children moving in unison and stirring a plume of dust. As I approached the disturbance, there in the center of this human mass, a man hobbled wearing only his under garment. Streaks of blood from his legs and torso cut multiple paths through his sweaty dust-laden body. His hands were tied behind his back with rope and his feet were shackled with iron anklets secured in the center with a chain resembling something left over from the slave trade. A guard prodded him with a long stick as the man shuffled past my front door. The spectators stoned and beat him with sticks, chiming in with heckling and laughter. My neighbor explained this to be a type of punishment for criminals or thieves called rogues. As I watched the villagers' gleeful participation, the punishment seemed more like entertainment.

I soon learned how justice was carried out in this remote village. The victim of a crime reported it to one of the two clan chiefs, Chief Manuel or Chief Ahmadou, who, with the tribunal of elders, then located the perpetrator and lay judgement. Most crimes were of either adultery or theft. Some wrongdoers were fined; those who could not pay, succumbed to the public beating and stoning. The duration of the physical punishment depended upon the crime or when the tribunal believed the reprimand was sufficient. Surely, shame and embarrassment were effective tools to keep order as this man would eventually return to his home. My neighbor said the rogue escaped from his crude windowless jail cell and was mocked and stoned for further punishment.

I only witnessed a public beating one other time during my first few weeks in Zorgowee. A woman, who committed adultery, was paraded through the village in her panties with only a small wrap around her waist. The villagers, including the adulteress's mother, mocked and stoned her. I never questioned the right or wrong of that dreadful custom, but I fully understood the power of shame. My mom impressed upon me long ago, "Don't bring out our dirty laundry for everyone else to see." In Morgan, you keep private family matters private, if you can. In Zorgowee anyone's life was everyone's business.

My life was in a fishbowl—from my window I could see all the activities and, of course, they could see me. The village of Zorgowee and all it encompassed became my entertainment for the next two years. Back on the farm, the arrival of our black and white TV unlocked our front door and the world came in. Now, I could open my front door, but this time, the world was at my doorstep; I was on the continent of Africa.

My African Family

With everything foreign to me, I needed to master navigating my village, its surroundings, and daily life in general. I needed a guide. After meeting Jacob's family during my first trip to Zorgowee, he introduced me to Martha, my Liberian English and Gio tutor. Young, gregarious and huggable, Martha warmed my heart with her curious eyes and prominent mouth. Her buck-toothed smile seemed to cover her entire face. I found her smart, a little frisky, and the best dressed Gio woman in the village. She wore the most beautiful lappas, the two yards of African fabric wrapped as a skirt. A matching tailored top completed one of her many fine outfits. I never once saw her bare head without a fabulous head tie of one full yard of fabric. The better dressed the woman, the larger the head tie.

At about twenty years old, with only a fourth grade education and a fair understanding of the English language, Martha helped me develop a good command of Liberian English, and it didn't take long to acquire key phrases and intonations. Short sentences were more sing-song in nature. My favorite phrase was, "I hold yur foot, ya," meaning, I beg you. "I'm coming to go, ya," is to say I'm leaving. "I say, you looking fine-o," indicates you're looking great. Another common one was, "I go walk about," meaning I'm going for a stroll. "No my, ya," equals never mind or sorry. This "lappa is dear-o," translates as the cloth is expensive. "She got belly-o," means she is pregnant. Adding "o" or "ya" to the end of a phrase gave it special emphasis, and I could always add them to any sentence and it would fit in perfectly as Liberian English.

Familiar English words took on new meanings. "Runny belly" equals diarrhea and "dry" is their word for being too thin from illness. "Torch" means flashlight. "Bock, bock" simulates a knock on a wooden door that doesn't exist in a thatched hut or used to let people know you are entering their space. Words like "vex" and "zoot" are certainly in our dictionary but not commonly used as in Liberia. "Zooting" applied to men or women wearing truly fine clothing.

Being a visual learner, I struggled with the unwritten Gio dialect. We plugged away weekly, nonetheless, with minimal success. Together we worked on a few key Gio phrases. I could say "Hello," "How are you?" "I'm fine," "Where are you going?" "I'm going to walk about," and "Thank you." I wrote them down phonetically for my reference: *Babua, aahoo, co mama, dimasaduo, igomey, a go goumpia, iswoudou.* The villagers loved when I spoke Gio more than anything else.

Beyond her language tutoring, Martha imparted some of the most valuable aspects of the Gio culture: their traditional customs and practices. There were several tricks and clicks I rehearsed to become proficient. I sucked my teeth to show disgust or distain. A handshake in Liberia is mandatory with every meeting. I never witnessed a nonoccurrence. The Liberian handshake provided a unique challenge when the middle fingers of two people met resistance when exiting a traditional handshake to create a "snap-click." It took me a good week to master the technique. To add deep respect, one must bow slightly while grasping the forearm with the free hand during a Liberian handshake. To the contrary, when the middle finger of the shook hand caressed the palm of the other person, it indicated a sexual connotation. I received this gesture several times from Liberian men in sexual pursuit and quickly withdrew my hand in disgust.

After a few weeks, I integrated many of these customs and gestures. Salutations often dragged on for minutes as each person greeted another. Before conducting business or mere socialization, one must ask about the welfare of their mother, father, brother, sister, cousin, children, aunt, uncle, or anyone else of importance. Care must be taken to never rush or skip this custom, otherwise a grave insult occurred. I made sure to complete all my greetings with respect.

Martha guided my understanding of marriage and relationships in the village life. But none so much as when she informed me, after our second lesson, that she was Jacob's mistress. Polygamy, accompanied by a mistress on the side, was commonplace for many men in Liberia. I wondered why Martha was not married and only a mistress.

By our third meeting, we both became emboldened to talk about personal things. Martha asked, "Miss Sue, why you not married-o?"

"Well," I stammered, "I wanted to first come to Africa to help people, like the people in Zorgowee."

Her contorted face gave away her confusion about my statement. "You have babies?"

"No, not yet."

"Me too-o. I been with Jacob for two year now and no belly."

"Is that why he not marry you?"

"Maybe. Having belly and babies is good for family. I think me not so good for family." She lowered her eyes.

I wasn't sure how to respond, except to say, "Maybe you will one day-o." It became apparent that a woman's infertility often led to her mistress status.

Over time, Martha became one of the women in Zorgowee with whom I could share my deepest thoughts, maybe because we were the same age, and like me, unmarried and childless. I told her about my letters from Doug and how I missed him. She pulled me through so many lonely times in my first weeks in Zorgowee. But when I told her we hoped to marry upon my return she gleefully queried, "You will marry you man?"

"Yes, I will. He gave me this ring as a promise," pointing to my pearl ring I wore every day. With that comment, all seemed right in the world for Martha and she could rest knowing I would have a man in my life.

To my knowledge, I was the only volunteer in our area who didn't hire a houseboy or house girl for *most* of my domestic tasks. It was ludicrous to pay for chores I could do myself such as cooking, housekeeping, cleaning fresh-killed chickens, just to name a few. But one difficult, dangerous task, and one heavily discouraged by Peace Corps, was washing clothes in the contaminated rivers. Living in the slow moving bodies of water were a host of diseases including schistosomiasis, and the Yar River in Zorgowee harbored this parasite. I abided by this rule because there were plenty of other tasks to keep me busy, so I hired Clara, the young sixteen-year-old girl who worked for the previous Peace Corps volunteer. I hated to think of her being exposed to a parasite, but she washed her clothes in the same river as we had no water wells.

Clara's sixth grade education gave her a good command of English. Physically strong with beautiful facial features and clear coffee-colored skin, she gracefully wore the common Gio trait of a slight part between her two front teeth. Quiet and unassuming, she entered my house at times and I didn't know she was there. I paid her $1 a week for doing my laundry including the laborious chore of ironing with a coal iron. Fetching the hot coals from a nearby fire, as well as trying not to scorch the fabric, took great skill that I showed little interest in mastering. Clara was a godsend and I couldn't have lived in Zorgowee without her help. She taught me how to cook chop and the ins and outs of the shopping in the local outdoor market. Clara taught me how to bargain and barter to stretch my $40 monthly Peace Corps allowance.

It was unusual for a girl of Clara's age to not be in school, married, or pregnant by that time, as most other girls were. Financial support from the previous volunteer in addition to the income I gave her would help Clara pay for living expenses when she attended high school in a nearby town in the future. I took her under my wing hoping she could choose a life for herself rather than a predestined path of a teenager marrying a man with one or more wives.

Within a few days of settling into my house another woman became a frequent visitor. Rita was about my age, single and without children. More educated than Martha or Clara, maybe to the eighth grade, she frequented nearby larger towns for days at a time, visiting her many lovers. She often spoke about her desire to join the Liberian Army. Unlike Martha, I rarely saw Rita dressed in Liberian lappas and head ties except for traditional holidays. She favored the Western clothing of pants or a short skirt and top. She never brushed her teeth with the end of a green twig like Martha or Clara, which she thought of as "too country." Rita used a store-bought toothbrush. Ironically, we had something else in common. She longed for the American lifestyle with no wish to be a village wife. I sought the continent of Africa with no desire to be a farmer's wife. Our dreams and desires kept us entertained, and I appreciated her willingness to spend time with me as we shared our deepest thoughts and feelings.

Martha, Clara, and Rita became a critical link in my understanding of the Zorgowee culture. We began to accept and embrace each other like best friends and family—my African family.

Sami, My Rock

One place was indispensable to all who lived in Zorgowee—Sami's Lebanese store. Sami was an Arabic man from Lebanon whose 100-pound, 5'6" frail frame made him look older than his thirty-seven years. His handsome Middle Eastern features of brown skin and black curly hair were highlighted by his kind gentle manner. He warmly welcomed me and his broad smile made me feel instantly at home.

Sami's store, only the size of a small two-car garage with double outward swinging doors, was much smaller than the ones I remembered in Monrovia. Without electricity or windows, even at high noon on a sunny day, its interior remained dark and dank. Sami explained that store owners avoided windows to prevent break-ins—"rogueing" as the locals called it. He scanned the shelves with his torch to show me his stock of nonperishable items: African fabric by the yard, sewing thread, razor blades, batteries, rubbing alcohol, soda, beer, canned goods, including fifty-five-gallon barrels of kerosene and gasoline sold by the bottle or gallon. He also sold sugar, flour, salt, and rice. Sami was the only person in the village to have a generator to produce electricity, and he turned it on a couple hours a day to chill his fridge to sell cold Coca Cola, Fanta, and Liberian Club Beer. The villagers relied heavily on Sami's store for these items. Additionally, he helped the local economy by selling his goods wholesale to the local Mandingo merchants, who in turn sold those items in their small shops or tables outside their homes when Sami's store was closed on evenings and weekends. Items such as bouillon cubes, salt, sugar, or tomato paste provided a small profit to the Mandingo people, who were not able to own land in Liberia due to their immigrant status. Sami had a big heart when it came to giving credit to those merchants when they could not front the cash. He was admired and respected by the entire village.

He began to invite me over for supper and taught me how to make delicious Lebanese specialties like hummus, baba ganoush, and traditional meat stews. I welcomed the diversion from the daily Liberian chop and rice. Later he invited me on his Sunday pigeon hunting expeditions in his 1966 Chevrolet pickup truck. I surprised Sami when he learned of my gun handling skills and I bagged a few pigeons with his shotgun on occasion. His houseboy handily cleaned those small birds for a nice meal.

I reciprocated his kindness with home-cooked American meals. My attempts to fatten him failed miserably as he seemed to lose even more weight while I lived there. For his birthday I made him a chocolate cake with candles and presented him with a hand-painted sign for his store: "Sami's Store." He thanked me profusely as if he rarely had such kindness bestowed on him.

Sami had a beautiful Liberian mistress, Nada. He had no intention to marry her because he hoped to return to Lebanon and seek a wife there one day. Nada, like Martha, dressed fine in her lappas and head ties. I started to notice a commonality about mistresses having a better life, working less, and being better cared for than traditional wives. Nada was one of the few mistresses to be fertile. She and Sami had a baby girl before I arrived, and their daughter was the most beautiful child I'd ever seen. Eleham's milk chocolate skin, loose curly black locks, and a quiet gentle demeanor mirrored her father. I rarely saw Nada and Sami together as a couple. They didn't live in the same home, and he always came to my house without Nada even though I invited her. I wondered if she felt their relationship was one of convenience or if she loved him, but I never asked.

Weeks passed and Sami and I became good friends. As the only two non-Africans in the village, we were welcomed by the locals and assimilated into the culture as best we could. He became my rock and confidant as unlikely as it may have seemed. Sami frequently told me about his war-torn homeland, of the bombings in Beirut, and loss of home and family. With little opportunity for young men in Lebanon, the turmoil compelled many Lebanese to become entrepreneurs throughout Africa. Only then did I begin to understand the reason for so many Lebanese in Liberia. Despite all that, he still planned to return one day. I shared with him my stories about Doug and the farm. Although Sami and I couldn't fully relate to each other's stories, we both understood our longing for family and loved ones.

Let the Clinics Begin

Due to the lack of proper care and treatment, most of the illnesses and deaths in the Zor Clan *could* be prevented. What this village needed was a doctor, nurse, nutritionist, health educator, and a fully equipped clinic...not just me, a twenty-year-old Peace Corps volunteer, the first ever assigned to this remote site. Sterile gloves or sophisticated fetal monitoring equipment like a Doppler or ultrasound were nonexistent. Therefore, we relied on education as our main tool. I knew most adults never reached the age of fifty and over half of the children died before the age of five, but I remained optimistic, hoping to make a difference in this remote clinic.

So with that, I eagerly introduced the free Antenatal and Well-baby clinics. Communicating to the villagers about our services for pregnant women and mothers with babies and children was the key to success. The women would receive nutritional education about maintaining a healthy pregnancy, and the children would be immunized for diphtheria, pertussis, and tetanus (DPT). Peter held general clinic on Mondays, Wednesdays, and Fridays while we established the Antenatal clinic on Tuesdays and the Well-baby clinic on Thursdays from 8 a.m. to noon. No need for afternoon clinics because most of the villagers worked tilling the fields, carrying water and firewood from noon till dusk. Women with babies tied to their backs or others up to nine months pregnant toiled alongside everyone else.

CARE donated vegetable oil, powdered milk, and flour to our clinic. Cooperative American Relief Everywhere was a not-for-profit organization started during World War II to provide humanitarian relief food packages to the war survivors in Europe, which later became known as "CARE packages." After the war they continued their food relief assistance but expanded their efforts to include self-help programs to needy countries around the world. Our Peace Corps Health Education Program, in conjunction with the Liberian Ministry of Health, chose to use the food supplements in two ways: we portioned the donations to those who came to our Antenatal and Well-baby clinics and performed food demonstrations as healthy examples of their use.

Shortly after my arrival, the Ministry of Health supplied our clinic its first ever stock of DPT vaccine. We now had two lures to encourage attendance—free food *and* vaccines. Perhaps these were like the grocery store gimmicks that snagged my mother's attention every week in Kanton. She always went to the store that gave her S&H green stamps that she could later cash in for a place setting or fry pan. There were major differences however—promotions of vaccines, milk, oil, and flour could prevent someone from getting sick or dying.

Once Peter and I arranged the schedule, the day and evening before each clinic, we walked through the village to spread the word about my new role and what services we offered. Peter's white nurse's jacket and my blue pin-striped uniform designated the importance of our calls. Our visits were welcomed and were crucial in my understanding of family life. Peter confirmed my optimism when he said, "The people talking all over bout our clinic. I think it will be good-o."

"Yes, I'm sure it will," I said. Though I was hopeful, I also had many misgivings. Other parts of Liberia provided trained midwives or doctors and equipment in their clinics to perform physical examinations to determine gestation or delivery progression. Zorgowee had none. Conducting antenatal physical assessments and exams were not requirements for my Health Education Group. Peter was never trained to do these. Had he possessed these skills they would not have been used because males were never allowed to be present during a birth or to perform antenatal examinations in the Zor Clan.

My LPN training gave me a rudimentary knowledge of obstetrics and minimal experience of external abdominal examinations to determine gestation. Clearly, I needed to develop those skills to assist in the physical assessments. When our vaccines arrived, we were also given a fetoscope, a type of listening device. About eight inches long with a metal trumpet-shaped hollow horn on each end, the fetal heart tones were conducted through this device when the wide end was placed against the mother's belly and the smaller end placed to one's ear. Unfamiliar with this device, I practiced the use of the fetoscope. It aided significantly in our assessments.

We documented each woman's name, gestation, blood pressure, temperature, and other pertinent information. I asked our first patient, Matta, to lie on our exam table, a higher version of a kitchen table. No cushion, no crinkly exam paper, no stirrups, no gloves, just good hand-washing technique in a basin with lye soap and water drawn from a bucket—that was all we had. My hands shook with nervousness as I placed them on her taut round abdomen. She said, "I make belly three times-o." To palpate her abdomen, I ran my fingers from the tip of her pubic bone to the top of the fundus (the uterus). I located those two points on her abdomen and then measured a two finger-width spread for each month. Without diagnostic tools, my measurements were only an estimate. She was about seven months pregnant. Before I listened with the fetoscope, I explained the use of the contraption as not to alarm Matta and placed it to my ear and auscultated all areas of her pregnant belly. Once the fetoscope rested closest to the fetus' heart, I heard it most prominent over the right lower side at about 144 beats per minute, a normal fetal heart rate. Matta and I were both elated as I shared the news. She gave me a big smile in return and said, "Thank you, ya," at least five times.

My second patient was Younga, Jacob's wife. Her exam revealed this to be her first pregnancy at six months and uneventful thus far. The third woman, Ester, in her fourth month with her fifth pregnancy had only two living children.

Peter translated her message, "She want dis baby to live-o."

"Peter and I will do all we can do to help you, ya," I told her via Peter.

"One baby die before one year old and her last baby die the day he born," Peter interpreted.

I took her hand, "I am so so glad you are here-o. Come every month and we will teach you good good things to help yur belly."

Peter interpreted in Gio while I taught the principles of cleanliness, good hand-washing, and eating plenty of greens, meat, chicken, eggs, and peanuts to make their bodies strong. I also gave them each a cup of oil, flour, and powdered milk. I explained ways to integrate this into their diet to add nutrition. All women nodded and gave me the typical respectful Liberian handshake. I, in turn, bowed with respect.

Over time I practiced and eventually my auscultation skills greatly improved. Soon I could easily detect the fetal heart tone and rate: differentiated between the mothers' at about 60-80 and the fetus' around 120 to 160 beats per minute. However, with only the touch of my hands on the abdomen, distinguishing between the fetus' head, butt, and extremities was challenging. With body fat on Liberian women being nearly nonexistent, palpating their abdomen was like feeling body parts through a ballooned membrane. In time, I became proficient and confident in detecting the full fetal outline.

I suspected many challenges ahead, but I saw a dim light at the end of the tunnel, and I announced to myself, "Let the clinics begin!"

One Step at a Time

In contrast to the modest beginnings of the Antenatal clinic, the Well-baby clinic was a challenge from the start, as I struggled against Liberia's infant mortality rate. By the fifth Well-baby clinic, I walked in at 8 a.m. to find the waiting room filled with chaos. At least ten sick, crying, squirming children were held by their stressed mothers. One baby vomited in the corner while another mother squatted her child outside the back door with diarrhea. Another child perspired with a high fever fanned by his mother to cool his hot body. Peter and

Duo, both overwhelmed, ran from one end of the clinic to the other trying to create order and treat the patients. According to Peter, a new gastrointestinal bug hit the community. My idyllic vision of teaching all the knowledge I possessed to attentive mothers in a calm clinic education room vanished at that moment.

Clearly, the name Well-baby clinic was a total farce. Soon I became embarrassed by my ignorance. Before my arrival, families never brought children to the clinic when they were *well*, so this must have been a confusing concept for them to understand. Additionally, villagers never experienced or understood preventive vaccinations before. I knew DPT vaccines could *not* be given to the babies in the presence of illness. In the five weeks we carried the DPT vaccine, we never gave even one immunization. I couldn't worry about vaccinations to keep them well—they first needed to *be* well. "Educate, remember, I'm not here as a nurse." I lectured myself. "You have a captive audience, so work with it."

I reflected on the information I gathered from my home visits with Peter those first weeks, and one home visit stuck in my mind. We entered a family's home where we found a thin ill one-year-old boy with his pregnant mother and his father, Jason.

Jason told us, "He be sick many day o. He not eat and only runny belly. He getting so so dry-o. We mus feed him every day."

The father picked up the squirming child, swaddled him tightly in a blanket to contain his flailing arms and legs, leaving only his head exposed. Over his lap, Jason lay the boy on his back, tilting the child's head downward. The father then took a clump of cooled cooked rice, formed a ball in his hand and proceeded to push the wad of starch down the wailing child's mouth. The child choked and coughed.

Startled, I leaned back against the wall. I tugged on Peter's arm and momentarily forgot all my Liberian English and said, "Please ask him to stop and have him bring the boy to the clinic tomorrow. We can help him."

Peter explained in Liberian English. He also described the danger of choking and aspiration pneumonia in a way the mother and father could understand.

When we left, Peter explained this was a long-time tradition in the Gio culture. He concluded that choking, aspiration, or death had occurred in Zorgowee from this practice. He tried to teach families against the custom, but with little understanding of illness they assumed only food would cure the ailment.

That afternoon I went home and invented the "Stuffing Baby." From my dad, the inventor and master of "creating something out of nothing" and from my maternal artistic talents, I combined those skills to create my classroom materials. With a small cardboard box from Sami's store, I draped it with a child's tank-top, inserted a cardboard head at the top with an open mouth, and inserted cardboard arms and legs in their appropriate spots.

The next morning, Jason brought his child to the Well-baby clinic. Along with several other mothers and their children gathering in the waiting room for medical treatment, my captive audience learned about the "Stuffing Baby." This seemed only logical as my audience all came in with sick children. For a child unable to take solid foods I taught them how to boil drinking water, cool it, and then make a saline-sugar solution to help combat dehydration. With Duo interpreting, I demonstrated and explained the stuffing practice and how force-feeding can lead to coughing, choking, and death. Then I modeled how to feed properly. Chatter arose among the parents.

Duo informed me, "Tis how it always done, you mus push da food down-o."

I shook my head and asked him to interpret as I demonstrated with a small child in the clinic, "Sit the child up like so and have the child take small, small with a spoon. Sugar-salt water is good-o. Bring them to clinic and we can help them." Uncertain how many really understood, all I could do was try. The stuffing tradition certainly preceded me and I knew I could only make baby steps.

After a week, Jason's son greatly improved and began eating normally again. Maybe they learned much more than I had expected.

Even though malaria was the next most frequent childhood illness in our clinic, most villagers were unaware of the link between the disease and the anopheles mosquito. There were three defenses against this nighttime predator: buy mosquito coils that needed to be burned nightly to ward off the insect, buy mosquito nets, or take the weekly medication of chloroquine. All of these were either too costly or unavailable for an average family of ten earning about 50¢ a day. The few malaria tablets we had at our clinic were for curative treatment only—requiring just a few pills—not for preventive maintenance. We were not supplied the quantities for the entire population, which required a weekly dose.

This left me with one tool—inexpensive prevention—teach them the link between malaria, the mosquito, and how they breed in stagnant water. I constructed a "Mosquito Chart," a felt board made from a baby blanket bought at Sami's store that I secured over a stiff cardboard backing. I then sketched, cut out, and colored images of a shovel, a stagnant body of water, an old rubber tire, a mosquito, and an ill child—all easily recognized by the mothers. The images were backed with tape that stuck to the blanket like a felt board to illustrate the teaching. Moving the images on the felt board told the story of malarial prevention. With Duo interpreting, I demonstrated how mosquitos breed in stagnant water, followed by the importance of discarding rubber tires that trapped water, and filling stagnant water holes around the villages. Mothers reacted, talked among themselves, and elicited more questions. I was pleased with their response.

Duo interpreted to me, "Miss Sue, da mothers say dey will do it-o."

In the following weeks I toured the village, monitored success, and taught ways to eliminate sources of stagnant water. Setting a good example, I secured screening material atop each of my rain barrels to prevent mosquito breeding. I saw many improvements throughout the village in those first weeks.

The information I gained from performing home visits provided a firsthand account of how families lived and what they ate. This was crucial for my training. Generally, all women breastfed, but I found one woman who used the Western approach of bottle-feeding her baby. When I inspected the baby bottle during a home visit, larvae squirmed at the bottom. The mother didn't understand the dangers so I worked with her to link this practice with the illness of her infant. If the mother could maintain adequate nutrition, breastfeeding an infant was also more cost-effective than bottle feeding. After a brief lesson and a few home visits, she returned to breastfeeding, reinforcing the need for others to continue to follow their traditional practice.

With birth control non-existent and multiple pregnancies of no concern to the mothers, due to the high mortality rate of infants, I discovered another reason to encourage breastfeeding. By default, the women learned breastfeeding their children as long as possible could delay another pregnancy. Undoubtedly, they didn't know the science behind the practice, but through trial and error, pure necessity and convenience, breastfeeding was the most effective contraceptive they had.

Our Well-baby attendance gradually grew over the early months. Not all present were without illness, of course, but I seized the opportunity to educate. On September 28, 1971, only four months after my arrival, I wrote in my diary: "Had the most spectacular of all clinics. Thirty-six babies and 80 percent were well; therefore, twenty-eight were vaccinated." All in one day.

We required the children to return healthy to the clinic— three times, a month apart—for their series of DPT shots, by far our biggest challenge. Similarly, I asked the pregnant women to return monthly for their checkups. Putting food on the table was a mother's daily priority, not worrying about a follow-up DPT injection for her child or have her belly checked. Their understanding of time, day, or date was not dictated by clock or calendar, but rather sunrise, sunset, rainy or dry season, and their farming needs. To ensure their attendance for follow-up vaccinations or antenatal visits, I often visited up to twenty-five homes the night before the clinic. I didn't mind because I could meet the entire family and visually identify newly pregnant women or unvaccinated children.

Our clinic jumped into the modern era in my fourth month when we received a kerosene refrigerator from the Liberian Ministry of Health. At last we could store supplies of DPT vaccine in larger quantities for the children. Before our refrigerator, any leftover vials reconstituted for the day needed to be discarded. Now we could save even more lives with more doses to prevent diphtheria, pertussis, and tetanus.

My joy only lasted a few days. When I returned from a weekend visiting Peace Corps friends, I was disgusted to find Peter had taken our clinic refrigerator to his house for personal use. That day, I lost my temper. I yelled at him for at least twenty minutes insisting he return it immediately. Sheepishly, he hauled it back the following day. Angry beyond measure, I now added "monitoring Peter" to my to-do list.

Despite those setbacks, the Antenatal clinic also grew steadily, often with ten to fifteen women in attendance. Ester delivered a healthy baby girl, and three months after Younga's first clinic visit she delivered at home with a local midwife. I made a home visit to her and her healthy baby boy and found Glyee and Sawee, Jacob's other wives, in the household providing her plenty of support and guidance. Younga enjoyed my enthusiasm with her newborn and demonstrated how to secure him on my back by tying a lappa around my torso. Scared at first, I paraded gingerly around the house as I learned to trust the mere fold of the cloth to safeguard my delicate cargo. I often wondered how the women worked in the fields, chopped wood, and carried pails of water on their heads with a baby on their back.

"Oops," I exclaimed, as a warm trickle of baby urine dribbled down my back.

Younga grabbed the little guy from me to cradle him in her arms while he finished urinating outside. Diapers did not exist in Zorgowee. Releasing the child from their backside crib periodically and holding him or her in the strategic position for both urination and defecation demonstrated a wonderful lesson in potty-training—African style.

Over time, some villagers coming to the clinic called me the "white-woman doctor." I didn't have the credentials nor experience to hold such a title but soon realized why Peter was given the clout he had. Eighty-five percent of the population had no education. Those who *did* were given power.

Bartering, Bickering, and Bush Taxis

Beef was nonexistent in Zorgowee; there was neither a butcher nor a reliable meat source, and I had to find a way to acquire protein. A few goats were raised nearby but were often carried to the larger market in the next town to fetch more money. I could locate fresh roasted ground pea and bony, a salt-dried sardine-type fish, but my Midwestern stomach yearned for meat. In the whole village only Sami and I had refrigeration for food, so for the remainder of the population, fresh meat or fish must be killed and eaten on the same day. In addition, meat was the most expensive food and a delicacy for Liberians.

Luckily my house sat on the main thoroughfare at the edge of my village, and on this route I was able to secure fresh meat being carried by the locals. The telltale sign of an antelope hoof or live bound chickens protruding from an enameled basin balanced on a villager's head were indications of protein being taken to the roadside to sell. The African antelope, known as the dik dik, is much smaller than an American deer and often hunted with a snare trap, while chickens were raised domestically in villages accessible only by foot.

"I say, come ya, I want to buy da meat-o." I yelled from my front door to catch their attention. I purchased the hind quarter of dik dik for $1.25. Grateful for my butchering skills learned on the farm, I threw the dik dik on the kitchen counter, and with a sharp knife removed the hide and de-boned the leg. I made stew for the day and froze the rest for later.

A fresh chicken sold for $1.00. I had never decapitated a chicken before, so I asked a neighbor boy to do it. As a kid on the farm I held many thankless chicken-duty jobs: gathering eggs in the dust-filled chicken coop; washing chicken shit off the eggs we sold for 19¢ a dozen; fending off attacks from the

big cock in the yard who jumped me with his dewclaws pointing toward my face; or picking pin feathers from the chicken
carcass and degutting them. Here in Zorgowee, with my be-
headed carcass in hand, I happily plucked, degutted and cut it
up into recognizable pieces, glad to have fresh protein for my
Liberian chop.

The locals were eager to share their seasonal delicacies. I
remained uncertain about sampling them, though I tried everything once. Well, almost everything. After the first few
seasonal rains, insects came out of nowhere. The Liberian
termites, in their breeding frenzy, swarmed the evening skies,
later to devour any tasty wood they could sink their chops into. But when nighttime came, the villagers prepared by
placing a lappa on the ground with a lantern in the center.
Masses of termites, attracted to the light, fell for easy collection on the awaiting cloth. Fried alive to a crispy nugget, they
became a wholesome protein. Although not awful in taste,
maybe like a carrot, the crunchy wings and legs in my mouth
turned my stomach.

Later in the season, when trees were felled to clear-cut
fields for farming, the hunt was on in the belly of the palm
trees for the palm weevil grub. A rare treat—rich with protein,
potassium, and calcium—the white, round plump grub measured about the size and length of my small finger. One day
Peter and Duo came to my house carrying a basketful of these
writhing disgusting critters. Peter demonstrated popping a live
one into his mouth all at once and swallowed quickly. "Don't
bite 'cause the insides will go across the room-o." He went on
to say, "Dey taste like coconut and da fried one taste like
meat-o." They both laughed when I refused to stomach a
squirming raw grub. I was certain they tasted like my dad's
fried calf brains.

Zorgowee's daily market, off the main road, consisted of
three to four tarps on the ground and a couple of wooden tables selling a handful of items: fresh greens, ground pea,
bananas, pineapples, onions, rice, Maggi cubes (bullion), and
tomato paste. No market could be without its staple of palm
oil. Villagers harvested palm nuts from the palm tree, cooked,
beat, and strained them to extract the orange oil, their main

source of cooking fat. In its raw form, palm oil was a strong pungent saturated fat that I soon became accustomed to. The strained pulp could be made into the most delicious palm butter soup, a favorite among volunteers. Eventually, no chop tasted good without hot Liberian pepper *and* palm oil.

Zorgowee's market and Sami's Lebanese store couldn't provide everything, so I traveled eight miles by public transport to Sanniquellie, a large town of about 5,000 people. There I found larger Lebanese stores with items such as pots, pans, plates, and other housewares. Sanniquellie boasted a Catholic Mission with a school, public schools up to high school, a hospital and clinic, and a daily outdoor market. Sixteen other Peace Corps volunteers lived and worked there and I looked forward to their camaraderie and Western socializing.

The Sanniquellie Saturday grand market found locals in their finest clothing and where they wanted to be seen. It was a spectacle to behold, a festival of sorts. Villagers, ironsmiths, weavers, potters, and craftsman of all types came from far and wide to sell their wares and produce: vegetables, rice, brass figures, handmade cutlasses, leather hides, mats, baskets, and clay pottery. Some vendors came from the neighboring Ivory Coast and Guinea borders to market items unique to their areas, such as tie-dyed fabric and woven baskets. I looked for my protein fix of the freshly slaughtered leathery beef from cattle who walked 200 miles from the north. Whack, whack! The butcher's forceful axe met the flesh and bone of the carcass hanging from a ceiling rafter of the market building. After what sounded like a massacre, he moved to a finer instrument, the cutlass. Before any food preparation, one carefully removed the shards of bone fragments.

Learning from the locals, I quickly gained the expertise of bartering and bickering, and became skilled at getting the best price. Rule of thumb: always offer half of what they ask. My most prized acquisition was a sixty-pound life-size bust of a Fulani woman from Mali carved of solid Mahogany. The price started at $75 and after walking away three times, including sleeping on it overnight, the Charlie (the name given to peddlers selling these artifacts) found me again and begged me to take it for $25. My Fulani woman landed in a lovely spot in my house in Zorgowee. In the end we both won—he made a sale and I got a good price.

Bigger purchases of shoes or clothing required a trip to Monrovia, one to two days by taxi or 170 miles away. But more frequently I shopped in an area the locals called LAMCO (Liberian/American Mining Company) in the town of Yekepa, a mine rich in iron ore deposits. From Zorgowee, on a good day, transport via two different taxis could often take over three hours. LAMCO employed a large Scandinavian contingent. Its grocery store was filled with the best imported cheeses, chocolates, and wine to please their palates. Peace Corps volunteers took advantage of this treasure when we traveled there at least once or twice a month to shop or catch a good movie. I purchased any Western cooking ingredient within my budget. With those options I became a known baker among my Peace Corps friends. In addition, LAMCO boasted a state-of-the-art hospital to meet the European standards of its employees. We also took advantage of their Olympic-size swimming pool every time we could.

I had only three options of transport in and out of my village: catching a ride with Sami in his Chevrolet pickup; a "bush taxi," often a simple Toyota Corolla; or a "money-bus," a Datsun or Toyota pickup. No taxi or money-bus drivers lived in Zorgowee, so I was at the mercy of transport passing from the north from a larger village near the Ivory Coast border, or those coming from the south from Sanniquellie. To catch a ride, I waited by the roadside, full of anticipation. When dust arose from the distance, I signaled the "slow down" hand gesture as the vehicle full of passengers screamed by like I wasn't even there. I sadly returned home one late afternoon after waiting the entire day without any vehicle passing by with an empty seat.

In the beginning, I was a novelty and often men gave me their spot in an available bush taxi or they allowed me to sit in the front seat instead of packing four in the back of the crammed vehicle. But as months passed, my princess image faded and I became one of the locals. Soon I was relegated to pushing and shoving like a commoner to secure a seat. Nonetheless, I happily shed my crown.

I preferred a bush taxi to a money-bus. The money-bus belied its name, except that it was all about the money. The "bus" was fitted with an open-sided canopy and a bench on each side of the bed for passengers. A rack on the top made room for extra produce or luggage. The more people in the vehicle, the more stops we'd have to make. Often the gas tank had only enough fuel to reach our destination, and no room for a spare tire—it only reduced space for potential payload. If we started in Zorgowee with a full money-bus, invariably there were one to three people who got off, partway to my destination, to hike to their small walk-in village. Then ten minutes later, we'd stop and pick up any other villagers waiting on the roadside at their make-believe taxi stand. The goal was always to have a full taxi. If it happened to be market day, the ride was prolonged even further with the loading and unloading of goats, chickens, gunny sacks of coffee, rice, cassava, ground pea, and firewood. But I shouldn't expect much for my eight-mile 25¢ ride.

The most memorable ride to Sanniquellie for Saturday market entailed an hour wait to get a bench seat in the back of the money-bus with five adults flanking each side. In between the benches, lying on the floor, were three gunny sacks of cassava, produce wrapped in four cloth bundles with four small children perched on top. On one side lay two motionless live chickens with their legs tied. I sat next to a woman who breastfed her newborn during the entire ride. More produce, luggage, and two live goats were strapped above us on the canopy rack. Our money-bus had two young helpers who rode open-air bronco-style on the rack to secure the load and help to calm the goats.

With four people in the front seat, fourteen of us in the back, two helpers on the canopy rack, we were twenty (twenty-one if you counted the newborn) heading to market in this Toyota money-bus. At 25¢ a pop, the driver made a killing with the paying passengers, not to mention an extra charge for payload. It was *all* about the money.

Oh yes...the goats. Halfway to Sanniquellie they decided to relieve themselves, providing an unexpected warm shower. An hour and a half later, traveling only eight miles, I dragged myself out of the Toyota bed to find my skin dredged in a film of red-laterite dust over a thin misting of goat urine. Give me a bush taxi any day.

Bonding

Even though three Peace Corps volunteers preceded me in my small village, I remained a novelty to many. Not only did my American accent amuse the villagers but also my Western dress. I wore short skirts, popular back home, or long pants that were never worn by the women in my village. But my skin color interested them the most. The women were particularly intrigued with my whiteness, while I was equally captivated by their blackness. Their skin, so beautiful, so clear and dark black, was much darker than the first black boy I saw in Omaha almost ten years earlier.

A few weeks into my life in Zorgowee, Martha and Rita came by for a visit. After we chatted a bit in Liberian English, they asked if they could touch my hair. Martha wanted to plait it into cornrows. I no longer used rollers or fussed with my locks. After a couple inches of growth since Nebraska, I often held it back with a rubber band. So, when they offered to coif my hair, I immediately undid my band and turned my chair. Martha combed and braided...combed and braided some more. Four hands caressed my shoulder-length brown hair and my scalp welcomed the gentle pulling and tugging. The silkiness of the strands would not hold the braids, and Martha redid several rows.

With some trepidation I asked, "Martha, could I touch your hair?" I yearned to feel the beautifully coiffed cornrows clinging close to her scalp. She eagerly agreed and my fingers rolled over a texture like that of a soft braided cotton rope. I smiled and cherished the closeness we felt.

But I suspected they were up to something when they spoke in Gio, so I couldn't understand. Finally, with their muffled laughter and shifty eyes, my suspicion grew.

Martha sheepishly said, "Miss Sue, we want to see yur breasts." Both giggled uncontrollably.

Upon my arrival, my initial shock at seeing bare-breasted women in public diminished as it became commonplace upcountry. Now a few weeks into my assignment, bare-breasted women were old news and I often didn't notice. Women's breasts in Liberia possessed a particular function: to feed their children. They breastfed upon demand while cooking, working in the fields, gathering firewood, riding in a taxi or anywhere else. I never witnessed any taboo or modesty about this part of a woman's body. The more babies a woman bore and breastfed, the droopier her breasts. But surprisingly, saggy mammary glands were not scorned, but revered as a sign of a fertile and respected woman.

I had mixed feelings about showing mine to Martha and Rita. I recalled the teasing I encountered in my childhood and how ashamed I had felt about my new developing buds. My Catholic upbringing taught me to believe breasts were off-limits and only to be seen by your husband. Now at age twenty, I had two African girlfriends asking to see mine. In the five seconds that I contemplated this momentous request, I weighed the pros and cons wondering what my family and God would think. Even with so much at stake, I said, "Yes."

"Ooh," "aah" and lots of talking in dialect, giggling, and hand-over-mouth gestures as I raised my shirt and unhooked my bra. Compared to their breasts they must have thought mine looked like two inverted white-enameled bowls each topped with a little pink button. As I stood there topless, surely their inquisitiveness was satisfied. But, no, now they wanted to touch them. And so...they did. After a few moments they seemed content and quickly departed saying their goodbyes. The giggling and laughter gradually faded as they frolicked through the village.

After my two African girlfriends left I clothed my naked torso and sat alone in my house reflecting on what had just happened. Although I abandoned my wish to join a convent at age eleven, the cloak of Catholicism followed me everywhere. In my self-imposed confessional that night I asked, "Would I go to hell for showing my breasts to anyone except my husband?" Somehow I knew God would not wrongly judge the Liberian women for adhering to their culture. For me, however, bare breasts were not a part of my upbringing. Though I believed I had sinned, I felt God's forgiveness.

Those first weeks and months in Zorgowee changed me forever. I began to think differently about being alone and my privacy, a mostly Western phenomenon. For privacy, we close our windows and doors, wear clothes to cover our bodies and build fences around our homes. That day my African girl-friends imparted a valuable lesson: I was no longer ashamed of or embarrassed by my body.

Loving-business

From the first week I arrived in my village, Liberian men came to my front door daily and often more than once a day asking the same question. First, so kindly, they introduced themselves. "My name is Moussa, Joseph, John," or whatever, followed immediately by, "I want to make loving-business." No flirting, no courting, no nothing, right to the brutal point. The telltale sexual handshake, often by educated Liberian men, was a precursor to the verbal query. Multiple sexual requests by the same person were not uncommon, because in Liberia, "No" meant "Maybe." Persistence was their virtue. If our Peace Corps training had alerted us to the loving-business pursuits, I do not recall it.

Village men made no distinctions. The man could be married or not, a local farmer, market vendor, town leader, or head of the clinic. Those of higher prestige waited longer to pop the question. For example, Peter—my clinic colleague—waited about three months before he asked me for a sexual favor. Since I had a daily working relationship with him, I told him I needed to think about it—like maybe the rest of my life.

After weeks of constant loving-business inquiries, I made up a story of my marriage, leaving my awaiting husband back in the States and flashing Doug's pearl ring. All to no avail. In fact, my antics made their conquest even more appealing. However, I never felt physically threatened. Harmless and sweet, they asked, but as far as I knew, Liberian men never forced or harmed a woman. All women in Liberia were subject to this treatment, including my Peace Corps peers.

A young schoolboy, about age sixteen, wrote me the most precious love letter, I put it away for safekeeping in case I wondered if I were ever loved.

Gowee Town
Oct. 3

Dear Miss Sue,
I want you to please note that I have had a burning desire of love for you from since I saw you two weeks ago for which I thought it wise to write you. Due to this fact, I could hardly sleep because some love is equivalent when a drum full of gas has been set on fire. Therefore, to be very precise, I wish to inform you that I definitely admire your entire out fit for which I ask you to become my love one. Hoping to hearing from you a reply praying to be favorable, I extend thanks in advance.

Sincerely yours,
Joseph

Only two men in Zorgowee never asked me for loving-business, Jacob and Sami. Jacob may have felt an obligation to Peace Corps to keep a professional landlord relationship. As frequently as Sami and I socialized, a romance could have developed, since we hung out together often for meals, parties, hunting, or trips to town. But he never once asked me for or alluded to sex, and for that I respected him greatly. Rumors were rampant in Zorgowee that we were doing loving-business, and I didn't care. Stories of others' loving business were often fabrication or just plain gossip; the main form of entertainment in my small village. Their speculation never fazed me.

A multitude of African and a few Western men were interested in me, but I declined. Some volunteers labeled me a cold prude. Even if I could locate birth control, I must uphold my virginity for Doug and my religion. And besides, I didn't want to shame my family with an accidental pregnancy.

However, Dr. Mattie, a Liberian doctor from LAMCO, harassed me from the first time we met. He had already asked me for sexual favors numerous times. One late afternoon he approached me on my turf when his fancy Toyota sedan pulled up outside my window. "Oh no! Not Mattie," I said, sucking my teeth in disgust.

Being courteous and polite, following Liberian protocol, I let him in. We gestured with the traditional Liberian handshake, but when his middle finger caressed my palm, I jerked it away. His blunt requests for loving-business in the past did not work, so this time he came bearing gifts: two dozen eggs, a frozen chicken, bacon, and a bottle of gin. Mattie was harmless. Maybe I could keep his gifts without giving something in return. Two can play this game, I thought. I refused to drink, while he proceeded to get inebriated. We sat on opposite sides of the table. Darkness fell and his loving-business pursuit continued.

"I know you love me too," he whimpered like a sick dog.

Fed up with his nonsensical begging, I said, "Mattie, you need to go now. It is getting late."

He reached over the table and caressed my arm and pleaded, "Miss Sue, I beg you ya, you are so beautiful."

"No!" I stated again and withdrew my arm.

"I know you...you know...you want me too," he slurred over his words. He stumbled to an upright position and lunged to my side of the table. I arose and moved quickly to the opposite side. The game of cat and mouse was on. I had no fear of his harmless drunken-self. Besides, my landlord, Jacob, lived right next door. He would come immediately if I called his name.

After three trips around the table, Dr. Mattie tired and slumped back into his chair. I declared, in no uncertain terms, "You must go now and take yur gin with you, ya."

I hoped he'd leave the eggs, chicken, and bacon, and he did. Off he drove into the night, kicking up the dust as he sped off in his fancy-ass sedan. Relieved but angry, I was tired of fighting off the men. "I hate African men. I hate Liberia."

I had much to learn about men, but understanding the dynamics of the African male took another trajectory. Just when I seemed to grasp the culture, I met a special dignitary from

Monrovia. That day the clan chief, Manuel, summoned me for the arrival of the diamond commissioner who planned a visit to Gorton. This small walk-in village, about a two-hour journey from Zorgowee, was the home of a well-known diamond mine operation in our region. Rare diamonds, up to two carats, had been discovered at this mine and were the main interest of the commissioner. He came periodically to collect his cache of these precious gems.

I reached the chief's house around 11:00 a.m., and an unfamiliar eruption of firearms acknowledged the diamond commissioner's arrival. A pair of four-wheel-drive Toyotas stirred up dust as they entered Zorgowee carrying eight gunslinging soldiers in Army fatigues. The village honored his arrival with braided palm fronds lining the edges of the main road. The chief set up a table with four chairs outside his house and motioned for me to sit. The chief sat to my left, Jacob to my right, and directly across was the commissioner. He was a slight man, wearing a military brimmed hat and green Army fatigues. Rarely did a woman attend such an event and I did not take the invitation lightly. The commissioner was of the Khran tribe and therefore we all spoke in Liberian English as the common language. After the Liberian greetings and introductions that went on for more than fifteen minutes, the chief's cook came from the kitchen with specially prepared chop—hot pepper goat soup with rice. Traditional custom often served the meal in a large enameled bowl and each person ate from the common vessel with their right hand. However, due to this upscale event, we were each given our own bowl and tablespoon.

Even though I was not the honored guest, they served me first with the most prestigious portion of hot spicy goat meat in a tomato-based broth poured over rice. I stiffened when my eyes focused on a stewed goat's head, complete with a jawbone, cartilage, and teeth neatly placed on the mound of rice as the pair of eyeballs stared at me from my bowl. My hunger quickly turned to nausea. The cracked skull allowed me the privilege to feast upon the brain, my dad's favorite. I had watched Liberians consume goat heads in the past, and even suck the jawbone, but I couldn't. I flaked off a couple of shreds of goat meat from the outer skull and mixed it with lots to rice to soften the blow of the flaming hot red Liberian pepper; and I ate *very, very* slowly.

The diamond commissioner became friendly and asked me about my work, where I lived in the village, and how long I planned to be in Zorgowee. I answered appropriately but briefly, as I knew he had other tasks on his agenda. After more Liberian small talk at our table asking about how everyone's wife, mother, father, and children were, we finished our meal. I then noticed at least fifty villagers surrounding us, standing within arm's reach of our executive table. Out of curiosity, locals stopped their work to come from the clinic, school, and their homes to see the visitor.

Suddenly the commissioner yelled a command to his soldiers in his Khran dialect, unknown to anyone in Zorgowee. Before I could blink, the soldiers ran into the crowd of villagers who scattered like a school of fish being scooped with a net. Within seconds the eight soldiers commandeered eight young strong Mandingo men. Separating the Mandingos from the Gio or Mano villagers was easy because they wore long Muslim robes and prayer caps. The captives resisted but were easily subdued by the soldiers' clubs and threatening rifles. The Mandingo men were quickly stripped of their upper clothing. Speechless and appalled, I wondered why the chief, Jacob, and the commissioner invited me to witness this dastardly act.

From the commissioner's truck, two soldiers retrieved a hammock, specially made for his visits to the diamond mines in the bush.

"Jacob, what are they doing?" I asked.

"The commissioner walks only small, small. He is carried in his hammock when he go to da small villages," he explained.

"Will he keep the Mandingo men?"

"No, dey go back to der house when dey come back to Zorgowee," he replied.

My shoulders dropped with relief.

The hammock fashioned from hand-woven vines with two long poles attached on each side became the commissioner's temporary throne. The four bare-chested Mandingo men functioned as porters each resting a pole on one shoulder, and once the hammock was in position, the commissioner climbed in. The four other captives were placed in reserve to relieve the first porters for the two-hour hike each way. Without permission I snapped photos to document proof of what I had witnessed.

With all the chaos that occurred I became distracted from the real reason for my special invitation to meet the diamond commissioner. Weeks later, after other stopovers to Zorgowee, he made multiple excursions to my house seeking loving-business. His high status meant nothing to me and I sent him on his way. I scolded myself for my stupidity, thinking that my initial invitation had to do with honor. It had everything to do with getting in my pants.

Never a Dull Moment

Life continued to unfold in front of my house and left me little time for boredom. Rainy season brought its own form of entertainment with tropical deluges filled with thunder and lightning. The relentless rain pounding on my corrugated-tin roof caused many sleepless nights. My rubber boots, rain hat, jacket, and umbrella were useless; no one used such items in Zorgowee or in the hot tropics for that matter.

During dry season the village came alive. One day I awakened to hear a commotion of maybe ten men gathered across from my house preparing to build a new mud and stick home to replace a neighbor's round thatched hut. In a mere ten days, using local materials, a few tools and their own resourcefulness, they completed the construction of a home like mine. Dad would have marveled at their inventiveness.

These men placed tree saplings, four inches in diameter and ten feet long, upright, about a foot apart in a cement foundation. The saplings were crisscrossed with strips of bamboo creating a horizontal lattice joined by twine stripped from palm leaves. Once they completed the base structure, they constructed a hip roof frame topped with corrugated tin roofing that was nailed into place. When the hand-constructed wooden frames for the windows and doors were completed, the bamboo-latticed walls were ready for the next step.

A group of about five men dug a large pit adjacent to the house and tilled the red-laterite clay soil to which they added water and mixed to attain the consistency of mortar. With bare hands, they picked up the mortar-like mud and hand-slapped, hand-troweled it into the walled lattice. Men worked on each side of the wall simultaneously to artfully work the mud into all the crevices. After days of curing and drying, the walls could be plastered with real cement. For those who could not afford that luxury, the mud was smoothed to a flat wall-finish. Some homes were crudely completed and the sliding hand prints on the outside walls created its own art form.

The owner purchased only a few items including nails, hinges, locks, tin roofing, and cement to construct this home. However, to save money, all could be made of indigenous local materials by substituting mud, thatched roofing, twine, and saplings.

No matter what materials were used to construct the houses, bugs, also, made them their home. Accustomed to insects on the farm, I cohabitated with the daddy long-legged spiders in my playhouse and the flies who coexisted with manure. African critters from the tropics were big and quick. I found the three-inch, non-poisonous spiders cunning and relentless, coupled with the speed of a mouse. Scary bedtime stories were created from spider tales, as these creatures move only at night. When surprised or threatened, their only defense is to jump—as much as four feet. One morning as I opened my kitchen window, a giant spider hurled right onto my face. Before I could respond, he scurried under the fridge escaping his fate.

But my archenemy, a saucer-sized spider I called Big Daddy, frequented my bedroom just before retiring. One evening I found Big Daddy on the wall three feet from my bed. I slithered past him to gather my weapon. With one fell swoop of my trusty broom, I missed him by two feet. He ran under the bed. I chased him out and back up the wall he dashed. My arms trembling from the last foiled attempt, I took another careful aim. This time I only missed him by one foot. Under my dresser he took refuge. After thirty minutes of prodding and poking with my broom handle, I could not blow his cover. Tired and exhausted, I turned off the Aladdin's lamp but my racing heartbeat prevented any sleep. I sensed an uneasiness in the air, and after fifteen minutes I grabbed my torch to survey the room to find Big Daddy right above my bed. Quite aware of his jumping abilities, I swiftly arose and swung the broom at the critter again with a miss. He fled out the bedroom door. I slammed it shut and stuffed a towel under the doorjamb, knowing I'd have to deal with him the next day—and deal with *them*...the rest of my stay.

On the other hand, the cute harmless three-inch geckos, who ate small insects and mosquitos, were sweet and welcoming as they scurried on the walls each night. However, I suspected Big Daddy ate the geckos for dessert.

The villagers held a healthy fear of the numerous deadly snakes found in our region. The death of a young schoolboy who fell victim to a poisonous snakebite still haunted me. Right from my front door I witnessed the funeral procession with his wooden casket hoisted on the shoulders of men, followed by wailing villagers. I had plenty of cockroach and spider stories but I feared snakes the most. I narrowly escaped death on two occasions when I missed stepping on a poisonous cassava snake and the deadly head-no-tail snake—a black nocturnal varmint with no differentiation between the head or the tail. Day or night one must always be vigilant. I never found a snake in my house, as some had. To avoid their stealth-like approach, I hired a boy to keep all grass, weeds and brush away from my house by twenty feet.

My earlier fantasy of a two-year camping experience in Liberia now seemed ludicrous. Whether in my house or just a few feet from it, I never experienced a dull moment.

Country Birth

"Younga Ti, come quick, Bendu, da head midwife call you. Let go, ya!" Rita yelled through my open window without even bocking. Bendu's call could mean one of two things: a troubled birth or my wish had been granted. Since my arrival five months earlier, I asked the head midwife if I could observe a country delivery. Time, patience, and trust were elements that must fall in line for me to witness such an event. Indigenous midwives were chosen by the head midwives and elders in the villages. Their knowledge and skills were handed down from generation to generation. None of the midwives in Zorgowee were formally educated or able to read or write, but they were highly respected. Having an outsider observe their practice must be carefully discussed and reviewed by the midwives. Even though I witnessed births before as an LPN, observing a delivery in Zorgowee would be instrumental in the development of my future midwifery classes. I understood that teaching new knowledge must begin with my understanding.

Rita and I rushed to the scene an hour before sunset. "Susan, be patient, be calm," I lectured myself, promising to not interfere with the process or jeopardize their trust. Out of breath from the fifteen-minute jog toward the edge of Zorgowee, we came to the entry of a large round thatched hut. Bendu met us at the front door when we bocked. She sent Rita home and only I entered.

As I made my way in the windowless round hut, maybe fifteen feet in diameter, a wood-burning fire in the center provided the only flickering illumination. Near the fire, a totally naked woman moaned in labor on a woven palm mat placed upon the earthen floor. Sana, the young sister of the pregnant woman, the only English speaker in the hut, warmly greeted me. She told me Fanta was in her final stages of labor.

Stunned by the number of people in the small room, I wondered, why so many? Eight women filled the hut, many in their twenties to forties, five being midwives plus her sister and mother and the laboring woman. When I asked Sana the purpose of the number of midwives, she explained that by observing and assisting in multiple births, they learned valuable skills; the more experienced midwives mentored those with less. I soon appreciated how the transfer of knowledge occurred in a culture of unwritten rules.

I knew two of the midwives, Bendu, the head midwife, and Larta. Each wore a colorful lappa wrapped around the waist and another around the chest. Their skin glistened with sweat from the ninety-degree heat and smoke-laden atmosphere. As Fanta lay in the traditional delivery position, on her back with her knees bent and feet on the floor, she faced away from the fire. The dim light made it impossible for me to visualize the birthing progress.

I clocked the spacing of her contractions at about ten to fifteen minutes apart. With no torch or lantern for adequate observation, I asked if I could bring a lantern from home and they agreed. I rushed back to the hut in the dark with my trusty kerosene lantern lighting the way.

After five minutes Fanta stood and I saw her upright for the first time. Liberian women appear enormous when pregnant because of their short stature, maybe 5'3" at best, slim bone structure, narrow hips, and little or no body fat. The baby pooched out front like a huge beach ball. Fanta's naked frame supported the tiniest pelvis I've ever seen for anyone about to deliver. Her belly button protruded probably two feet from her spine. Could this baby be too big for her pelvis? I kept my question to myself promising not to interfere. Fanta lay down again on the mat.

After another set of contractions, she arose and took hold of her mother who had been sleeping on one side of the hut. They walked in a circle as if in some sort of stupor. Fanta again lay down and the midwives began to bring bowls filled with soaked leaves, roots, and stems. Bendu rubbed the leaves between her hands, then added cold white ashes from the fire to create a white paste. She straddled Fanta between her legs and brushed her hands down both sides of the pregnant belly. Bendu uttered Gio phrases, three times, while painting white chalk-like streaks from the top of Fanta's protruding belly down to the floor.

"Sana, why da midwives do dis?" I asked.

"Dis is what we call 'country medicine.' Dis medicine is from da bush. It is good good for da baby and da mother," Sana said. "It make da baby come head first and come straight down."

The indigenous midwives used no Western medicine or treatments in their deliveries—only country medicine herbs and rituals, their traditional cures. With contractions in shorter intervals now, Fanta appeared more uncomfortable and arose again. She walked about the hut to the four different points and put her hand on my shoulder as she passed. A tingling sensation rushed from the touch of her fingers to my toes as I sensed the honor and privilege of my invitation.

Fanta sat on the mat. Without communication, two other midwives repeated the same ritual of leaves, roots, stems, and ashes over Fanta's body. One midwife made three sweeping strokes on Fanta's back from neck to the floor while the other made it down the sides of her abdomen to both legs. Fanta's moist ebony skin now had chalky white symbolic streaks down all sides of her body and her pregnant belly as well.

Between contractions and country medicine rituals, the women joked and laughed among themselves. Then suddenly, silence fell over the hut as the older Christian midwife, who did not believe in country medicine, said a prayer. According to Sana's translation, she asked God for a safe delivery. Along with the one Christian midwife, Fanta revered Allah, her Muslim God, while the other midwives were animists embracing country medicine beliefs. Eight women gathered with a harmonious blend of religions, country medicine, and three different tribes (Gio, Kru, and Mandingo) in one Liberian hut all working toward the same goal. While the midwife prayed, I, too, talked to God to give me patience.

The smoke, flickering fire, and rituals placed me in a trance. In and out of my consciousness, I wondered if a safe delivery could be possible with Fanta's seemingly prolonged labor and small pelvis. Abruptly, I pulled out of my stupor when Larta took a drink of water and literally spat the water on Fanta's belly. The laboring woman arose again and stooped as she passed through a small doorway to a second room about eight feet in diameter smelling of freshly cut wood, rice stalks, and chicken poop. Fanta had walked into the storage room for firewood, unhusked rice bundles, and live chickens. Fortunately, there were no chickens present that night. The rice bundles were stowed up in the ceiling rafters. However, remnants of the room's contents were scattered about the dirt floor. Fanta sat directly on the floor facing the wall as if not wanting anyone to observe. Sana and I followed her. I squatted on the floor leaning against the wall while the heat and smell gripped my stomach. I slumped near Fanta wondering how many more times her pacing would continue.

Sana said, "Fanta have many baby-o. Four, all living."

Only in her mid-twenties, Fanta, certainly a strong fertile woman with multiple pregnancies, could deliver quickly. I still had doubt. Suddenly I heard a "kerplunk" in the corner. "Oh shit!" I blurted. It sounded like the baby popped out. From my squatting position I jumped upright and rushed to the main room for my lantern. Upon return I found her amniotic sac burst, splashing fluid against the wall.

The other women came into the small room and positioned Fanta on her back away from the wall. Sana sat with Fanta's head and shoulders on her lap. Two midwives squatted on each side of Fanta holding her bent knees and feet apart while one other supported Fanta's back with her left foot—a perfect position for delivery. No need for stirrups when human bodies can do the task. Bendu sat in position between Fanta's legs to receive the baby.

As if corking a bottle, Bendu placed an old piece of cloth with her big toe directly on Fanta's anus. Sana heard my gasp, witnessed my raised eyebrows, and said in a faint whisper, "Da midwives believe da baby can come by da rectum, not the good way. Da toe will help da baby go da good way."

Normally, in the U.S., an episiotomy (a small surgical incision at the vulva) would be performed to prevent a possible tear all the way to the rectum as the baby exits the birth canal. If any midwives had witnessed this type of tear before, it may have appeared that the baby came out of the rectum and not the birth canal. My nursing knowledge also helped me understand that the toe plug could also prevent any accidental feces from interfering with the birth. An enema prior to delivery to help decrease the possibility of fecal contamination was often routine in the U.S., but clearly, not here.

Fanta's mother and the other midwife grasped each of Fanta's hands. I squatted near the delivery end, waiting— adrenaline pumping and fatigue banished. A few times Fanta yelled out her sister's name as if still in her delirious state. All the women laughed jokingly. I chuckled, too, just to feel comradely, but I was terrified at the entire situation.

One midwife approached with an empty palm oil bottle and cap Fanta had thrown in the bucket of water about an hour earlier. She motioned the cap over Fanta's breast, then over her belly and dropped it to the floor between her legs. She did the same motion with the bottle. I asked Sana what this meant and she said no one knew. Fanta just told her to do it with the meaning known only to herself. No more unusual than our homegrown superstitions when we believe in rabbit's feet or wearing special colored socks to a high school football game to bring good luck.

I estimated the nine of us sat in our respective positions in that crowded room for the next two to three hours with her contractions coming every two minutes. As a nurse I knew delivery was imminent, but there seemed to be no visible signs of progress. They were not performing internal digital exams which would reveal the progression of the dilation of the cervix I was accustomed to. With the current sanitary conditions and no surgical gloves or even hand washing observed, I was relieved to not witness any internal examinations.

My conflict, about what to say or do, heightened. Fanta lay directly on the dirt floor with chicken droppings and God knows what else. And now the delivery seemed stalled. I repeated to myself, "Susan, remember your promise, remember your promise," but I could no longer sit silent. I would regret it forever if I did. I chose the less direct route by sharing only with Sana my concern regarding the lack of progress.

"Sana, Fanta must go to the hospital. The delivery has gone on too long with no baby. Her hips are too small-o."

"Miss Sue, all of Fanta's four babies have come dis way. She take time-o to deliver da baby. No my, ya."

Sana's reassurance gave me no peace of mind as my skepticism had peaked. No longer able to contain my thoughts and let the mother and the baby die, I immediately suggested Sana tell the midwives my possible conclusion and she be taken to the hospital in Sanniquellie (about eight miles away) before any other complications arose. She complied with my request and translated my concerns. All five midwives softly smiled, shook their heads, and told Sana to tell me their message, "Da head coming-o."

Fear overcame me and I decided to look for Peter and ask for his advice, my only other medical consult. Trembling and anxious, I ran from the hut and found him at home and as we returned I reviewed the situation. When we approached the hut, they denied Peter's entry as it is taboo to allow a man in a country delivery setting. Peter agreed with my conclusion even though he could not examine her.

Before he returned home, I asked to borrow his stethoscope to auscultate for the baby's heart tone to determine any fetal distress. I passed the threshold of no return as I already broke my vow of silence. The kind and forgiving midwives allowed me to listen to Fanta's abdomen with the stethoscope for as long as five minutes. I moved the bell of the scope to at least twenty different points on her huge belly straining to hear a fetal heartbeat of any kind about 120-160 beats per minute; I could only hear the mother's at about 90 beats per minute. I now became even more concerned and informed the midwives via Sana that I could not find the baby's heartbeat.

They seemed disinterested and said, "Da head coming-o."

I looked with the dim light but could see nothing. I sat on the dirt floor with my back collapsed against the thatched wall and could only think of all the terrible things that could happen. I trembled with fear and prayed, Dear God, please help Fanta and her baby, please.

As I wiped sweat from my face, Bendu asked me to look. It appeared to be the hair of the baby's head. Unsure in the dim light along with an undetectable fetal heartbeat, my enthusiasm flattened, I could only imagine a stillbirth.

Another forty-five minutes passed before a certain observance of the crowning of the head. Bendu took a goopy concoction of cooked okra and dribbled this over Fanta's birth canal and the baby's head as if to lubricate the opening. I knew there was no aseptic technique in this country medicine treatment. Oh Lord, please help this mother and baby.

Within moments as Fanta moaned and pushed, the banana shaped head came out. No breathing noted as of yet, which can be totally normal. After a few minutes of more laboring wails, the shoulder delivered and then the rest. Thank God, the baby, a big boy, began to breathe, but ever so faintly. They pricked his feet but he didn't cry—possibly due to total exhaustion from the hard labor and delivery.

Bendu then patted a black-colored country medicine paste of herbs and ashes all over his body and placed him on a large banana leaf and one over the top, covering him completely. Then she tapped the top leaf with another making the baby cry loudly, helping him to clear his airway. Fanta then grabbed my hand tightly and I hers. "Praise the Lord," I murmured, as I wilted with relief.

I didn't care that my assumptions were wrong and that I acted as if I bestowed the knowledge of all Western medicine. I cared that Fanta and her baby boy were alive.

Within minutes of the delivery, Fanta moved to a squatting position as Bendu reached beneath her. In the dimly lit room, I couldn't see for certain, but it appeared she either reached her hand inside Fanta's birth canal or pulled on the umbilical cord to hasten the expulsion of the placenta. I knew for certain Fanta bore down *without* the presence of a contraction, which is not recommended. This action could cause partial removal of the placenta which in turn could lead to hemorrhage and possibly death of the mother.

Within five minutes the placenta delivered. Fanta attempted to stand but wobbly from exhaustion and blood loss, she sat on the earthen floor near the wall. Her mother offered Fanta cooked rice which she refused.

About fifteen to twenty minutes later, the cord had still not been cut. Normally the cord is clamped immediately after the baby is born and before the placenta is delivered. My mind continued to race, thinking of further complications of blood loss and infection.

The placenta and the umbilical cord, still attached to the baby, now lay on the earthen floor of the dirtiest room in the hut; the baby still sandwiched between the banana leaves. Bendu took the cord from the dirt floor and draped it over a twig she found nearby. With twine stripped from a palm frond she tied the cord on either side of the twig, then took a rusty razor blade from a square cloth satchel and cut the cord between the two ties. I said nothing as she made the cut. My mind was filled with concern about tetanus or any other infections. I took a deep breath to contain my fears; I had already been wrong tonight. Why should they listen to me now?

Two midwives bathed the baby boy with the warm water from the wood fire and wrapped him in a cloth. Bendu shouted a Gio phrase four times with every one responding in harmony "Aahooo!" Sana said this informed everyone in the village of a joyous delivery of a baby boy.

Soon, another midwife began to dig a hole in the corner of the room where Fanta delivered. There she carefully placed the placenta with the cord on top. She scraped the blood and other remains from the earthen floor along with the cleansed banana leaves to deposit them in the hole then covered it with dirt, leaving no signs of a delivery.

When I gained the wherewithal to look at my watch, what seemed like a twelve hour ordeal had only been five. Completely exhausted, I turned to thank Fanta, Sana, Fanta's mother, Bendu, Larta, and the other three midwives for allowing me to witness this event. They, in turn, thanked me.

The immense privilege bestowed upon me to observe their traditions and customs of country birth with five indigenous midwives was pivotal in my true welcome to Zorgowee. I sensed a bridge of trust had been built. The following day I documented my full description of the delivery because, as far as I knew, no written account of a Gio country birth existed. But I had yet to witness the closing paragraph: would the mother and baby live?

With the 1970 child mortality rate at 60 percent from birth to five years of age, traditionally the baby is not named for one to two weeks after birth. Also, the highest death rates among young women were from complications after delivery. So, as I made my home visit to Fanta and her baby boy a few days after his birth, I entered the familiar hut with some trepidation knowing he or she may not be past the window of danger. To my surprise, both were happy and healthy.

"Fanta, what will you name dis fine, fine baby boy?" I asked.

With her sister translating she replied, "What is yur father name?"

"Paul John," I said.

"Paul John is da name of my baby boy, for you, ya." Even with my inexcusable meddling from inaccurate medical knowledge, I was being honored. Meek and humbled, my respect for the people of Zorgowee grew by the day.

A few days after the delivery, I used Peter's stethoscope in the clinic and could not even hear a blood pressure. I discovered the ear buds were plugged, causing my inability to hear the fetal heart tones. And the wildly beating heart I thought was Fanta's was actually my own pounding out of my chest from adrenaline.

After the window of risk passed, Paul John grew into a healthy little African baby boy of the Mandingo tribe in Zorgowee, Liberia; and Fanta became a proud healthy mother of five. In my next letter home, I wrote to Dad telling him of the honor Fanta bestowed upon him. I hoped he appreciated the fact that a little baby boy in Africa carried his name from a people and a culture he did not understand. But as weeks passed I never heard a reply.

Indigenous Midwives

Witnessing Fanta's birth, in the presence of her supportive family and the local midwifes, helped me understand my village culture. Education is important but cannot or should not undermine wisdom and experience. I naïvely valued my nine months of practical nurses training over and above the years of indigenous midwifery expertise. Now humbled, I was the one who needed to learn. If I proceeded with awareness instead of arrogance, my teachings could be an adjunct to their current traditional country medicine knowledge. Observing Fanta's delivery with the indigenous midwives gave me specific ways I could improve the outcome of the maternal morbidity and mortality statistics. I wanted to develop a midwifery training course, not an expectation of my Peace Corps training. I believed as a practical nurse I possessed enough background to make a difference. I *could* do it and I must. However, my foolishness in interfering in Fanta's delivery may have cost me their respect.

A couple of weeks passed when I approached Bendu and, with the help of Peter as translator, said, "I thank you ya for calling me to see Fanta giving baby-o. With respect, I want to make school for the midwives to teach them good good things to help them."

"I think dis is good-o. We can learn new things," Bendu happily agreed.

"Oh, thank you Bendu. How many midwives you want to come?"

Bendu counted on her fingers and held them up. Ten plus two.

I said, "Twelve," repeating her hand gestures.

She nodded.

We went on to discuss how and when, and we agreed that teaching all the midwives together would be the best option, despite the three different dialects. In addition, she thought an official midwifery course would encourage camaraderie and raise their level of respect in the community. Acquiring the same information at one time would also decrease confusion among the midwives.

Gathering twelve indigenous midwives together for four weekly, ninety-minute trainings had never occurred before. Bendu notified all the midwives and informed them they were responsible for bringing their own interpreter, while Peter arranged the clinic schedule to accommodate the classes.

I never taught a class before let alone developed a curriculum in a foreign culture. Overwhelmed, I didn't know where to begin, how much detail, what to cover or what not to cover? How long could I keep their attention with three interpreters speaking at the same time? All the midwives were unschooled and unable to read or write. I must strip the curriculum down to basic sanitation principles and teach about preventable complications. My primary goal—to save lives; even if only one birth out of hundreds.

First, I focused on general sanitation, and Fanta's delivery gave me the basis from which to work. I wasn't aspiring for a sterile environment, just clean and aseptic, as we call it in nursing. Good hand-washing became the foundation. Next there must be a place to deliver besides the earthen floor, followed by the tying and cutting of the cord. All must be as clean as possible. However, these concepts required supplies, and I must develop a list of items where all could be purchased locally. Sami's Lebanese store, within walking distance of each village, had the stock supplies I needed.

I developed a midwifery supply kit comprised of five items: A bar of lye soap, a bottle of isopropyl alcohol, a square yard of plastic tablecloth material, a packet of straight-edge razor blades, and a spool of white thread. The soap could be used for washing hands. The reusable plastic tablecloth provided a delivery mat on the floor and would be cleaned with soap and water between deliveries and then sanitized with the alcohol. The sewing thread could be tripled, used only once and soaked in alcohol before tying the cord. And lastly the razor blade, used only once and must be sanitized with the alcohol before cutting the cord. Five basic supplies for a total cost of about $1.00, a lot of money to a village midwife. The average income for an entire family might be 50¢ per day; I could only hope they would see the benefit.

How to convey these complicated topics became my biggest challenge. Would images even work when teaching someone who had never been in a classroom setting before? One flipchart given by the Peace Corps provided me with some guidance. Lessons learned on the farm never had written procedures when it came to harrowing the field or delivering pigs or calves. Show, not tell, must be my emphasis.

From the boxes I collected at Sami's store, I constructed a cardboard two-dimensional display of a life-size image of a woman's vulva with her legs spread and a separate cardboard baby, complete with umbilical cord made of rope with an attached cardboard placenta. I hand-cut, glued, sketched, and colored these images as close to their real size and appearance as possible.

A month later, we held our first midwifery class. Here, progress was about to meet head on with traditional customs. Twelve indigenous midwives, each dressed in their finest lappa, top and matching head tie, sat in a crescent row of three adjoining benches in our clinic education room. Behind them stood three men, the interpreters for the three dialects; Gio,

Kru, and Mandinka. Men were prohibited from being involved in deliveries, so how would men as the interpreters work? I knew we were treading on unbroken ground, yet my confidence surged knowing how much this meant to them. One of the Christian midwives prayed at the beginning and the end of each class. I needed that blessing and strength more than they knew.

I selected the five most common delivery and birth complications: prolapsed cord, placenta previa, breech, postpartum hemorrhage, and blue baby. I stressed prevention, praised their expertise and when they were to seek help.

I began my first class greeting everyone first in Gio, "Babua."

"Aahoo," all twelve with three interpreters chimed in together.

Then I spoke in my best, unadulterated, Liberian English I knew to date, "I say, I thank you, ya, for coming from yur village and leaving yur family today to come to midwifery school. Thank you for all the good good work you do for da mothers and babies of the Zor Clan. Yur chief and Peter thank you too, ya. I want to teach you new things so more mothers and babies can live a good good life." I paused after each sentence for the three dialects to be translated all at the same time. They each, in turn, thanked me, which gave me hope.

I stood nervously in front next to a table with my crude three-piece life-size cardboard display of the woman's vulva, the baby with umbilical cord and placenta. I began by moving each object through its normal delivery journey. As soon as the images moved and came to life, faces lit up as "oohs" and "aahs." The two-dimensional display now became 3D. Eyebrows raised and giggles ensued as I began to maneuver all the props, replicating complications and how to prevent them or actions to take if they couldn't. Some began talking among themselves as I progressed with the demonstrations. I left time for questions and answers after each session. Their queries and comments were appropriate and focused, assuring me they *did* understand.

As I gained more confidence with each class, other instructions including clearing the baby's airway, caring for the cord after delivery, and delivering the placenta became easy to demonstrate with the props. I carefully explained the use and care of the supplies.

At our fourth and final class I presented them with their own starter midwifery kit in a small shoe box with a hand-crafted certificate of completion. Their reaction to my $1.00 gift box to each of these twelve midwives was as if I had given them a $20 gunny sack of rice and a free trip to Monrovia. Bendu presented me with a gift from the women: a small bowl of rice, an egg, a live chicken, and 50¢. "Iswondon," I said as I accepted these gifts with honor and grasped my forearm to bow with respect while I shook the hand of each midwife.

After the presentation Bendu unexpectedly announced she and the midwives had spoken, and with their completed training they would now ask for money from the family, maybe $1.00 per delivery, at least enough to replenish their supplies. Her idea was unprecedented. Peter recommended we bring this idea to the Zor Clan Chief, Manuel and the Mandingo Chief, Ahmadou for discussion. The following day Bendu, Peter, and I met with Chief Manuel and Chief Ahmadou, each wearing their chief's gowns and caps. During the fifteen minutes of official greetings, I never dreamt my teaching could garner such attention from the clan chiefs.

Bendu began the discussion, "Chief Manuel and Chief Ahmadou, Younga Ti teach us good good things for the mid-wives to help da mothers and babies in the Zor Clan. She give us things to make the mothers and babies safe." She displayed her midwifery kit as the example. "Dis box cost $1.00 from Sami's store. We beg you ya, to make it known to the clan dat the midwives want $1.00 for every baby born by midwife. Dis money will go to buy more for the midwife box. I beg you ya." She bowed her head in respect.

"Yes, Chief Manuel and Chief Ahmadou, I think dis is a good good plan-o," Peter elaborated.

Chief Manuel and Chief Ahmadou leaned and whispered to each other briefly as the three of us sat across the table from them. Then Chief Manuel replied, "Chief Ahmadou and I think dis is a good good plan. Tomorrow all baby born by midwife must pay $1.00 or in food for dis service."

Pleased with the decision, I only hoped asking for some form of payment would not be a barrier to care. Once the midwives learned cause and effect regarding my teachings, maybe each could save just *one* baby or *one* mother. And if they did, I had succeeded.

Some weeks after the training, Bendu reported the midwives were using their supplies and most families were either paying for their services with money or in kind. The midwifery kit gave the midwives prestige. More importantly, it provided safer deliveries, what I had been striving for.

Comrades and a Role Model

Despite my love and admiration for my village, I periodically sought comfort in the homes of like-minded Americans. I frequented Sanniquellie where sixteen Peace Corps volunteers lived, most being schoolteachers, rural development workers, and one health educator. I often visited on weekends in the beginning and less often as I became habituated to Zorgowee. Maggie and Pam were most kind, generous, and supportive, offering their homes to me each time I came. Maggie, a teacher from Colorado, and Pam, a health education volunteer from Oregon, each lived in country almost two years and were well-seasoned volunteers. Pam, a Catholic Italian-American, and I attended Mass on the weekends. She understood my strict religious upbringing and never made fun of my prudishness.

Volunteers gathered for entertainment, shopping in LAMCO, traveling the countryside, or taking in an occasional local film. The simple pleasure of a 10¢ movie projected on the whitewashed wall of a vacant building gave the locals and volunteers a cheap escape from a day's challenge. While we endured the hard wooden benches, a Bruce Lee Kung Fu film roused the locals with screams and jeers. Toilet tissue, protruding from my ears, dampened the yelling and the generator blasting outside the back door.

Most weekends found Peace Corps group meals, pinochle card games, or some reason for a party—either a volunteer arriving, leaving, or visiting. We often wore vibrant colored dresses, tops or shirts, custom-made by local tailors for only a few dollars. Except for one or two black volunteers, all the women wore long flowing hair down their backs, me included. Our gatherings included Liberian chop as the main course and fresh baked American goods for dessert that satisfied the volunteers. Taped African highlife and American music filled the host's house with local favorites of Club Beer and Senator's Brand Rum, flowing freely. I chose rum and Coke with lime. I never acquired a liking for beer and found the tepid yellow foamy drink nauseating. Often volunteers from nearby towns and villages would hear wind of a party and the crowds grew to thirty or more.

During those parties, I met Tom, a Peace Corps teacher from Virginia who lived in the small village of Zapa on the road to LAMCO. He arrived in country two months before my arrival and was the only volunteer in his village with one Lebanese store. Our comparable living situations gave us many common stories and experiences to share. We instantly fed off each other's energy. His beautiful head of wavy red hair and freckled skin made him a standout among the Liberians. We talked of plans to visit each other's villages in the future.

I also met Jim, an agricultural volunteer from the village of Kpain, over an hour south of Sanniquellie. As a stockbroker from Yonkers, he acquired an unlikely Peace Corps assignment: teaching villagers how to breed and raise pigs for profit. As soon as he learned of my Nebraska farming background, he invited me to see his pig project for which I hoped to give my expert advice because I knew a good quality breeding boar when I saw one. His 6'4" frame had an uncanny ability to consume many bottles of Club Beer with no apparent effect. Jim showed a great interest in travel and we shared the possibility of exploring East Africa together in January. We vowed to keep in touch to coordinate our epic adventure.

Pam introduced me to an older married Peace Corps couple, Ruth and Harold Jacobson. They arrived in country a month after me and were assigned to Gbedin, a village over an hour south of Zorgowee. Harold worked as a mechanic for the Liberian-Chinese Rice Project. His curl-tipped handlebar mustache, stocky, Norwegian stature, and bowed legs added to his uniqueness in a crowd of "Kwi Po's," as we white people were called. Harold could fix anything including tractors, pumps, and vehicles. Like my dad, he machined his own replacement parts when needed.

Ruth, too, stood out from a crowd of Peace Corps women. Her short-cropped grey hair and black-rimmed glasses attracted special attention. Ruth worked as a health educator in the village clinic staffed with a dresser and basic supplies like that of Zorgowee. Ruth did not have the health education training we did in the Virgin Islands; however, as a registered nurse, she took it upon herself to fill a different role. Ruth delivered babies alongside the midwives, sutured wounds, and performed as much medical care as she could with few supplies. For items she lacked, Ruth negotiated procurement of these supplies through the Liberian Ministry of Health or purchased them herself.

I met the twosome at a few Peace Corps parties. Even though they were thirty years my senior and older than my parents, they quickly adjusted to the Liberian culture. Ruth, an avid seamstress, crafted her garments out of Liberian tie-dye or lappa material. Harold proudly wore his tie-dyed dashiki tops with machine embroidered collar and sleeves. Despite a receding hairline, he soon took on a more youthful appearance when his hair grew long. I couldn't imagine my own parents adapting in this way.

Ruth invited me to visit when I traveled through. So, one weekend on my taxi excursion to Monrovia I spent two nights with them in Gbedin. When the rice project generator shut down around 8:00 p.m. we sat around the Aladdin's lamp while their houseboy, John, and house girl, Agnes, cleaned up the supper dishes from our hot peppered Liberian chop. Ruth and Harold financially supported Agnes and John's high school education. Most girls past puberty were often pregnant and married with little chance of attending school, so Ruth and Harold gave Agnes a better chance for education. Their kindness and generosity impressed me.

They were from Washington State and had two grown daughters with three grandsons. We were amused at our connection to practical nursing as Ruth had taught at a local college, training practical nursing students. Her mother was also a practical nurse. The following morning, I joined Ruth on two home visits: one to a mother with a newborn that Ruth helped deliver a few days earlier, and the other to a young boy with a hand injury that she had sutured a week before. As we entered each thatched hut, I stood in awe of her skill and knowledge while observing her gentle and kind manner.

Ruth and Harold exemplified the qualities of mature, openminded, capable individuals who possessed unparalleled integrity. They exuded confidence and compassion with a worldly flair and wholeheartedly cared about the Liberian culture they did not fully know or understand. Smart and expert, without pretense, they applied their skills to their community. Ruth and Harold could easily have been the parents of us younger volunteers, yet they blended in wherever they went as if no age gap existed. Many of my peers cherished their wisdom. Soon other volunteers and I looked to them as mentors. They gave me the best example of unconditional caring and generosity, and I treasured their non-judgmental character.

During my work in Zorgowee, I often questioned my actions and wondered what my role model, Ruth, would do. I wanted to emulate her wisdom, education, and confidence so I could be like her someday. After a few months in Zorgowee, I sensed my limited practical nursing knowledge restricted my interventions when I couldn't identify symptoms of an illness earlier to ward off consequences. My nine months of practical nursing training provided simply the means to learn the procedures, leaving little time to understand why I did them. Practical nurses did what we were told by an RN or a doctor and never made decisions on our own. I could not do the tasks Ruth did in Gbedin. She taught me that I could be a critical thinker, be assertive, and do the right thing within my capability.

A vision of my future began to gel the longer I worked in Liberia: I planned to continue my education and become an RN. When Ruth and I met a few weeks later she encouraged my vision and told me she only had a three-year nursing diploma and planned to get a BSN once she returned to the U.S. I could hardly imagine a woman over fifty years old returning from Africa to obtain a bachelor's degree. She had a plan and a goal. If she could, I knew I could.

My Soul Sister

I hosted my first Peace Corps party in Zorgowee three months after my arrival. Clara helped me prepare three kinds of chop: palm butter, ground pea soup with chicken, and collard greens with beef. We made sure to add plenty of hot red Liberian pepper to make our nose run and eyes water, because, well, that the way it's meant to be eaten. She cooked one huge pot of rice at her house on an open flame in a cast-iron pot because I ran out of burners and cooking vessels at my house. I baked pineapple upside-down cakes and peanut butter cookies for dessert. Everyone brought their own beverage of choice; Club Beer filled most of the coolers.

I invited my soul sister, Rainbow, via our monthly correspondence. I was elated when she arrived from Zwedru. We hugged and talked nonstop until others arrived. I had not seen her since our swearing-in ceremony. I also invited my Liberian friends and coworkers: Sami, Jacob, Rita, Clara, Peter, Duo, and others who intermixed with my twenty Peace Corps friends. Zorgowee had not witnessed so many white people in its village at one time. With plenty of batteries to power my boom box, we danced to African highlife music and American classics. The Beatles, Marvin Gaye, and Neil Diamond played into the night. We consumed chop, and beverages flowed freely. My living room—dimly lit with kerosene lanterns and my Aladdin's lamp—provided the perfect ambiance for the house packed with swaying bodies. However, four hours into the party, Rainbow began to concern me. Drunkenness transformed her personality. My bedroom soon became a venue for the men she entertained.

The party closed down by 3:00 a.m. and some friends with vehicles returned to Sanniquellie. The remainder, including Rainbow, spent the night wherever they could find space in my house. The floor with a blanket accommodated most of them.

The following morning after the visitors departed, Rainbow told me of her passion for sex and men. She lost count of how many she slept with in Liberia—two during my party. I was clueless about how to respond. I just listened. Soon we abandoned the man-topic, because I had nothing to share, and chatted about our lives before Peace Corps, our village experiences, and our love of life.

Rainbow seemed to embrace a boundless life, a free spirit of sorts. With our grand differences, our special bond mystified me. After Rainbow returned to her village, we sent each other notes via the Peace Corps courier who passed through monthly.

A few weeks later, I spent the weekend at Pam's in Sanniquellie for some R&R. That Saturday night the town generator shut down at its usual time of 10 p.m. and we retreated to our twin beds, turned off the Aladdin's lamp and stared into darkness reminiscing about the week.

Pam said in a tentative voice, "I have something to tell you."

"What?" It took all my strength to ask as I feared for some bad news from my family.

Her message echoed off the black ceiling. "Rainbow is dead."

Shock and disbelief pierced me. I lay motionless as tears rolled from the corners of my eyes. Images of Rainbow flashed through my vision like a movie in the infinite darkness. I saw her John Lennon-type glasses, her long wavy brown hair, and sweet carefree smile. I heard her laugh...my soul sister.

Pam's voice trembled as she continued, "Last week Rainbow was medevacked by plane from Monrovia to New York where they placed her in a psychiatric ward. Because of her delirious state, they secured her in a straitjacket. When the staff returned, Rainbow had partially untied the straps and strangled herself."

"Strangled. Dead." Whether accidental or not, Rainbow was gone—gone forever.

I never found out what transpired before they medevacked her to New York. I sent my condolences to her mother in Texas but didn't receive a reply.

Many weeks later, frequent flashbacks of Rainbow haunted me. I questioned our strange friendship more than before and wondered why we were ever attracted to each other. That fun-loving person may have been tortured from the inside out. Maybe...maybe she wanted to be like me, more circumspect, less daring. And in some dark way, maybe I wanted to be like her—free and uninhibited, without so many rules and constraints. As different as we were, we never judged or criticized, but loved and cared for each other. In total, only a few precious days together bonded my eternal love for Rainbow. I cried many times thinking of this lost soul knowing all she probably wanted was unconditional love and acceptance. *Just like me.*

Tragedy to Affection

On July 23, 1971, three months after my arrival, the political future of Liberia was upended. President William Tubman died of an illness after his twenty-seven-year reign. After so many years of Tubman's control, his death filled the country with uncertainty. His Vice President, William R. Tolbert, assumed power in an apparent seamless transition. Tolbert's leadership style, different from Tubman's, created a ripple effect of changes throughout the country. Within weeks, Tolbert announced a new head tax and the promise to move "Liberia to Higher Heights." I assumed he meant improvements.

By late 1971, after only a few months in power, President Tolbert mounted pressure on the foreigners in Liberia. He dictated new rules for all non-nationals owning businesses—including the Lebanese—to leave their small towns and relinquish ownership of their gas stations, restaurants, and stores. The Peace Corps and its volunteers were not impacted by this new policy. The entire village of Zorgowee depended upon Sami's store for our basic needs such as fuel, rice, and non-perishable items including supplies in the midwifery kits. All over Liberia, villages and towns relied on the Lebanese stores. All we could do was wait and see.

Shortly after President Tolbert assumed power, a tragic incident occurred. Marsha, a Peace Corps volunteer, was slain in her village by a person brandishing a cutlass—the same village in which Ruth and Harold lived, half an hour south of Sanniquellie. This news reverberated throughout the world because murders of volunteers were unheard of. Liberians and Peace Corps volunteers were in shock, and the news traveled quickly upcountry. The day following the murder, two Sanniquellie volunteers arrived at my door to tell me of the news and encourage me to return with them for safety. I refused. The villagers in Zorgowee were concerned I would abandon my village out of fear. I assured everyone— Zorgowee, the volunteers, Peace Corps administration, and my parents—that I felt safe and protected in my village.

In my first five months in Liberia, human birth and death were now a part of my life. The political future of the country was yet unknown. I witnessed the tenacity and strength of life juxtaposed with the fragility and fatefulness of loss that can be out of one's control—so many hard lessons that can never be acquired from a textbook. Through these experiences I discovered my small village wanted me and cared about me. Zorgowee began to feel like home. I became a part of the Zor Clan, its people and the culture. To me and many who felt its love, Zorgowee became affectionately called Gowee. And so, from that time forward, Gowee was its name.

A month after Marsha's killing, Martha, Rita, Clara, Peter, Jacob, and Sami all expressed how proud they were of me, knowing I had no plans to leave our village. Their affection affirmed our love for Gowee and her people as well as their love for me. As this affectionate bond developed, the non-English speaking villagers called me Younga Ti. To those who spoke English, I became Miss Sue. To the Peace Corps volunteers, I was known as Gowee Sue. To Sami, and only Sami, I was Susie.

Surprise Pregnancy

The direct correlation between sex and pregnancy was not commonly known to some villagers, especially young girls. Why should I be surprised? At age eleven I believed divine intervention caused pregnancy. Not until high school did I make the entire correlation and only in my nurses training did I fully understand the physiology.

Six months after my arrival in Gowee, Clara, my house girl, age sixteen, missed her period. After a doctor's appointment in Sanniquellie, it was determined she was four months pregnant. We were shocked at the news.

I asked Clara, "Who is the father?"

"What do you mean?" she asked.

"Are you sleeping with a man?" My voice steeped in anger. I wanted to know who this guy was. I knew how relentless the African men could be in their sexual pursuits, and I wanted to give him a piece of my mind. "Do you know that loving-business causes belly in girls?"

"No, I do not know."

"Who did you sleep with?" She refused to give me any sort of answer, just stared out the window.

Donning my parental hat, I used the tool of shame that was effectively used on me back home. I threatened to write Clara's Peace Corps friend, Sally, hoping that would embarrass her enough to tell me her lover's name.

Clara avoided me for the next two months. Only then did I realize how absurd and punishing my behavior had become. I was becoming my dad and mom, for God's sake! I woke up one morning to realize I would alienate her forever if I didn't end my interrogation. I finally stopped and began a more compassionate approach. She benefited from my concern, not from my threats. Even if girls and women knew how pregnancy occurred, they had few methods of prevention. My caring approach slowly normalized our relationship.

Three months later a villager notified me Clara had gone into labor on her family's farm. I rushed to boil thread and take some midwifery supplies, but by the time I arrived she had delivered a healthy baby boy by a midwife I had previously trained. Her family rejoiced and was pleased the "white-woman doctor" had come.

Not long after her delivery I talked to her about the relationship between loving-business and pregnancy. Ironically, my message to her was no different than the one I received from my dad. With no reliable birth control available to Clara, I told her to "push the men away." I never discovered who fathered her child and she had no intention of marrying him.

Extended family members often care for young children, so with help from her parents, funds from her Peace Corps friend Sally, along with wages from my domestic work, Clara supported herself and kept her eyes set on school. I was very proud of her.

The Honeymoon's Over

Two years earlier, I had been enchanted by the television commercial depicting a young female volunteer walking through her village trailing happy African children. Now I asked myself if she experienced death, relentless loving-business encounters, loneliness, and despair. I wondered if she witnessed beatings and stonings, as I had.

My diary became stained with my frequent tears as I chronicled my miseries. I longed for anything familiar: a hot shower, a hamburger, fresh cow's milk, and springtime. Five months into my induction into Gowee, my Peace Corps honeymoon was over. The day I arrived in my village I sat on the foundation of my house shedding tears of joy. Now my days were filled with loneliness and despair. Clinic goals that fell short of my expectations, my soul sister's death, and constant loving-business pursuits took an emotional toll. I had no one to hold me and tell me it would be alright. I refused the comfort of a lover that Rainbow readily accepted. Maybe this Peace Corps experience was a mistake. Were my parents right? My strict Nebraska upbringing taught me right from wrong, white from black, good from bad, and heaven from hell. Many of those beliefs were in direct conflict with my remote village experiences. My new life wrestled with my old. My past found little room for gray or brown, discovering the truth, being a non-conforming Catholic, and God forbid, being myself. My feelings of hopelessness and depression mounted. The downward pull on my once jovial emotions scared me. I fought those feelings, but still I often cried.

U.S. mail came only once a month to Gowee via the Peace Corps courier. A single piece of correspondence became important. I cherished any communication from Doug, my parents, family, and friends and spent many nights answering their letters on my blue aerogram stationary (a lightweight foldable air letter) that often took three to four weeks in transit. Mom wrote monthly about local news and her constant worry about my safety in Africa. I told her mostly of good news and adventures. I certainly never mentioned the snakes, bugs, and illnesses or about my loneliness and depression. Dad never personally wrote. Only rare messages from him came via Mom.

One day I received a delightful letter from a friend who enclosed local newspaper clippings. The articles included my nursing graduation photo and described my work in Liberia. Peace Corps provided a press release to the local papers and my community chose to recognize me. I now ranked among the frequently published wedding and birth announcements and alongside the local boys who had joined the military. My parents never wrote to tell me they read the announcement. I hoped it made them proud. Who was I kidding? Neither one of them supported my work in Africa.

Doug's letters became less frequent and less informative. I wondered if he would be waiting for me upon my return. News from friends and family members told me Doug no longer attended junior college but instead worked as a bartender and a filling station attendant. The Vietnam War was winding down and a draft lottery had been initiated the year we graduated. I didn't understand the war or how it would impact him, and I needlessly worried about so many things out of my control. Crazy as it seemed, out of desperation—to save myself and our relationship—I wrote and asked Doug to visit me in Liberia.

About two months later, Doug replied by letter that he *was* coming to visit. I reread his words several times stating he planned to arrive sometime in the New Year. Another farm kid from Nebraska hopping on a plane to Africa, but to see me? I believed he was serious. After a few attempts to make contact via radiogram in Sanniquellie, I confirmed his arrival two months hence, mid-February, after my return from the East Africa vacation that Jim, the Peace Corps volunteer from Kpain, and others had planned.

I was eager for Doug to meet everyone in Gowee, including my new African family and Sami, of course. They were excited when I told them of his impending visit. I felt some trepidation about his arrival. My doubts, riddled with anxiety, soon overtook my joy. I spent many sleepless nights wondering if he would be the same. Was I the same person he remembered? Would he like Liberia, the people and the culture as I did? Had my feelings for him changed? Had I made a mistake asking him to come? Before I confronted the answers to my questions, I submerged all that into my work and planning my vacation. I packed for my four-week retreat from my duties. East Africa beckoned.

PART IV

EAST AFRICA

Kings and Dictators

Annually, my peers vacationed in droves to explore the vast African continent. The exodus occurred during December and January, teachers' holiday break, and the peak of dry season—devoid of the heat and tropical rains. Travel books were unavailable to guide our passage through these foreign lands, and a detailed map was impossible to find in Liberia. Travel agents in Monrovia were somewhat helpful, but word-of-mouth from those who explored the well-traveled routes before us were our best guide. In mid-January two other volunteers, Jack and Betty from Monrovia and a Catholic Brother, Nathanial, joined Jim, my friend from Kpain and me on a direct flight from Liberia to Ethiopia where we began our four-country, four-week tour of East Africa.

We arrived in Addis Ababa, Ethiopia's capital, on January 17, 1972. The streets greeted us with opulent gold-laden Ethiopian Orthodox churches that were contrasted starkly with the poor begging children who surrounded us each time we left the hotel. Wealth and poverty stood side-by-side in the city, something unfamiliar to me in Liberia.

The current King, Haile Selassie, at age 82, reigned as Emperor of Ethiopia for forty-one years. Selassie's leadership had mixed reviews, but most Ethiopians revered him in the face of anti-colonialism sweeping across Africa. Never colonized under his rule, Selassie helped modernize Ethiopia with school and police reforms, and instituted a new constitution centralizing his own power. There was evidence of common human rights abuses including imprisonment and torture of political prisoners. However, respected by the international community, he met with many heads of state including Mao Zedong of China and attended the funerals of President John F. Kennedy and Charles de Gaulle.

During the time of our visit, a prolonged drought that led to famine, ever-worsening unemployment, and an increasing frustration with the government's inability to respond to the country's problems began to undermine Haile Selassie's rule. Despite the country's fragile stability, and no warnings to avoid travel there, we arrived two days before Ethiopia's biggest religious celebration of the year—Timkat, the Feast of the Epiphany.

Priests from all the neighboring towns gathered annually in Addis Ababa for a convergence on the main church. The parade of patriarchs was mesmerizing. Each wore magnificent vestments of shimmering brocade varying in color to designate their specific region. Their shoulders supported a massive three-sided headdress. Only a shadow of their faces could be seen. Each priest sat on an elevated throne carried by up to six servers followed by a processional of attendants wearing elaborate white flowing robes with gold-embossed hems. Descending from their thrones, the priests gathered for the chanting ceremony. Servers held bejeweled umbrellas shielding the patriarchs from the African sun. The smell of burning incense wafted from the swinging censers. I sensed my privilege and honor to walk alongside and photograph the parade of priests during Timkat.

From Addis Ababa we flew to Kampala, Uganda's capital. Idi Amin Dada, the new dictator of Uganda, overthrew Milton Obote in a military coup d'état just twelve months prior to our arrival. In that short amount of time, Amin became notorious worldwide for his human rights abuses, political repression, ethnic persecution, and corruption. As tourists, we were not discouraged from traveling to Uganda. However, we remained alert and limited our foolishness.

Under Amin's rule, the value of the local currency plummeted, making the criminal black market money exchange a lucrative side business. Amin required all money transactions and exchanges be made at the banks, in the local currency of shillings. Few did that, even given the risks.

The locals immediately spotted our white faces peering from the open airport bus windows when we arrived at Kampala. Americans equaled U.S. dollars, a hot commodity in their stagnant economy. We were accosted by a mass of hands waving in front of us even before we stopped, saying, "You want money? Missy, Mista, money. Dolla, Dolla?" We moved with hesitation, not knowing the black market rate. Solicited at least twenty times between the bus and our hotel, people tugged on our bags and clothing. An East Indian merchant covertly offered a money exchange when we purchased a cold drink at his store. The known reputation of Idi Amin caused us to proceed with caution. After freshening up in the hotel, Jim and I thought our safest bet would be a money exchange with the Indian store merchant. We believed an indoor transaction would be less conspicuous for procurement of shillings rather than on the street, in full view.

We ventured back to the East Indian store under a stealth-like cover to purchase a candy bar. We nonchalantly approached the counter and Jim whispered to the merchant, "We'd like to buy a candy bar and change some money." Without another word between the three of us, the merchant tilted his head for us to follow him into the back room. I broke into a cold clammy sweat in the African heat and followed Jim blindly and innocently. I wasn't certain if our actions could be considered illegal because money exchange was occurring almost everywhere, some even in public.

"I thought we were going to limit foolishness," I whimpered to Jim. He told me not to worry. Besides, in a previous life he'd been a stockbroker, so he knew something about gambling.

The merchant avoided eye contact as we sheepishly followed him. He led us to the back of the store to a large window-fronted office. Opening the door, he motioned for us to sit and pulled the curtains. I sensed we could be in danger.

A club to the head and he'd have our money and passports. I became mute and nodded for Jim to proceed so we could get the hell out of there as soon as possible. Words spoken in a whisper made the legality of our money exchange transaction seem questionable.

Within moments we had a bundle of shillings in a plain white envelope and exited the store with a phony who-me? type of look. With loot in hand, twice the amount we would have gotten from a bank exchange, my guilt quickly vanished as I joyfully contemplated our next Ugandan adventures.

We encountered many armed checkpoints as we traveled throughout the country. As a Catholic, I had no skill at hiding my remorse, when police scornfully flicked through my passport to match my face and check my visa. I might as well have had "Black Market Offender" written across my forehead. I wiped the sweat from my marked brow each time the police waved us through. To relieve my lingering guilt, I enacted my mobile confessional—making the sign of the cross on my chest and saying, "Bless me Father for I *may have* sinned..." God is a forgiving being. I, however, may have to settle for purgatory.

As we departed Kampala several days later, news reached us at the border that a group of foreigners had been detained for illegal activity. We also heard of the harsh punishment, and even death, that Amin inflicted upon the East Indians— the ill-favored foreign merchants. About seven months after our return to Liberia, Idi Amin expelled all East Indians from Uganda. This dictator meant business.

The Nile and the African Queen

Exploring Uganda was worth the risk, even under Amin's rule. Jim and I traveled together on the next leg of the trip while the others would join us later when we would begin the game preserve safaris in Tanzania. I wanted to see the headwaters of the Nile, to experience the longest most magnificent river in the world. The Nile is 4,258 miles long, fed primarily from direct rainfall including thousands of small streams from ten countries. Jim and I chartered a taxi to find its source up the road to Jinja, where the massive Lake Victoria cascades into the beginning of the White Nile. Lake Victoria is the world's largest fresh-water tropical lake—26,000 square miles in size. Liberia had nothing of this magnitude.

Our travels continued outside Kampala to Masindi with a boat trip on the White Nile toward Murchison Falls. Our lodging included canvas tents with cots in a campground on the bank of the Nile. My first indication of danger was rifle-wielding camp guards; guns kept the wildlife at a distance, away from the tourists. Hippos, of most concern, can run as swiftly on land as under water and kill intruders who enter their domain. I wasn't too scared, because in some way, it resembled a glorified Disneyland with its mechanical animals playing on the tourists' fears. However, during the night I heard hippos fighting in the river, and a guard fired shots from his rifle to chase one back into the water after it approached our encampment. Twice that night, the roars of the lions woke me. These were not plastic animals like Disneyland after all. I joked to myself to ease my anxiety thinking our canvas tent would merely serve as a napkin for a hungry lion.

The following morning, I snapped photos around the park compound while waiting for the boat ride up the Nile, when fifty yards ahead of me walked an adult elephant. I swung my 35 mm SLR camera up, adjusted my zoom lens, and telescoped the focus in tight on her eyes and trunk. I adjusted a few settings taking more shots. What a majestic animal and so close, I mused. I retracted the zoom and realized her whole head filled my lens. I jerked the camera from my face and focused my eyes on this creature walking calmly on the sidewalk straight toward me, not twenty feet away. Was she on the attack? I didn't wait for an answer as I jumped into the bushes. She calmly strutted by. This may have happened before with other ignorant tourists. The elephants in the compound seemed habituated to humans, though I later found plaques warning us about the elephants—which I hadn't bothered to read. The guards were especially cautious around the hippos and lions. They raised their guns instantly at their sound or movement.

Jim and I, along with several other tourists, boarded a flat-bottomed boat for an epic ride on a calm portion of the White Nile, about fifty yards wide at our entry point. Akiki, our captain and guide, a thin short framed Ugandan, appeared six feet tall with his commanding control of our watercraft. In the comfort of our boat we motored within feet of marabou storks, secretary birds, gazelles, foxes, and elephants. I wondered if this could have been the perfect spot to see flamingos, but there were none. Then I saw what appeared to be a twenty-foot plastic crocodile lying motionless on the bank of the river with its mouth gaping open. "Oh great, Disneyland props, I don't want to pay money for this," I told Jim. Just as those words left my lips, Akiki revved the motor and the crocodile raised up on all fours, ran toward us and dove under our thirty-foot boat. My heart skipped when the croc's wake caused our vessel to rock for over a minute. Several more times on our route, the corpse-like monsters woke from their stupor and ran into the water for safety. My newfound fear and excitement of Africa rose to a more realistic level. Even though I felt safe with the guides, I now gained a healthy respect for the dangers surrounding me.

The river began to widen and more grassy vegetation clung to the shoreline. We met a swell of movement in the river accompanied by the grunting and splashing of bobbing heads. In the heat of the day, up to fifty hippos kept cool at the river's edge. Akiki assured us we would keep our distance. I zoomed in to capture remarkable photos of fighting bulls and moms protecting their babies. We motored past the edge of the group when a massive bloated dead hippo floated past, upside down with four legs pointing upward like a stuffed animal. "This could be the result of an earlier battle," Akiki surmised.

Gently we rolled up the river. Jim said, "Hold that pose," as he framed a portrait of me gazing over the railing of our boat. He said, "You look like Katharine Hepburn in *The African Queen*. That movie was actually filmed on the Nile in Uganda."

I held my pose as he snapped the photo. "I've never seen the movie but I've heard of it." I certainly felt like an African Queen that day.

We enjoyed another few moments of calm water with wildlife wherever we looked. Then all eyes stared ahead to the sudden change in scenery. A sheer mountain wall came into view with a white mist rising from the river soaring a hundred yards into the sky. The calm White Nile became more turbulent with eddies swirling around us. The silty brown water turned white with clusters of floating foam as large as our boat.

With skill and confidence, Akiki negotiated the currents and whirlpools of foam resembling a huge draining bubble bath. My fear subsided when the wind cleared the mist for us to see a full view of Murchison Falls. We saw the falls from the top a few days earlier, but experiencing its force while at its base filled me with awe. My camera shutter clicked and my movie camera documented this torrent. I then lowered my devices to turn my attention fully to the visual beauty that lay before me.

Filled with contentment I told Jim, "I am happy, I have seen everything." The river tour was only halfway over and I had already gotten my money's worth from seeing the hippos, elephants, crocs, and hearing the lions roar at night. I relaxed in my bench seat for the trip back. We returned more quickly now as the boat flowed with the river's current.

The sudden slowing of the motor stirred me from my contented serenity as I looked up to see all the other tourists with cameras and binoculars pointing left of the boat.

"Come quick!" Jim called out.

We were back at the same spot where we discovered the bloated dead hippo an hour earlier. About twenty hungry crocodiles had found the hippo carcass. Huge jaws clamped on the hippo's tough hide then spun until they broke off pieces of flesh. The guide informed us that crocodiles cannot chew; they swallow their prey whole. When the prey is too large, they must clamp and spin to rip pieces they can swallow. I rolled the movie camera for this phenomenon because a still picture could never tell the story. Clamp, spin, rip, chomp, and swallow, over and over again: a feeding frenzy of epic proportions.

That night I lay less securely in my tent than the night before. What would be in store for us on the next leg of the trip?

Could Kenya or Tanzania top everything we had seen in Ethiopia and Uganda?

Finding the Pink Flamingos

We gathered in Arusha, Tanzania, to join our travel friends from Liberia and begin our guided Land Rover safari. Our guide, Thomas, a local from the Maasai tribe, drove us to the rim of the Ngorongoro Crater. He explained the crater formed two to three million years ago when an approximately 19,000-foot volcano exploded and collapsed upon itself. Fossilized evidence proved humans roamed this volcanic area of northeast Tanzania around the same time as the eruption.

The motor of our nine-passenger Land Rover moaned as it strained to reach the top of the volcanic rim. My heart raced in anticipation. We switch-backed up the dirt road about three to four miles with an elevation gain of 4,000 feet. When we leveled off, my mouth gaped in wonder. "Oh my God." Below me lay an extinct volcano with the deepest unbroken, unflooded caldera in the world. This 100-square-mile basin of lush green flat grassland surrounded a 2,000 foot-high volcanic rim on which our Rover now stood.

I wiped the dust from my eyes to clear my vision and gazed upon slow moving clusters of wildlife roaming the grasslands, as if God had opened Noah's Ark years ago and released all the African animals into this gigantic rich pasture. How could all these animals, about 25,000 according to Thomas, live together in one huge natural enclosure? After pausing to capture this moment on film, we proceeded from the rim and descended onto the floor of the caldera. As we drove closer, I began to see the outline and colors of all the incredible wildlife: herds of thousands of wildebeests, cape buffalos, gazelles, and zebras as well as smaller numbers of lions, hippos, hyenas, foxes, rhinos, and elephants. Thomas informed us that depending on the season, the animals migrated freely in and out of the caldera. As we arrived on the volcanic floor, our Land Rover slowly separated the herds like Moses parting the Red Sea. Habituated to the tourist vehicles, the animals essentially ignored us, knowing we were protected and safe in our wheeled fortress. However, Thomas carried a loaded rifle by his side, just in case.

About a quarter of the way through the caldera, a clump of six-foot tumbleweeds formed a large circular compound. When we reached the barrier, Thomas stopped and yelled a local greeting, "Supai." As if a gate opened, two clumped weeds lifted and out came a man from the local Maasai tribe. They spoke in their native tongue, Maa, for a few moments using hand gestures accompanied by laughter when more family members came out to greet us. Three women wore colorful cloths wrapped around their bodies and beaded jewelry adorned their necks and arms. Two men wore shorts with cloths draped over their torsos. Thomas encouraged photos. We took their pictures and paid them for the privilege. He went on to explain the tumbleweeds were actually barbed branches from the acacia tree and stacked in a circle surrounding their five-hut compound to protect them from the lions. Dad would have been impressed by this African barbed wire fence.

Inside the compound stood a small herd of domestic cattle used for milk and bloodletting. Thomas explained how the men use an arrow to pierce the jugular vein and drain blood from the live cattle to drink—an excellent source of protein. Without harm, a plaster of mud and cow dung would heal the wound nicely. During the day the villagers left their protected compound to graze their cattle, hunt and gather. Probably up to 400 Maasai lived in the Ngorongoro Crater at that time.

I marveled at this atmosphere of harmony with which 25,000 wild animals and hundreds of humans could live in a 100-square-mile natural enclosure. It is no wonder the Maasai named the area Ngorongoro which means "Gift of Life."

We continued our drive and my head spun looking out all the windows—front, back, side, or standing up to peer from the opened sunroof. Wildlife and photo opportunities surrounded me. Thomas alerted us to look to our left. We stopped to witness a pride of lions and lionesses with their young, devouring a recent zebra kill not thirty feet from our vehicle. Our presence never even provoked their attention. As I leaned out the window to take my photos, my lens cap fell to the ground. I reflexively opened the door to retrieve it and only then did ten lion heads and ten pairs of eyes focus solely upon me. My internal gasp became the bloodcurdling truth—I had become instant prey. Astutely, Thomas told me to close the door and we moved on, adding to the probable hundreds of other abandoned lens caps on the Ngorongoro Crater basin floor.

Our destination was Lake Magadi at the far end of the caldera. At high noon, the equatorial sun beat mercilessly upon us, cooking the grassland to over 100 degrees Fahrenheit. The heat and flat terrain generated a layer of thermal waves of incredible color, distorting the green grass, blue lake, and sky in the distance. My dad once explained how the Arizona heat could bend light, colors, and images into a mirage. In the baking sun, the caldera created a wave of colors that *must* be a mirage, as a base layer of green danced with colors of blue, and above shimmered an overlay of brilliant pink with what appeared to be rose petals dropping from the blue sky. The Land Rover's bumpy ride on the potholed road didn't help my focus as I strained to see what the kaleidoscope of colors could be.

The closer we came, the ripples of color began to dissipate. The rose petals falling from the sky now brandished wings, and the shimmering overlay of pink at the base became clumps of cotton candy walking on long chopsticks. We drove closer. I blinked again and the heat waves radiating off the caldera subsided as the bands of colors flattened into an image I could have never imagined. Lake Magadi overflowed with thousands of pink flamingos.

We approached the deafening sounds of honks and squawks, water splashing and wings whispering through the air with landings and takeoffs. Even as my senses overflowed with the cacophony of sounds and magical images, my unconscious mind flashed back to my Nebraska childhood memory of the four pink flamingos in the framed print at Louie's Italian Restaurant. I wondered about them ever since I was eight years old, where they lived and if they could fly. No need to wonder anymore. But instead of *four* pink flamingos, there were thousands. Thousands in the lake and many more in flight with telescoping necks guiding their direction, long legs as rudders and black markings on their wings. God created these magnificent creatures to live in the wild, to fly, and be free. A serenity of indescribable proportion overcame me.

I never expected to see flamingos in the middle of an extinct volcano in East Africa surrounded by thousands of wild animals. "This place really exists," I said to myself. "This is what drew me here...this is why I came to Africa."

Primal Instincts

That night and the following day, the intoxicating sights and sounds of the Ngorongoro Crater swirled in my head. We still had more to see and do in Tanzania, as we pressed on to the famous 5,000-square-mile national park called the Serengeti.

As we entered the park the next day, the vastness of the plains interspersed with clumps of trees and shrubs made the trained eye of our guide, Thomas, even more critical for spotting wildlife. Many locals found an income in tourism protecting the wild animals rather than hunting or poaching. Thomas seemed as excited as his passengers to make the discoveries. Among hundreds of different types of wild animals, we spotted the elusive cheetah on a treetop eating a gazelle carcass twice her size. She dragged it there to eat in peace, away from the hyenas or other scavengers. We watched a pride of lions stalking a lone wildebeest, a great white rhino wading in a mudhole, ostriches running on the plains, hyenas fighting over a leftover carcass, giraffes grazing on the tree-top branches, and baboons coming within feet of us as we ate our lunch.

As a seasoned scout for deer, coyotes, and pheasants with Dad on the farm, I took the helm, next to Thomas, to watch for wildlife. The mirage effects of the sun continued to make it difficult to determine illusion from reality. Scouring the terrain, I spotted many clusters of trees surrounding us in the distance. However, one cluster, straight ahead, seemed to be moving right to left. I pointed it out to Thomas who zeroed in and drove directly toward it.

I asked, "What is it?"

He said, "You will see."

Our Land Rover headed off the dirt road and bounced over potholes, avoided small bushes, and dodged downed tree trunks. Within minutes, Thomas estimated the moving clump of trees to be a herd of 100 elephants. "It is not every day that we can find them," he exclaimed with delight. "They are now in migration searching for water and food." We approached them cautiously in our Rover as he warned the females can get protective and aggressive, and our vehicle would provide little safety from the herd.

Thomas drove to the back of the herd as they slowly moved in unison. "We don't want to anger the lead female in the front," he informed us.

"Look, look," Thomas said as he nearly jumped out of his seat with exhilaration.

In between the dust billowing from their bushel-basket size feet, at the rear of the pack, staggered a baby elephant. We watched with astonishment as the group of pachyderms gently coddled a one-day-old newborn with its dangling umbilical cord. The baby wobbled and struggled to keep up with the pack. Its mother, sisters, and aunts all surrounded the baby like a natural buffer, nudging it forward. An adult trunk under its belly guided him. Thomas clarified that only the females protect the baby this way. Most impressive were the four females bringing up the rear who all walked backwards, swaying their heads and trunks back and forth as they moved.

Thomas saw my furrowed brow and mouth agape. "This is how they prevent any lions that may attack from the rear of the herd and between the adults' legs," he explained. Primal instinct guided these gentle giants as they sheltered their young from harm.

The Cradle of Mankind

Our safari through the game preserves came to an unwanted end, and we parted ways with some in our group. Two others and I made our way by public transport to a beach retreat for a couple of days. Our hot and sticky journey began with the daily departure of our public bus from Arusha, Tanzania, to Mombasa, Kenya. Full to capacity, we were fortunate to get a

spot on the thirty-seat diesel transport. Its interior was deco-
rated with beads and tassels hanging above the windshield and
colorful painted emblems on the windows that made up for
the puke-green paint job on the exterior. In Africa the vehicles
have an appearance of being poorly maintained but will often
run for decades until the floor rusts out. I purposely sat in the
middle hoping to land on the axle, just in case.

Our eight-hour journey to the Kenyan coast traversed the
East African savannah of the Rift Valley. This region seemed
more prehistoric and ancestral than West Africa. Only eighteen months earlier I'd read in my bedside encyclopedia that
the Rift Valley was the Cradle of Mankind—where man began. I recall tracing my finger across the map of Africa. The
enormity of the continent eluded me then. But as I gazed from
the dusty bus window, I began to gain perspective on the
vastness of the Rift Valley that lay before me. A perfectly
straight one-lane dirt road narrowed into a single thread then
disappeared on the horizon. Distant plumes of dust rose from
vehicles ahead but size determined how vehicles negotiated
this narrow band of road. Our driver, behind the wheel of our
green diesel bus, held the lane while smaller vehicles swerved
into the loose dirt to avoid a near collision.

We sat among local Maasai villagers of all ages. Men and
children wore common Western pants and shirts. The women,
with their high cheek bones, beautifully plaited hair, colorful
dress, and exquisite beaded jewelry adorning their arms and
necks, caught my attention. Determined not to look like a typical tourist, I failed miserably nonetheless, wearing my khaki
pants, shirt, and sandals with a camera hung around my neck.
The villagers timidly cast glances at the three white-skinned
foreigners.

A mother held her two-year-old son a couple of seats behind me. Not feeling well, he cried and squirmed in her lap
until he finally vomited. Possibly, motion sickness, but when I
looked at the floor, I guessed wrong. The vomit writhed with
eight-inch long white spaghetti-shaped roundworms. My gaze
turned to the window in an effort to save my own stomach.
The child calmed, and I could only hope they were taking him
to a clinic for treatment. At the single village on our journey,

the bus halted for a rest stop. After they cleaned up the floor, the mother and child departed and we drove on.

I dozed off and on for hours. Any change in speed disturbed my slumber. Unexpectedly we slowed to a crawl, I raised my head to view the barren terrain without a village or town to warrant a stop. I prayed for no flat tire or mechanical issues. The desolate landscape held nothing except the road, sparse one-foot-tall leafless shrubs, and thousands of square miles of dust and dirt. The parched earth had not seen rain in months.

When the bus came to a complete stop, the driver opened the door and the chatter among the passengers fell silent. Their hush was warranted when an unsuspecting seven-foot Maasai warrior boarded the bus. He walked toward me, scantily clad with a G-string, a beautifully beaded red sash draped from one shoulder, a seven-foot spear in his hand and dark black shiny skin with reddish finger-painted streaks covering his entire body. His hair twisted into long dreadlocks, plastered with more red paint, smelling of earth and animal fat. He wore two metal, beaded anklets. With no empty seats, the warrior stood in the aisle four feet from me as the bus resumed its route.

I looked back at what could have been called a bus stop. There was nothing there. Where did he come from? How did he know a bus was coming? How long had he waited? Where was he going? I sat in awe of his presence. Clearly, even the locals responded to something magical and regal about him. Even though our family Bible stated that God created mankind from Adam and Eve, conceivably, I may have witnessed the true beginning of mankind in that most magnificent warrior.

He rode with us for forty-five more minutes and suddenly, without gestures or communication, the bus began to slow, then stopped. The warrior stepped off the bus as majestically as he had entered. The door closed. As our bus wobbled on toward the Kenyan Coast, the Maasai warrior walked into the savannah of the Rift Valley... surrounded by miles of nothingness.

PART V

GOWEE, MY VILLAGE

The Farm Boy Visits

The epic sights, sounds, and experiences I witnessed during my East African vacation quickly faded two days later while I anxiously waited at Robertsfield International Airport for Doug's arrival from Nebraska. I wanted him to love Liberia as I did. But would he? Had I changed? Had he changed? Maybe he would try to persuade me to return with him to marry. I'm sure that's what my parents wanted, anything to have me out of Africa. Even my friends wrote me of Doug's excursion to Liberia and wondered what this farm boy's intentions were— a mystery and certainly the main gossip back home. "Well...I'm not leaving Liberia," I muttered to myself, "and I'm not going to marry, at least not now."

The jet engines roared and tires screeched on the tarmac and then the Pan Am door opened. Among the multitude of black faces, I saw the handsome, tall, 6'2", lean man I remembered. His thick blond hair was much longer and he sported a new goatee. My legs quivered with joy and fear. In amongst the other passengers, we kissed and embraced. I sensed something amiss with Doug. He has jet lag, I told myself, and that was true. Travel time from Omaha to Liberia, on his first ever flight, had taken nearly thirty hours.

We caught a ride with Jim, my East African travel partner, as he drove us in his pickup from Monrovia to Sanniquellie.

On the long ride upcountry, I pointed out areas of interest and the cultural nuances, especially when we encountered the traditional thatched huts, bare-breasted women, babies on the mothers' backs, and villagers balancing loads of wood or rice on their heads. Doug held my hand but asked few questions. He kept his gaze toward the taxi floor and seldom glanced out the window the whole ride up to Sanniquellie. I was disturbed at his indifference that was so contrary to my first experience in the country.

We said goodbye to Jim in Sanniquellie and I commandeered a taxi to Gowee. We jammed into the backseat along with a mother breastfeeding her infant and a man holding a bound live chicken between his legs. We said little to each other and Doug continued looking down most of the ride. Just before sunset the taxi dropped us off by my house. Once inside, I gave him a quick tour and warmed leftover pasta. I intended to avoid African food for the first few days.

"I brought you a gift," he said as we sat at the table in the light of my Aladdin's lamp.

I worried he may have an engagement ring. As much as I loved Doug, I sensed myself changing, unsure now of marriage. He reached in his suitcase and placed a twelve-by-twelve inch box on the table. My blood pressure instantly dropped when I found the contents to be an inflatable red chair. I said with a broad smile, "Oh, wow, well, thanks so much. Comfortable furniture is hard to get around here."

Doug stepped outside to light up a cigarette while I did the dishes. I hated smoking, but not wanting to nag, I said nothing.

As bedtime approached, we entered my room and stood with the bed between us. He took off his shirt and jeans and dropped them to the floor. The dark room hid my nervousness as I slowly removed my handmade yellow Liberian dress and draped it over a chair. We climbed into bed in our underwear and entwined in each other's arms. When the full length of our bodies lay together for the first time, the sensation was surreal and tender. He gently caressed my long hair. Our kisses were warm and passionate. For me, romance at a physical level developed a new meaning of love. However, my promise to keep my virginity intact remained paramount, and our underwear proved to be a sufficient chastity belt. We held each other closely until sleep overcame us.

The following morning our smiles told everyone what the village had hoped for: Younga Ti now had a lover. I proudly walked Doug through Gowee introducing him to Peter, Martha, Jacob, Rita, Clara, and Sami, and everyone else who came by. All graciously greeted him and commented how tall and light (blond) he was. I sighed with relief when not one man solicited me for loving-business during Doug's visit. "You will not be alone now," Martha said happily.

Over the next several days, Doug continued to sit, disengaged, in my house or smoke in my hammock in the palaver hut, showing no interest in coming with me to the clinic or on my home visits. This man with whom I found comfort and contentment seven months earlier now seemed foreign to me. In Nebraska our perfect relationship was built on similarities. Now he seemed uninterested in my work and all the things I loved about Liberia. Had I made a mistake asking him to visit? Many villagers asked him to stay and work in Gowee because they thought his presence would make me happy. When he told them he needed to return to his job back home, truthfully I was relieved. I *would* be happy for him to stay if he loved Liberia as I did, but that was not the case.

Conversations about our friends and family only magnified how much I had changed. Most of our classmates were married and pregnant or with one baby on their hip. Marriage and babies were not my priority. My main concern was helping people in my village to lead healthier lives. That's what I cared about.

As time passed, Doug and I visited LAMCO, swam in the pool, attended Peace Corps parties in Sanniquellie, and hiked to small villages. Sami extended his kindness by inviting us over for meals and pigeon hunting on Sundays. Three weeks into his stay, frustrated with his indifference to the culture and his smoking, I blurted, "I want you to stop smoking. It makes me sick to smell it on you."

"I smoke outside. But, if it makes you happy I'll stop," he said begrudgingly.

Going straight to the heart of the matter, I asked, "Do you like…Liberia? Zorgowee?"

"I don't want to live here, if that's what you mean, but it's OK. I'm not sure why you like it here. People are poor and the children don't even wear shoes. Heavens, you don't have electricity or indoor plumbing. When you finish your service let's get married as we planned."

"Well, I'm thinking about it."

"What do you mean? You're still wearing my pearl ring."

"Yes, but I'm thinking of continuing my education when I return to the States. I want to become an RN."

"I thought you would be done helping people. When you come home let's just get married."

Not knowing how to respond, I turned the focus back to him. "Why don't you go back to school? You know the Vietnam War could be in your future."

"I don't care about the war. School is not my thing. Besides, I like working in the bar."

Clearly, I came to Liberia because I wanted to; he came because he wanted *me*. The tension of his final three weeks ebbed and flowed. The passage of time crawled and we never brought up school or marriage again. He did stop smoking off and on, except when Sami offered him a cigarette. I was no longer sure we were even a match going forward. I remained hopeful that the bond of us sleeping together would somehow change us both for the better. He told me of the women he had dated and I told him of my dates—zero. I probably could have mentioned the Peace Corps trainee, Steve, as a date in the Virgin Islands when he took me out to eat one evening. However, I never had any plan of being without Doug back then. Our relationship cooled during those final three weeks.

On the eve of his departure, our intentions were entrenched. Doug remained determined to marry me once I returned home in a little over a year. I stood committed to follow my educational path. The following morning, I arranged our taxi rides from Gowee to Monrovia so he could catch his departing flight the following day. We endured a dusty hot ten-hour ride, and by sunset we entered the traffic mayhem of the capital. Our final dinner at Oscar's by the ocean provided a bittersweet ending to his visit; we still cared about each other but neither of us got what we had hoped for.

The $7.00 hotel room on Peace Corps wages sufficed for our last night together. In our dank room, decked out with a sagging double bed, one nightstand, a mildewed bathroom, and a lightbulb dangling from a ceiling wire, passion filled the air. My Dad's voice rang in my ears just as it did when I was eleven, "Boys cannot control themselves and I will never trust you." I didn't want him to be right. Making a good decision about boys, men, and sex was something I was sure I could do. Certainly, my behavior was outside Dad's approval, but our underwear served as protection. Neither could I forget the community rejection that my two pregnant high school classmates encountered nor my parents' condemnation of those girls. I feared the wrath from Dad and Mom much more than I feared the wrath of God. God would forgive me for my behavior; my parents never would. As hard as it had been over those six weeks, I believed I had kept my promise and my integrity intact.

The following morning, we said our stiff and reserved goodbyes on the tarmac of Robertsfield. As Doug boarded the Pan Am flight, he turned to meet my eyes and each of us waved halfheartedly. I felt empty as the flight departed. The vision I once held of a long life with my high school sweetheart all but vanished into the jet stream.

I struggled emotionally in the weeks following Doug's departure. I knew what I *didn't* want but wasn't at all sure what I *did* want regarding an intimate relationship. I was taught to date men only as a prelude to marriage. With most of my high school friends married and many of my Peace Corps colleagues hooked up with someone, I felt all alone.

Shortly after Doug departed, I mustered the courage to write him these words: "I don't think we have a future. You are a good person, but I have changed too much." In my heart and mind, I began to let Doug go. I suspected we both knew this was the beginning of the end of our relationship. Yet I continued to wear his pearl ring.

My Salvation

After Doug's departure, my despair grew to an all-time high and I reverted to simple methods of comfort. I ate, cooked, and ate. Sweets gave me a great sense of well-being: I baked pineapple pies, upside-down cakes, cinnamon rolls, cookies, doughnuts—sometimes three different items at a time. One day I ate an entire cream pie in one sitting. I mastered cooking the local cuisine. My favorites were ground pea soup and collard or mustard greens with deer meat. Alcohol became another comfort tool. However, I couldn't hold my liquor; one or two drinks did me in. With food, alcohol, and lack of exercise, along with the sweltering heat and humidity, I watched the pounds mount—at least twenty. I was the heaviest of my entire life. I made the dreaded "weight chart" just as Mom had kept. I set my goal at 125 pounds, my weight at high school graduation. Two pounds lost and five pounds gained; it was a never-ending battle.

Even though I rarely found myself alone in Gowee, I was incredibly lonely. Sketchy reception faded in and out from my battery-powered short-wave radio, my source of companionship and my link to the outside world. I positioned the tin-foiled rabbit ears in the direction of Monrovia to catch a clear sound of the *Voice of America* broadcasts and the British accent of the BBC correspondents who comforted, entertained, and provided me company as darkness fell precisely at 6:00 p.m. News of the Vietnam War aired on the radio every night, but by 1972 American military involvement began to decline. I knew little of that conflict other than my second cousin returned from Vietnam with his legs blown off above the knees. My brother, Bob, was fortunately deferred because of an old football knee injury. As I sat back in Doug's red inflatable chair, I wondered what was in store for him. Vietnam seemed so far away. Besides, I had my own battles to fight in Gowee.

Once the radio news broadcasts were over, I listened to African highlife music transmitted from Monrovia. The West African sound swept over me with its infectious melodic, up-tempo, syncopated rhythm. The guitar solos seemed to sing and undulate, and I reflexively swayed to its beat. At Carnival

in the Virgin Islands a few months earlier, I could only respond with restrained movements. In Gowee, I could let go.
During evenings of the full moon, drums emanated from
nearby huts and flooded the village with sounds from the talking drum, a handcrafted hour-glass shaped wooden cylinder
that could modulate its pitch of the leather drum head by
squeezing the tension cords between the drummer's torso and
arm. A skilled player could mimic speech with this drum, and
the villagers responded. Often Martha or Rita summoned me
to dance to the rhythm of that magical drum.

Daily diary entries became a nightly ritual—my salvation
and best friend. After my evening meal by the light of the
Aladdin's lamp, I chronicled the events of the day and details
of my failures and successes, sadness, and joy, as well as rejection and acceptance. I often wrote in code, not knowing
who might read its precious words. I rarely documented my
innermost feelings. When I read the entries even weeks or
months later, I could recall every nuance that lay between the
lines. My words retained memories that were never captured
with a photo. I looked forward to the comfort of my pen and
paper every night.

My self-inflicted despair seemed minuscule compared to
the daily difficulties of the people in Gowee. The thin fragile
line between life and death rarely seemed to affect the value
of their precious existence. The villagers easily found happiness with rice in their belly and a roof over their head. Their
resilience was remarkable. I had so much more to learn from
my people in Gowee.

Making a Difference

Each month our clinic saw seasonal surges in reported deaths
and illnesses, and I often wondered whether any of my efforts
made a difference. Patience was a virtue I seemed to have lost
somewhere in Nebraska. How many mothers and babies did I
help with my midwifery training? Did the villagers encounter
fewer bouts of malaria? Did parents stop stuffing their sick
children? In our remote setting, we had no way of measuring
mortality or morbidity outcomes directly. The only tangible

markers were our monthly reports of Antenatal and Well-baby clinic attendance and DPT vaccinations which I faithfully submitted to the Ministry of Health in Monrovia.

Peter and I patched up our relationship after my angry outburst over the refrigerator incident. We continued to diligently spread the word about our clinics. Our efforts paid off when twelve months after my arrival, our weekly antenatal attendance numbers were in the twenties with the highest being thirty-three pregnant women recorded in one four-hour clinic. As time passed the villagers became comfortable coming with their sick *and* well children to the Well-baby clinic. Gradually our rate of a complete series of three DPT injections per child soared.

With great surprise, Gowee became the most successful clinic among my peers in the Health Education Program, demonstrating the greatest percent of improvement in Antenatal and Well-baby attendance and completed DPT vaccination rates. Some of my colleagues had better supplied clinics with equipment, electricity, doctors, nurses, and trained midwives; therefore, *our* success was even more remarkable. After my first year, Ms. Picket, my Peace Corps supervisor from Monrovia, recognized our efforts by inviting a host of national and international visitors to our clinic, now labeled a "model rural clinic." I'd never drawn this much attention before, except when I was valedictorian of my high school graduating class (albeit in a class of sixteen graduates).

All that year important international guests toured our clinic including three separate visitors from Washington, D.C.: Joe Blatchford, the Action Director; Don Hess, the Peace Corps Director; and finally, a U.S. Senator. Liberian dignitaries also visited, including the Minister of Health and Dr. Walton, the Regional Director of Health, who brought doctors and public health officials from Japan and the U.S.

As I led those delegations through our clinic, our measurable success seemed more real and my farm-girl tenacity seemed to prove itself. Within the first six months of landing in-country, three of my Health Education colleagues terminated for a variety of reasons. An additional three transferred to other posts within Liberia. By the end of my term, of the eighteen who completed the Virgin Islands training, only eight finished the full two years of service—a 44 percent attrition rate. I realized with some pride I had succeeded beyond my wildest dreams.

Prior to my arrival, our clinic was a mere shell, but since then we were gifted a fetoscope, kerosene refrigerator, baby scale, sterilizer, microscope for examining stool samples, vaccines, plus CARE milk, oil, and flour. We could only hope for more. Maybe with our success and international attention we would receive more supplies and medicines for our clinic.

Morbidity and Mortality

Basking in our clinic's success was short-lived. In September 1972, I entered in my diary, "three babies died in our small community today." Before coming to Liberia, I had never known of a baby or young child who died. In Gowee, infant mortality remained heartbreakingly commonplace. Not all deaths or their causes could be confirmed, with sketchy data collection coming from nearby walk-in villages. Most likely the death rate was even higher due to under-reporting. Malaria, dysentery, measles, respiratory infections, and malnutrition were some of the main causes of mortality in the Zor Clan. "The starving children in Africa," as my mom used to say at the dinner table, rang true that day. Due to the high infant death rate, a mother often had up to twelve pregnancies with only five living children. With the unavailability of birth control, pregnancy was easy to achieve. Staying alive was not.

When a village death occurred, immediate wailing commenced. Outward crying and howling filled the air from men, women and children, both young and old. No one refrained. Grieving could last for one to two days, shorter for an infant death and longer for an adult. The deceased lay in a simple wooden casket or a shroud of lappa for a ground burial. Once the grieving subsided, villagers quickly resumed their daily lives. Ironically, back home, we grieve longer for a lost pet. Death in Gowee seemed so familiar that in order to cope they focused on life rather than sorrow.

Reality was tackling my idealism. And reality was winning. During that month of September, deaths rose by the week. I hit an all-time low when my diary notations became marked with tears of sadness and helplessness. I said to myself, wait. Aren't tears forbidden? Greisens don't cry. Maybe you are a sniveling weakling. There I sat in my village, 6,000 miles from my parents, with shame buried deep within me. But crying was all I had. The unabashed flow of tears gave me a sense of cleansing my pent-up grief—unresolved sorrow from my failure to meet my parents' expectations. I had wanted to save the villagers from death and disease, and now I failed to meet my own lofty goals in Gowee.

At other times outbursts of anger filled my diary; anger toward the Liberian government for not doing more, or for Peter being selfish and egotistical. Later, I cringed with disgust to learn the government was even less supportive than I imagined. Dr. Walton, supervisor of Peter and Duo, visited our clinic one day and handed each of them an envelope, saying, "This cash is for you. It is at least two months' salary." Later, both confirmed this was their first pay since my arrival eighteen months earlier.

Prior to President Tubman's death, government workers like teachers, soldiers, and healthcare workers were paid somewhat regularly. However, wages appeared to have nearly stopped after President Tolbert came into power, and I made a naïve assumption that Peter, Duo, and the two schoolteachers were getting paid. The Liberians described Tubman as a President who left a few crumbs for the locals. Tolbert rarely left any.

Humiliated by my lack of awareness, I felt remorse for yelling at Peter who asked the people for large sums of money and took the clinic refrigerator home. Similarly, my disappointment embarrassed me when the grade schoolteachers didn't show up the day I taught my health education class at the school or when they asked the students for money. These government workers needed to eat too. I was ashamed of my ignorance and even angrier at the system.

While death and illness plagued Gowee, there was no better person to begin with than myself. I worked to become a healthy role model for my community. Good hand washing, taking my antimalarial medication every Sunday without fail, boiling and filtering my drinking water, protecting my food from flies, and washing and peeling all my fruit and vegetables were part of my daily life.

I had three points of access to health care: Sanniquellie at their local hospital; at LAMCO with its Western-type clinic and hospital; or the Peace Corps office in Monrovia with its own doctor and nurse. Access to these options could take hours or days depending on the level of care required and the availability of transport.

Despite my compulsion to prevent malaria, I contracted the parasite three times in my two short years. My blood tests confirmed I had contracted three of the four types found in West Africa: *Plasmodium vivax, P. ovale* and *P. malariae. Plasmodium falciparum*, which affects the brain, is the deadliest, and the only one I did *not* contract. All Peace Corps homes had screened windows, but when traveling to areas where I did not have that luxury, I used the dreaded mosquito coil, a form of incense that smoldered throughout the night, releasing a stench of caustic smoke to ward off the insects. Nonetheless, screens and mosquito coils had failed me. Luckily, my three bouts of malaria were successfully treated and placed in remission. Only after leaving a malarial area, can the final medication be given to fully kill the parasite. (After I left Liberia, the mutation of the parasite made the current treatment of chloroquine ineffective and a new medication was prescribed.)

My virgin immune system rebelled violently and became hypersensitive to all the bugs in Liberia. I had some symptom or another at least monthly. Notes of runny belly, gas pains, fever, malaise, cough, and headaches filled my diary. At one point, I suffered a two-month period of severe malaise including a host of intermittent symptoms. While on a visit to Monrovia, I complained about my condition to the Peace Corps doctor who ordered stool, blood, and urine samples, including a chest x-ray. The results determined I not only had streptococcal and staphylococcal infections but also trichuriasis, commonly known as whipworm. It appeared all my germaphobic treatment of water, fruit, and vegetables had failed.

During a seven-day hike with Peter to six Zor Clan villages for clinic outreach, I encountered a multitude of other parasites and varmints: a tarantula atop my straw mattress, a scorpion on my path, and a nest of driver ants who crawled up my pants legs and bit me voraciously. Upon my return from the trip, Martha removed a jigger with eggs from my big toe, Rita found scabies nits in my scalp, and my body was marred with multiple bedbug bites.

Along with other volunteers, I succumbed to numerous ailments. The Peace Corps did its best to train and prepare the volunteers, but by my sixth month I encountered most every illness in the Peace Corps handbook, including pneumonia, and hoped my immunity from the newly formed antibodies along with the gamma globulin injections were sufficient to ward off any other illnesses.

Our lack of easy access to reliable health care, along with battling our own illnesses, created deep bonds among volunteers. As the only volunteer with nursing skills in our remote locale, I was often utilized for various clinical tasks. Emboldened with my meager knowledge, I diagnosed my peers with various non-life-threatening disorders including dysentery or bladder infections and provided injections of gamma globulin every six months. All volunteers were given a Peace Corps cache of medications, so treatment often occurred with favorable outcomes. I repeated the nursing motto: Do no harm.

All my scars from the farm couldn't hold a candle to Liberia's diseases. I never wrote home about most of the illnesses, and certainly not the deadly ones. Mom harped that Africa was a dangerous place, and I didn't want to give her the pleasure of thinking she was right.

Diamonds and Near Death

Tom, my Peace Corps friend from Zapa, invited me to accompany him for a weekend outing to Gorton, the well-known village near Gowee that the diamond commissioner visited. Even though my village had a diamond mine, Gorton's was at least ten times the size, surely making our two-hour hike an adventure and an education.

Tom's houseboy, Alonso, a strapping fifteen-year-old, served as our guide to his home village. Alonso's khaki shorts revealed his muscular calves and I marveled at his Liberian sandals, handmade by a local cobbler. These sturdy open-toed shoes had soles cut from used tire treads with rivets attaching the straps made from the inner tubes. The luxury of wearing shoes indicated a villager with some form of good income. With his wages from Tom, he moved to Zapa to attend school.

We met in Gowee and began our hike with a plan to spend the night with Alonso's family in Gorton. En route, lush vegetation often fell across our path, and Alonso quickly slashed it with his cutlass to clear the way. Astutely, I wore long pants to add leg protection and plastic store-bought sandals in case we encountered rain. For his young age, Alonso was wise beyond his years. He was a walking medicine chest of knowledge. He pointed out a small plant called the fever leaf. Its boiled foliage created a tea that relieved febrile symptoms. Next, he showed us the bark of a tree that helped tame stomach ailments. With his cutlass he dug up the root of a shiny-leaved plant used to heal infected wounds. It could also act as an antiseptic. Another nearby root aided in curing snakebites. Alonso displayed a leaf to be crushed and consumed or spread on the skin to inhibit mosquito bites. "This one is used for toilet paper," he said, pointing to another broad-leaved plant. Vital information to have, because not all leaves should touch those delicate areas.

He identified other plants having medicinal qualities. From my nurses training, I was aware of herbs being used for such purposes, like foxglove to make digitalis for heart conditions. However, I had just walked through the pharmacy of my local community. So, this was how Africans survived for thousands of years without Western medicine. They were brilliant and resourceful. Maybe we could learn more from them.

We reached Gorton around 12:30 p.m. and about twenty villagers came to greet us. First in line was the village chief who introduced his three wives and ten children. We met Joseph, Alonso's father, and his wife and four children. Most of the women were bare-breasted with an African lappa tied around their waists and no head tie, indicating a hardworking community. All the children were barefooted and shirtless with shorts, except for one privileged boy who wore a tattered oversized t-shirt. For many, we were the first white people they had ever seen. Most of the young children hid behind their parents curiously looking at us. The older ones approached cautiously, and a few quickly touched my skin and hair, eliciting a few giggles. Alonso's family presented us with fresh bananas to revive our energy.

Gorton, a typical small village of about ten homes, consisted of seven round huts constructed of woven bamboo siding. Three rectangular ones were of mud block, all with palm-thatched roofs. Joseph showed us his new round thatched hut being constructed by the villagers. Most of the work occurred in the afternoon when the men returned from working in the diamond mine. He explained that up to twenty people could construct a hut in only a few days. Women and youth fabricated the woven siding and thatched roofing while the men cut the slender wood saplings for the roof and larger ones for the sides. Both men and women were skilled in the critical bark-stripping technique to create twine used to bind the entire structure together.

Joseph went on to tell us how wind and rain resistant the homes were. If a roof did leak, a mere hike to the bush to cut and fold a palm leaf resulted in an immediate repair. The downfall of wood and thatched homes were the termites who entered it from any exposed wood and could destroy the foundation within days. Families watched the wood constantly for the telltale signs of the termites who left their raised highway ridge-work. Joseph told us his new home might be done next week, hopefully before the rainy season began.

Smoke rising from many of the huts' cone-shaped centers signified the women preparing meals from wood fires. Most families cooked in the same hut where they slept, and the reason soon became apparent. As a nurse, I think of the asthma and other respiratory conditions that occur from prolonged proximity to wood smoke. However, there were benefits to reap. First, the smoke rising to the ceiling rafters and thatched roof warded off many opportunistic predators such as destructive termites, stinging scorpions, poisonous spiders, and snakes. Secondly, the rafters stowed husked or unhusked rice as well as dried meat and fish which the wood-fire heat helped to keep dry and preserve. With a Liberian's average life expectancy to be around forty years of age, my long-term health concerns of lung cancer or emphysema were the least of *their* worries. Parasites, germs, and childbirth complications are just a few of the culprits that kill in Liberia.

After our introductions and orientation to the village, Tom and I rested for an hour, then with Alonso and his father we headed off to the diamond mine, another thirty-minute walk. About a mile and half from the village we found the deep open-pit mine about the size of a football field. On the ridge of the mine stood one supervisor, and ten men with pickaxes and shovels worked deep inside the pit. Six men were from Gorton and five others from a nearby village. The mine was a source of income for the men and many came from a distance to seek a job grossing 50¢ a day. Depending on the size of a mine, as few as five and as many as thirty men labored at one time.

Most digging appeared to be random and disorganized, with smaller trenches dug within a larger pit, and only a few areas had evidence of terracing or methodical digging. Most of the men worked in muddy water up to their thighs. The echoing sound of a two-stroke gasoline powered pump drained the water to prevent the pit from entirely flooding during the excavation. Diamond mining in Liberia resembled the crude American gold panning days back in the 1800s that I once saw on TV. We watched Joseph's neighbor pour muddy water from a bucket over a homemade boxed screen to sift out any material. He further washed and filtered the gravel to reveal any diamonds.

While we watched them dig, wash, and sift the soil for about thirty minutes, two workers found two small diamonds the size of a small pea. We didn't know the value but understood that many found there were of industrial rather than jewelry quality. However, there had been rare discoveries of clear diamonds up to two carats found at the Gorton mine— the reason for the diamond commissioner's visits. The workers never kept the diamonds, relinquishing them to the supervisor when discovered. They wore little clothing, making it harder to conceal any stowaway gems. With my photos I documented the human face of this archaic industry.

Diamond digging was dirty, hard, and risky. Working in bare feet all day in the mud with pickaxes and shovels posed just one means of injury or infection, not to mention the collapsing of unreinforced dirt walls as high as fifty feet. Standing water left in the mines provided a perfect breeding ground for the anopheles mosquito, the carrier of malaria, providing a grave risk to nearby villages, like Gorton. Even though our visit was for pleasure and adventure, I couldn't help but contemplate this health hazard. But with the list of health challenges awaiting me back in Gowee, I relinquished my concern for the villagers in Gorton to my higher power—God.

Now about three in the afternoon, we walked back to the village thoroughly exhausted. Alonso's mother fixed us a wonderful meal of Liberian chop made with chicken and greens over rice. Chicken, a rare and expensive meat in the bush, was often freshly killed and prepared for special guests, like us.

With one cow on the premises and no latrines in the village, flies were abundant. These pests were a main source of disease in Liberia and I knew this well in my teachings to the villagers. Flies swarmed our plates of chop and I shooed them away with little success. My hunger raged, so I scarfed the food down with my nose running from the abundance of red hot Liberian pepper. No meal, now, was worthy without it.

Once nighttime fell, the chief's wife heated a bucket of water over the open fire. With a kerosene lantern in one hand and the bucket in the other, she motioned me to follow her to a small clearing at the edge of the village for my bath. She must have known my proficiency to wash and rinse my entire body with a half a bucket of warm water, because that was all I got. I won't ever take for granted the long hot showers I grew accustomed to on the farm. Water was a precious resource in Liberia; clean water was even rarer. As she returned, I stood alone fifty feet from the village except for the lone cow who approached my bucket of water. She took a sip, before I chased her away. I barely had enough for my bath.

I gazed up from my bucket to marvel at the thatched huts silhouetted by the few outdoor cook fires flickering in the night. The dark dense jungle at my back encircled me like a curtain in my country shower. I undressed, turned down my kerosene lantern and the light from the crescent moon reflected off my white naked body like a beacon in the African night. I never once worried about anyone looking. I had been in Liberia too long by then. And I was too tired to care.

The country cook fire, either inside or outside the hut, was like our television back home—the place where everyone gathered during and after meals. But instead of sitting in silence and watching the TV, the villagers talked, told stories, and laughed. In front of the fire, storytelling began and history was passed down to the generations. Children learned to respect the fire and set their roots of traditions and culture from the stories told. Tom and I sat around the crackling flames with Alonso's family and the chief while we shared our tales.

As the flames flickered, serenity overcame me. I sensed a connection to the hardworking villagers and their simple lifestyle. Their bond with nature and love of family resonated within me. It was that night my love for Liberia and its people grew deeper.

Bedtime approached and surely we displaced villagers from their beds as it is not uncommon for five to ten people to sleep in one hut. Tom and I shared one alone, each having a bed to ourselves. This four-foot by five-foot wooden bed frame was constructed of crisscrossed wood saplings, secured by twine, and topped with a woven palm mat. The bed was nothing special, but for bush standards I preferred it over the bare ground.

We lay down with all our clothes, covered with a blanket, and turned off our kerosene lantern. Just as I began to fall asleep, I heard the pitter-patter of feet in the woven-mat ceiling right above our beds. At first it sounded like one varmint; it stopped and started. Then after a few minutes, more joined in. Now I could hear as many as five in the ceiling. From the sound I suspected them to be large rats, not uncommon in the bush. Tom slept soundly as I lay motionless praying one would not fall through the ceiling mat onto my face. Maybe I could outlast their romping when they discovered nothing of value. My hunch failed. Now the sound of tiny scurrying feet became a frolicking dance. They were either playing or mating, and I did not care. I had enough. While debating what to do and who to summon, the scampering moved to the floor around our beds. Did Tom or I have any food in our bags which now lay on the floor? We could be in deep trouble!

"Jesus, Mary, and Joseph, if I did anything to vex you, please forgive me," I mumbled. If rats carry disease, I did not want it. Many rats scuttled on the floor around the bed in the sheer darkness, so I deserted my option of running out of the hut. Pretending to be brave, I didn't scream or awaken Tom. Besides, I am tough and the only white woman residing in an African village.

I dozed off and on for hours as the racket awakened and startled me. Then the sound of a rooster's crow jolted me upright as a dim light leaked through the thatched walls and under the one inch gap by the front door. I survived the night and I reached down to feel if I had all my toes. "Thank you, Jesus, for saving me."

Tom awakened and I told him about my horrendous night. He laughed and said he slept through it all. We ate a quick Liberian breakfast of beignets and instant Nescafé. Tom, Alonso, and I spent several minutes saying goodbye and thanking everyone for welcoming us to Gorton. We left for Gowee at 9 a.m.

About an hour into our hike, we sat to rest briefly and hydrate. When I stood from my palm-log bench, I could barely resume the hike as the sultry air drenched my skin. Maybe I suffered sleep deprivation from the rat circus the previous night. The two-hour walk seemed more arduous than the day before. I dragged myself back to Gowee.

Alonso left our company when we arrived at my house before noon and returned to Zapa by taxi. I took a quick shower to remove any remnants of rat droppings and immediately began to feel chilled. With little appetite, I pulled leftovers from the fridge for lunch. I could only manage a couple of bites of rice when I developed runny belly.

Still feeling cold, I located my thermometer and it registered 99.6 degrees, not a concern. Within minutes I began shivering and my temperature rose to 102 degrees and then 102.6. Tom reacted by taking care to provide me with fluids and aspirin. As my teeth began to chatter I tried not to bite off the mercury thermometer that now registered 103. We decided I needed to get medical care quickly.

It was now 6 p m, I knew Sami was in Monrovia and finding a taxi out of Gowee after dark was nearly impossible, I directed Tom to Malibako, the only taxi driver I knew who lived in town. Chances of him being home and available were slim. Even with my bouts of malaria, these symptoms seemed different. Malaria often presents with a severe headache, aching, and chills. This episode had no headache with terrible runny belly, plus it came on suddenly. After thirty minutes, Tom returned with the taxi and we drove off, blazing a trail of dust on the road to Sanniquellie in the darkness.

Tom decided my best option was go to Pam's house and confer with our Peace Corps friends on what should be done. I have no memory of the forty-five minute ride except that two people carried me out of the taxi. Once inside Pam's house, I became keenly aware of everything, but could not move or talk. Within minutes, two other Peace Corps volunteers surrounded me. I lay on Pam's bed trembling with my eyes open and teeth chattering from fever. Sweat saturated my dress and long hair. Pam assumed the challenge of reducing my fever and applied ice and 70 percent isopropyl alcohol directly to my body. My arms and legs convulsed wildly as three volunteers pinned me down in a four-point restraint. My convulsions may have been spurred on from the shock of the ice cubes and smell of the alcohol rather than the fever. Grave concern marked their faces. I was in an odd state of delirium—speechless with intermittent lucidity. I yelled, "Tom, Tom," the only words I spoke during those hours. Due to my combativeness, no one was able to take my temperature but my skin was burning from the fever.

Above my chaotic screams and wailing I overheard them discussing what to do next. The volunteers chose to transport me by taxi to Sanniquellie Hospital, where the doctor gave me two injections. I had no recollection of what they were; most likely one for malaria, always a safe bet. However, convulsions, diarrhea, and hysteria did not indicate malaria.

With no marked improvements in my condition, my friends reviewed other care options: stay at the Sanniquellie Hospital, back to Pam's to recover, or take me to LAMCO where we could find international doctors and better medical care. They decided to take me to LAMCO, thank God, my muted vote exactly.

Pam suggested we contact Dr. Gobbe, one of the Liberian doctors in town, who owned a lovely black Mercedes. At midnight he offered to drive me to LAMCO, forty-five minutes away. This was probably the only Mercedes in all northern Liberia, and for sure the only car available with an inflated spare tire, a full tank of gas, and functioning shock absorbers. Tom, bless his soul, offered to accompany me to LAMCO.

The two of us sat in the back seat of the black Mercedes while Dr. Gobbe sped down the curved, potholed dirt road at about sixty miles an hour. I looked out the window and the headlights flickered off the passing greenery like a carnival ride gone bad. Queasiness gripped me and I cranked the window down to vomit. Tom clamped his hands around both my ankles as half my torso hung out the back window. I needed air. I wanted to get out, plus I didn't want to soil Dr. Gobbe's Mercedes. I retched at least five more times, kicking and gagging. In between the puking, I noticed a conveniently placed napkin. When I used it to wipe the bile from my mouth, I discovered it was my entire tent dress worn like a scarf around my neck. I couldn't care less about what anyone saw below my neck, I had other things to worry about having left all my stomach contents on the red laterite road between Sanniquellie and LAMCO.

A team of medical personnel in white coats converged upon me after we arrived at the hospital. My memory lapsed when they heavily sedated me. Staff told me I vomited and had runny belly well into the next day while on continuous intravenous fluids. On the third day, my symptoms subsided, and they removed my intravenous needle to feed me a light breakfast, which all came back up. Later that day a nurse brought me a rectal suppository for my nausea, placed it in a cup with a glove on my overhead table and walked away. I donned the glove and gave it to myself. I hope that the Peace Corps got a discount for my hospital stay.

Five intravenous bags of sodium dextrose were administered within forty-eight hours to compensate for my fluid loss. The bedpan and emesis basin became my constant companions for four full days. The stool cultures revealed I had Shigella Bacillary dysentery, an intestinal disease as severe as typhoid fever, deadly if left untreated. On the fifth day, my symptoms diminished with medication, and I wanted to be released. The following day, in a feeble voice I said, "Doctor, I am so much better, ya. I am a nurse and have friends who are health volunteers. I hold yur foot, ya, to let me go." With reluctance the Liberian doctor discharged me. My volunteer friends accompanied me by taxi back to Sanniquellie where I stayed a couple more days before returning to Gowee.

I made a full recovery after about a month of weakness, but I had a new appreciation for how people die from tropical diseases. I was taught how flies transmit illness, but I had no idea that the ones who landed on my food in Gorton could have ended my life. Had I become ill in that remote village or been alone in Gowee, the outcome could have been different. I certainly owed my life to Tom.

Weeks after my recovery I came to an ironic conclusion. Sitting around the fire with the villagers in Gorton was the day I fell so deeply in love with Liberia. That was the same day I came closest to my own death.

Devils and Medicine Men

One afternoon, Manuel, the clan chief, put Gowee on full alert; all work and school activity came to a halt. Martha summoned me to follow her to the center of the village where I found walls of braided palm fronds around the open perimeter. At least a hundred villagers gathered in a semicircle, creating a stage for the event. Some stared out their windows, while others stood at the edge of the crowd to keep a respectful distance. I sat on a bench next to Martha. Across the courtyard two fearful beady eyes peered through the wall of palm fronds.

Suddenly gasps and cheers rang out. A human-like figure wearing a massive raffia skirt, about five feet in diameter, exited one of the huts. The creature wore a black wooden-carved Gio mask adorned with a crown of cowry shells. Metal teeth protruded from its smallish mouth. Over the slit-like eyes was a white-painted mask. Purple cloth covered its arms and torso then draped down the back like a cape. Atop its cone-shaped hat stood a foot-long red-leather cylinder that clasped a tassel of black and white goat hair. The Gio short devil had come to our village.

He twirled, spun, and dipped his raffia skirt until the red laterite dust created a magical aura around him. The masked figure rhythmically danced to the cadence of the hollowed-log slit drum. The short devil's entourage—a drummer, an interpreter, and two others to keep the crowd in check—accompanied him wherever he went. This was Gio witchcraft at its finest, and its power ran deeper than simply the fear of this scary creature.

The majority of the Gio were animists who believed spirits dressed as devils possessed witching and supernatural powers. Witchcraft played an important role in Gio beliefs, especially in circumstances for which they had no explanation, such as infertility or snakebites. They believed the devil's dance could rid the victim of this ailment. Or its spirit could bestow a good harvest of rice to a family for the right price. On the other hand, devils had the ability to curse and even kill their victims. Martha explained, "The devil make good or bad to any people. Just pay dollar, chicken, or rice and you get yur wish. If the devil witch you, people get sick or die-o. One husband ask da devil to witch his wife who did loving-business to another man. Man and wife both be sick-o."

The devil speaks his own language. No one else but he and his entourage can understand, and therefore the need for an interpreter. As he danced, the interpreter translated. He wished the village well with a good farming season. However, if anyone had other wishes they could pay a small fee. Those who had money gave 10¢ or 25¢, and I gave $1.00. With no wish in particular, I asked permission to take photos of the short devil and his entourage, and they agreed. Not ten feet from the devil, his spiny, silver teeth and white-masked eyes peered into my camera lens.

The superb dancing of the short devil, however, was surpassed by the tricks and magic of the tall devil when he visited Gowee a month later. That tall creature possessed an eeriness with his blank black mask lacking facial features. He wore a prominent cowry shell crown with six-inch long tassels dangling from his temples and a two-foot cone-shaped headdress topped with blond goat hair draped along each side. His raffia skirt, smaller than that of the short devil, allowed him freedom to perform his magic while dancing on five-foot stilts that elongated his long spindly legs to eight feet. The hand-woven cotton country cloth covering his arms and legs dangled beyond normal appendages. No human skin was visible, adding to his intimidating appearance.

The tall devil's magic was symbolized by his superhuman feats. With his soaring frame, he spun and dipped, then ran, skipped, and jumped. We became believers in his magic when he leaned forward almost to a face-plant before reacting to catch himself. I coined it the "dead-man fall." But he defied human capabilities when his sidekick laid flat on the ground, face up, and the towering twelve-foot stickman ran from twenty feet to land a wooden foot one inch from the man's head. The crowd oohed and aahed and gave more money. If he could perform these feats, he could certainly cast good or evil on anyone.

No one touched or spoke directly to the masked spirit. Villagers had to use his interpreter to communicate in the devil's language. With money in hand, I took photos of that mysterious phenomenon and movies of him performing a dead-man fall. The priceless photo of me holding the tall devil's hand with a baton between us kept the mysteriousness alive.

One day Clara summoned me for a tall devil sighting, and to my surprise I discovered not one, but two. They came from nearby villages inviting a supreme dance competition; each one sought to outdo the other with their dips, spins, jumps, and dead-man falls. The show went on in the daylight for hours. When they tired and took in as much money as the villagers could surrender, one devil summoned a money-bus and splayed himself atop the canopy like a grasshopper on top of a toy truck with his long legs spilling over the side. With his entourage inside the money-bus, they made the forty-five minute ride to Sanniquellie for his next show and more money.

While watching the tall devil mount the money-bus, I flashed back to St. Thomas in the Virgin Islands when I witnessed the tall stilted human dancing in the streets during Carnival. Only then did I naïvely make the connection to how the slave trade brought its culture from Africa to the Caribbean. The similarities were uncanny—a fully clothed human on wooden stilts. There, the commonalities ended. The Virgin Islands' cousin was unmasked and displayed joy and fun, but in Gowee, the devil possessed mystery, power, and intrigue.

Most villagers came to respectfully and curiously view the show. However, other regions of Liberia held different devil cultures and practices based upon their unique tribal customs. When the devil came to the town of a fellow volunteer, everyone in the village barricaded themselves in their homes with shutters closed tight and no one was allowed outside until he departed—which could be up to two days. The frequency of his visits caused undue stress to the volunteer and she terminated her service early.

Villagers turned more commonly to another form of healing to cure the plethora of ailments present in the Zor Clan—the powers of the medicine men. These few individuals dressed in normal clothing possessed special capabilities. Their craft, also known as traditional or country medicine, came in the form of potions, herbs, or rituals. Their role was like the midwives who treated only women and infants, but the medicine men had broader healing skills. Prior to Western medicine, these treatments and practices had been the main form of curative care for many parts of the world for thousands of years. The more current methods have probably been around for just a few hundred years.

Different from the short and tall devils, who only came to the villages periodically, the treatment from the medicine men could be obtained at any time—somewhat like a country clinic. For villagers who lived deep in the bush and farther from Western influence, the traditional treatment of the medicine men flourished. In the sixteen small villages of the Zor Clan that surrounded Gowee, some of the most powerful medicine men could be found. Peter and I traveled the villages by foot on a seven-day outreach clinic tour. Hoping to guide our way, I diagrammed a map of this previously uncharted area. The small village of Durlay, one of the farthest from Gowee (a three-hour hike), was known in the Zor Clan as the center of country medicine.

When conditions could not be explained in their culture, such as a miscarriage or malnutrition, the medicine men were empowered. When Peter and I arrived in Durlay, I succumbed to the power of the medicine man. I eagerly paid for his special treatment to make me dry (thin) and curb my appetite when I had failed to lose the twenty pounds I gained since arriving in Liberia. I purchased another to cure a cold virus. He concocted a unique mixture of herbs sewn in a small leather pouch for me to wear around my neck. I can't say for certain if either was effective, but the pouch of herbs gave me willpower and confidence. I thought twice about eating the whole batch of cookies and the cream pie when I saw the pouch around my neck. Even if it was a placebo, it worked.

I have little doubt that some country medicine was effective as I learned from Alonso on our way to Gorton. But I also witnessed the flip side of traditional country medicine—the toll it took in lives and money. To keep my impatience in check, I justified their local treatment, realizing Western medicine was too new and not easily accessible to everyone in the Zor Clan. Superstitions cultivated from the medicine men were compounded when people waited too long to arrive at a clinic or hospital and ultimately died there, perpetuating the belief that one would find death at the doors of those Western facilities. I blamed myself when I didn't observe villagers' symptoms early enough and heard of people walking to Durlay for treatment. I experienced the consequences of the traditional treatments so many times with snakebite victims and the high infant mortality from curable illnesses like diarrhea, dehydration, or malnutrition. Malaria, a preventable disease, could not be cured with country medicine. Not only could death result from this practice, but it could be quite lucrative for the medicine man who received money or food from the victims who could ill afford the treatment.

Medicine men dealt not only with illness but anything that created ill will. Property theft was commonplace. Everyone had something stolen at one time or another. If I left my door or shutters unlocked, something would be stolen. In my first month, my transistor radio was taken when a rogue entered an unsecured window. The medicine men could be of help or hindrance in the area of rogue business. Juju medicine, a special herbal concoction, can retard the rogue *or* the victim. Stories tell of the rogue sprinkling juju dust on the sleeping homeowner after a break-in to cast the victim into a deep slumber. After a suspected juju dust encounter, the entire house of a Sanniquellie volunteer was ransacked, stealing selected items while the victim slept through the ordeal. One volunteer had nearly all her valued possessions taken from her home. Fortunately, rogues were rarely violent upcountry.

I took steps toward rogue defense. At the market I purchased a perfect weapon, a fufu stick, used by the locals to mix a paste from boiled cassava root which is formed into an edible dough ball. The two-foot stick with a wicked carved half-moon at its base would give any rogue a second thought if whopped upside his head. This became my "juju-fufu" club. I assumed my house would eventually be a target and slept with my torch and weapon at my bedside. Only one window shutter had hinges to the outside making the remaining four shutters nearly rogue-proof.

One fateful rainy night I abruptly awoke to a crowbar violently splitting that vulnerable wooden shutter. I grabbed my torch and juju-fufu club for defense, but by the time I arrived at the window, my neighbor scared him away. I searched for wire to repair the shutter dangling on one remaining hinge and discovered the rogue had been in my outdoor latrine and storage shed searching for other valuable items.

For the first time, I felt scared to sleep alone. I had no personal fear for my life. I knew he wanted my possessions, and by God I was going to protect them. I slept with my juju-fufu club in the bed that night. The sound of the tropical rain pelted my tin roof and eventually soothed my raw nerves enabling me to fall into a fitful sleep.

My privacy was violated soon after my arrival upcountry with children peering in my windows and the constant loving-business pursuits, but now my personal space was violated. Later, I purchased a potion from the medicine men in Durlay to help me feel more mentally secure regarding rogue business. I began to understand country medicine culture much more fully than I initially expected.

Value of Life

Scaling a thirty-foot tree for palm nuts with bare feet, using a belt fashioned out of a vine, could lead to disaster. The men and boys who managed the task were quite skilled, and equipment failure was rare. I cringed at the news when I learned of a farmer who had fallen out of a palm tree and broken his back. Peter and I were summoned to his walk-in village, thirty minutes from Gowee, and found Abdou, lying in his round hut, paralyzed from the waist down. Abdou was a soft-spoken father of four children—ages two, three, five, and seven. He had two wives, one pregnant. His family was supportive and willing to do whatever was necessary. Unskilled at determining the exact extent of his spinal injury, Peter and I concluded that seeking evaluation and treatment at Sanniquellie Hospital would be his best option.

We approached the family regarding our plan. When they agreed, we sent a written message via taxi to the hospital to expect him, asking them not to demand money for his admission. The following day, with careful instruction to keep him lying flat, two family members carried Abdou on a sapling stretcher to Gowee and then headed to the hospital in the back of a mattress-padded money-bus. We were relieved knowing his care would be more successful in the hospital than in his village.

He returned two hours later because the hospital refused admission without the $10.00 fee. I was furious, but we could not give up on Abdou. Via taxi, I sent a note to Pam in Sanniquellie to spread the word among our Peace Corps friends for help. A week later Sister Catherine from the Catholic Mission in Sanniquellie offered her van to transport him to their airstrip for a mission flight to Monrovia for care. Again, the family agreed and Sister Catherine transported them to the mission airstrip in Sanniquellie. Surely, he would get the best care now, even better than the Sanniquellie Hospital.

Four hours later Sister Catherine returned with her human cargo. She explained the seats of the plane could not be removed for him to lie flat. Again, our efforts were thwarted.

A month later, with his condition declining, the desperate family took him to the medicine men in Durlay. The night I learned of Abdou's death, I grieved another preventable loss of life in our small community—four total that month. At the same time, I rationalized his demise, perhaps to preserve my sanity and survive my assignment in this remote part of Liberia. I questioned if Sanniquellie or Monrovia's medical facilities could have met his needs for treatment and physical recovery. Rehabilitation for a paraplegic or long-term care was not a health focus in Liberia. Treating acute conditions like diarrhea, malaria and pneumonia were more what those hospitals could handle. When I acknowledged the inadequate transport, lack of funds and insufficient level of care, Abdou's choice to stay in the village was probably the right one.

Through Abdou's death I gained a new perspective regarding human life in Liberia. People must have a role and a function for the greater good. The repair of a broken person— a paraplegic—comes at a cost, both monetarily and in family's commitment to provide care. When villagers lived day-to-day and meal-to-meal, caring for a condition like paralysis was not a viable option. Taking one to two people to care for Abdou would take those people away from providing for their family as a whole. I could never have imagined this challenge in the U.S. Eventually, my frustration turned to understanding, when I grasped what options and choices the villagers had. I never experienced human existence at a basic survival level until I lived in Liberia. Previously, my only knowledge of an expendable life had been with farm animals back home. Dad believed in "survival of the fittest." Even though Abdou's family did everything in their power to help him, he was beyond repair...for the time and culture in which he lived.

PART VI

WEST AFRICA

Planes, Trains, Buses, Boats and Taxis

The Nigerian Airliner began its nighttime descent into Bathurst, the capital of Gambia. I squinted, hoping to catch a glimpse of the city lights outside my window. The engines revved, landing lights lit, but I saw nothing in the dark. The pilot pulled back on the throttle and with a thump, the wheels bounced twice. Seconds later, blazing torches passed by my small window. My seatbelt gripped me as he slammed on the brakes. The aircraft door opened and a rolled staircase bumped the plane. I stooped under the small doorway to descend the steps and searched for a better perspective on my surroundings. Flames lined each side of the runway in the night—these were, in fact, our landing lights. The passengers and I grabbed our bags deposited on the tarmac while I combed the darkness for a terminal or building. A generator lit a few lights in a corrugated tin building erected to protect baggage from the elements. I speculated that we may have made an emergency landing in a small village. But, no, there Sara stood with her friends to greet me. "Welcome to Gambia!" they yelled.

In my second year as a volunteer, I once again hit the vacation trail, a much needed break from my challenges in Gowee. I planned to make a full circuit of West Africa: Gambia, Senegal, Mali, Niger, Upper Volta, Ghana, and Ivory Coast by plane, train, bus, boat, and taxi—all to be completed in about six weeks. Many other volunteers had taken this popular route. Sara, a Peace Corps volunteer, and her seven friends would accompany me for part of the trip. A dark-haired Catholic Italian-American from Virginia, Sara had been my roommate in New York before heading to Liberia, but she decided to transfer out of health education and took a teaching assignment in Gambia.

Gambia's colonial past, with its language, architecture, and infrastructure, possessed a Portuguese influence—its first European settlers. Later, when Britain colonized the country, English became the common language. The kind and gentle locals developed a specialty for crafting tie-dyed cloth. Carefully hand-tied fabric strategically dipped into sunken cement vats of dark-colored dyes created their beautiful signature patterns. Some of the finest tie-dyed prints in West Africa emerged in brilliant colors of red, green, indigo, black, yellow, orange, and purple.

The antiquated airport landing in Bathurst never dampened my excitement about my vacation that lay ahead. Sara took me and her friends to one of Gambia's incredible beaches. I walked fifty yards into the Atlantic Ocean and the breakers never rose above my head, contrary to the treacherous beaches in Liberia with deep undertows and rip currents.

A group of eight Gambian volunteers and I then traveled by ferry and taxis to Dakar, the capital of Senegal, a country once under French colonial rule. Dakar was known as the Paris of West Africa. Wonderful cafés and boulangeries lined the sidewalks. With only two French words in my vocabulary—*merci* and *bonjour*—I quickly learned *croissant* and *café au lait*, both pleasant changes from the Liberian beignets and instant Nescafé. The religious culture shifted from seeing an occasional Muslim in Liberia, to Islam as the predominant religion in Senegal. Light-colored robes, or agbadas, and prayer caps were the norm. Calls rang from mosque minarets five times daily to summon the population to prayer. The clean, tidy city maintained a manicured look with trimmed tree-lined streets. Taxis and buses navigated in an orderly way within the roundabouts without obnoxious honking. Dakar blended a bustling West African seaport of trade and commerce with the flair of French culture.

On our first full day, my travel companions ventured off to a market while I journeyed alone on a day-excursion to the island of Goree, a two-mile boat ride from Dakar. The small forty-five acre island off the coast of Senegal was known as the location of the House of Slaves (Maison des Esclaves), built by an Afro-French family about 1776. The last original slave house standing was now converted to a museum. The island's historical preservation depicted the horrors of the slave trade throughout the Atlantic world. Ships departing from the island often transported slaves as incidental passengers, but also carried the chief cargo of ground pea, peanut oil, ivory, and other commodities.

When I disembarked our boat, a fifty-foot-tall circular rock fortress greeted me. Armory, guns, and cannons, scattered strategically throughout the structure, had guarded the port against invaders from other European countries. Tall slits from windows were heavily barred. My legs became heavy as I trudged up the steps to read the placards and narratives, sensing something grave had happened in this place long before I was born. As I read of humans being chained and shackled, an air of sadness and despair hovered over me. As many as thirty men, fed only once a day, sat nearly naked in an eight-square-foot cell with only a small slit of window. Disease permeated the House of Slaves. Children were separated from their mothers who were jailed across the courtyard, far from their children's cries. Locked up in more oppressive, smaller cubicles under the stairs, the more rebellious Africans were fed seawater through the holes in walls to speed up dehydration and suffering. Another placard turned my stomach: "Young girls, Men, weigh station." Treated as pieces of merchandise, like gold or cotton, the Europeans sorted and priced the slaves by sex and weight.

I tried to wrap my mind around this historical slave-trade monster, a complex history with dozens of interplaying countries vying for the human commodity. My internal rage mounted. What compels such human cruelty, all for greed and prosperity? The slaves may not have known they built their own death chamber when they constructed the House of Slaves.

I continued to move through the museum, but abruptly stopped and widened my stance to steady my gait. My throat narrowed as I read the inscription on an arched doorway. "The Gate of No Return." Many perished en route to the Americas and those who lived, would never return. My high school history class did not cover this topic and my lessons in the Virgin Islands only scratched the surface. No written words or lecture, no matter how accurate, could have the same profound effect as the day I walked the path of slaves.

Pain, suffering, and loss of all the slaves who passed through the "Gate of No Return" permeated the air, soil, and walls. Could this be the reason the black boy in Omaha seemed so sad to me or why black people rioted in Birmingham? I wondered again why Dad hated black people so much. Maybe if he knew how the white man brought them to America and treated them like animals, he'd have pity rather than hatred or anger. These Africans never asked to come to America.

The pearly white cliffs, turquoise ocean waters, and clear blue sky of the island of Goree brought me no joy or pleasure. I departed with a heaviness as if I, too, had been shackled.

My travel companions and I regrouped in Dakar, and several went their separate ways. Sara and I, along with three other volunteers from Gambia—Matt, Karen, and Ned—continued on. We secured a sleeping berth for a two-day, one-night train ride from Senegal to Mali. The first day aboard the travel section of the train, I closed my eyes hoping to numb myself from the clickety-clack and squeals of the railcars. My butt ached from the jarring jumps and bumps as I bounced on the hard wooden seat. The train rattled through bluffs, plateaus, and vast expanses of intermittent vegetation. Every few hours we passed through small villages of about thirty to forty round thatched huts. Our train was heading toward the periphery of the Sahara Desert.

Our bedtime accommodations were far from what I imagined first class to be. We reveled in the idea that we avoided the hard seats for the entire sixty-hour journey. My sleeping berth consisted of a soiled two-inch thick lumpy mattress made for the size of a small child. Instructed to bring our own bed sheets, we hopefully limited the scabies and bedbug bites.

Ned, a tall handsome outgoing guy from New Jersey, could strike up a conversation with anyone. He invited me to have afternoon tea in the dining car at the front of the train. Now that was my vision of first class: white tablecloths and real china. The dining car consisted of ten booths with tables lining each side of the car, a great place to sit and view the scenery. As we entered, all the tables were occupied. One white woman motioned for us to join her.

Ned nudged me with his elbow and whispered, "That's Betty Friedan."

"Betty who?" I asked under my breath while glancing at the middle-aged woman with a prominent nose, salt and pepper hair, sitting alone in her booth.

"Betty Friedan is an icon of the women's movement, women's lib, feminism, you know?"

"Oh, yeah sure," I replied, not knowing what the hell he was talking about.

Ned and I sat across the table from Betty and ordered tea. They interacted freely while my only contribution was sharing about where we had traveled and where we were going. She planned to travel a similar route with her partner.

After our tea interlude with Betty, we returned to our friends in the travel section of the train. Not until Ned went on and on about meeting Betty Friedan, did I realize her significance. They discussed her pioneering efforts in the '60s and '70s, documenting and promoting women's rights and creating the second wave of the feminist movement, as well as being the author of the famous book *The Feminine Mystique*. Their discussion lingered in my mind even though I'd never heard of the concepts of women's rights, feminism, or women's liberation back on the farm. These were terms I didn't understand.

The further we traveled by rail into the Sahara, villages became sparser and the magnitude of the desert overwhelmed me. The environment became harsh, dry, and unforgiving. Accustomed to the tropical Liberian humidity for the past nineteen months, moisture now evaporated from my pores at an alarming rate. In Liberia, if one ran out of water or food, a stream could be found from which to drink, a root to forage, or a banana to harvest. With one miscalculation of nourishment while traversing the desert, death would ensue. The temperatures in the dry season soared to 120 degrees Fahrenheit midday with humidity hovering in the single digits. My skin shriveled like a dry sponge; I drank fluids constantly. I vowed never to take water, our precious resource, for granted ever again.

The train penetrated deeper into the interior of West Africa to the southern fringes of the Sahara Desert. We entered the landlocked Francophone country of Mali and two days later we disembarked in the capital of Bamako. Gone were the French cafés and boulangeries. No more roundabouts with fancy buses and taxis or white high-rise buildings with tree-lined avenues and streetlights—all of which I had appreciated in Dakar. It appeared the influence of the explorers never made it to Bamako.

Bamako's landscape consisted of one or two-story adobe structures, but the Grand Mosque, standing at five stories high and covering two city blocks, was an architectural marvel. The precolonial adobe mosque plastered with mud on the exterior looked more like a fort or castle with spires and towers. We wanted to see the interior, but only Muslims were allowed to enter. Open-air bazaars lined the streets with occasional goat and camel markets. One leg tied in a bent position kept the animals within hobble distance of their keepers. The taxi and bus station packed with hundreds of vehicles parked every which way appeared chaotic. No semblance of first come, first served, but rather, who could grab you first and sway you with the best fare. Sheer mayhem, yet excitement, surrounded me as I vigilantly guarded my belongings.

It was Christmas Eve in a Muslim country, with no visible trace of Christian religious symbols. Struggling to locate hotel lodging, we secured one of the last rooms in town for five of us. One bedside stand, a sagging double bed, and a tired bathroom completed our meager accommodations. Two others and I slept on the floor.

That afternoon we shopped for our holiday meal that consisted of salami sandwiches, potato chips, pickles, yogurt, ice cream, and beer. Beer can be found in a Muslim country but was often lukewarm. In our room a slow stream from the showerhead gently cooled our tepid drinks on the broken tiled floor. My revulsion for the lukewarm foamy yellow froth gradually changed when no rum and Coke could be found. This memorable evening with my four friends was filled with laughter as we ate our unconventional holiday meal atop our double bed. I snapped a keepsake photo of our Christmas Eve celebration. The following day we located the only Western-style hotel catering to expatriates and treated ourselves to a turkey dinner with chestnut dressing.

During our visit in Bamako, I met three new travelers: Barb, a Peace Corps volunteer from Senegal, and two British tourists, Gerald and Marshall. While discussing our travel plans over supper one evening, we discovered the four of us were traveling to Gao, Mali. We had three options for traversing the Sahara: gigantic lorries with direct routes only going north to Morocco (not my destination); a camel caravan, which could take more time than I had (besides, camels can be mean and cantankerous); or a large passenger paddleboat on the Niger River. The Niger River was the beating artery of life flowing into southern borders of the Sahara Desert. With its seasonal passage, we hoped to catch the final boat voyage at the end of dry season. We took the risk and opted for the boat with a stopover in the famous Timbuktu.

Timbuktu held a reputation in the Western culture as not really a city or town, but an expression for a distant or outlandish place. Timbuktu was not only a *real* city, it possessed a rich past as a regional trade center on the trans-Saharan caravan route in the 12th century, flourishing with its commerce of gold, salt, ivory, and slaves. In its Golden Age from the 13th to 17th century, the town's numerous Islamic scholars and extensive trading network made possible an important book trade. Together with the campuses of the Sankore Madrasah, an Islamic university, the book trade established Timbuktu as a scholarly center in Africa. During that prosperous time the population grew to an estimated 100,000. I had to see this place called Timbuktu.

Barb, fluent in French, was a godsend for negotiating taxis, boat tickets, and visas. Of my fellow travelers, only I required the Niger visa because my West African circuit had a stopover in Niamey, Niger, to meet a Peace Corps friend, Steve, from the Virgin Islands. Some countries allowed visas to be purchased in the airport upon arrival, while others required them beforehand. The Niger Embassy stated a visa before entry into their country was *mandatory*; however, it would take three days of waiting in Bamako. When we checked on the boat from Bamako to Gao via the Niger River, we were told it departed weekly and was leaving the following day. In contemplating the week's delay, we also learned it *could* be the final boat, as the river was gradually receding and it may no longer travel that route until rainy season, several months later.

The notion of an African river flowing into the Sahara Desert was baffling. The Niger River's unique course begins in southeast Guinea and runs directly away from the sea into the Sahara Desert forming the *inland* delta near Gao, the end of the riverboat journey. The river becomes navigable again when it turns south and gathers water resources once it reaches a few hundred miles into Niger. Much later it reaches the Gulf of Guinea known as the Niger Delta on the Atlantic Ocean.

The timing of our travel seemed risky when we heard terrible stories of other tourists sand barred in Timbuktu for five days until they could get released from the sand's grasp. While the desert sucked nearly every drop of moisture from my body, I never dreamt that a lack of water could affect my transport too. If I left Mali without a visa, I might miss my stopover to see Steve. If I stayed in Bamako to acquire a visa, I could possibly blow my chance to catch the last riverboat of the season. So, with my German stubbornness, I banked on forgiveness somewhere en route, hopefully in the Niamey airport. Besides, I purchased most of my other visas in airports before. Why should this be any different?

The following morning in the chaotic Bamako taxi stand, I said goodbye to Sara and my Gambian friends and joined my newfound travel mates, Barb, Gerald, and Marshall. All four of us jammed into the back seat for a forgettable seven-hour taxi ride to Mopti, to board the paddleboat to Timbuktu. Again, we met with hotel room issues once we arrived. As we set our bags down in our $20 room, the French owner told us it had been reserved for someone else. The four of us slept on saggy cots in the hotel office for $1.00 apiece, eaten alive by mosquitos. I hoped this would not be an omen for the remainder of my trip.

Timbuktu, a Place Lost in Time

On New Year's Eve, we boarded the triple-decker river boat in Mopti, Mali along with about 200 locals and a few tourists for our four-day voyage to Gao. The paddleboat was named the *General A. Sumaree.* I affectionately called the boat the General. It was a vintage variety with multiple coats of white paint covering rusted iron railings with a snow-white painted wooden exterior and green trim. Majestically, the boat waited at the dock with its twenty-some paddles at the rear readied to whip the turbid river. Some tourists, on a slim budget, traveled on the bottom or middle decks and slept on the floor. We took the top deck with sleeping berths, my first real bed since arriving in Mali a week earlier. Barb and I shared a room— steel bunk beds with bumpy mattresses. The claustrophobic chamber felt like a prison cell, but I felt no remorse because I could have been on the lower decks sleeping on a mat with the goats and chickens.

Once on board, we headed to the top deck café for a tepid beer. The diesel engine moaned, spewing dark smoke from its stack and soon the paddles began to slap the water to move us slowly down river. When the large town of Mopti vanished on the horizon, I finally relaxed knowing nothing could impede me now, not even the lack of a Niger visa. On New Year's Day, 1973, the auburn sun rose over the Sahara horizon and ripples glistened on the Niger River. An American couple, wrapped in a blanket, hugged each other on the upper deck. They waved as I snapped their photo. To see those lovebirds filled me with emptiness and a discreet yearning. I wanted what they had.

The following morning the sun rose over the Sahara Desert precisely at 6 a.m. After our breakfast of Nescafé and bread on the top deck, Barb translated the captain's message. The loudspeaker announced we were about to arrive in Timbuktu around 8 a.m. for a two-hour layover and any passengers who chose to disembark must return to the boat for a 10 a.m. departure.

As the General hugged closely to the sandbank and came to a gentle stop, the captain reminded us, one final time, to be back by 10 a.m. To my surprise, Timbuktu was nowhere in sight. The gangplank lowered onto the riverbank's edge as sheets of dried-crusted sand collapsed into the river and gently washed away. The height of the river a few months earlier, maybe twenty feet in some areas, left its mark imprinted clearly in the sand's history. A once forceful flowing river now bore the stress of the dry season with sandbars dotting our path downstream. The Sahara Desert nearly swallowed the General from both sides. Nothing but sand surrounded us except for a narrow and diminishing ribbon of water cutting a swath through the center of Mali.

Soon a few villagers in dugout canoes approached us from the riverbank to sell handmade bread, hot tea, and small trinkets. Five taxis and their drivers hailed in French for the tourist business just beyond the gangplank. "Taxi, Mesdames, Messieurs, Taxi, Taxi!" An eager taxi driver approached us to say in French that Timbuktu was about twenty kilometers away, and he would take us there. Barb took command to negotiate our taxi fare, then motioned for Marshall, Gerald, and me to get in. Off we drove with a tornado of sand dusting our trail. Within seconds I lost sight of the *General A. Sumaree* from the rear window, and ahead lay nothing but a bland tan color everywhere from earth to sky. This Midwestern farm girl needed a marker or something to rest her eyes upon. I found it unnerving to not know what we would find at the end of that road.

Thirty minutes later, several rectangular adobe homes appeared. The driver stopped and said, "Nous sommes arrivés!" At midmorning, Timbuktu was nearly devoid of people or animals. I didn't see one green thing, not one blade of grass, and only spindly leafless trees dotted the horizon. We walked the sand-covered streets, which reminded me of snowdrifts on the Nebraska farm. At least our snowstorms and blizzards were seasonal; in the Sahara, people dealt with sand and wind every day. Timbuktu became a white-out of sand. The sand blended with the homes, the homes melded with the streets, the streets blurred with the sky as it swirled with sand that fell back to the earth again. A few women and children swept the drifted sand away from their front doors, hoping to prevent the Sahara Desert from claiming another victim. With a population of under 2,000, Timbuktu was no longer a thriving hub of trade and literature, but instead a seemingly impoverished village gradually being consumed by the Sahara.

We walked the streets and came upon a mesmerizing door guarding an adobe home. I imagined the once flourishing life in the beauty of that intricately carved solid-wood door with bold hand-cast hinges, a rounded door knocker, and multiple inlaid silver decorations. Those wooden planks may have traveled hundreds and even a thousand miles from the rainforest to beautify and safeguard their home. As I proudly stood next to that magnificent door wearing my handmade African print bellbottoms with my newly purchased goatskin bag from Bamako slung over my shoulder, Marshall snapped my photo. Timbuktu was real. But behind that majestic door I sensed something so different from 600 years ago. I was overcome with sadness. Perhaps that was why Westerners refer to Timbuktu as a "distant place." Maybe, a place lost in time.

I hoped to mail my brother, Bob, and his family, a postcard from this iconic town. Barb asked, "Who wouldn't want mail from Timbuktu?" In Bamako I had purchased a stamped postcard of a boy fishing on the Niger River and completed a narrative of my journey in Mali thus far. We roamed the streets looking for the lone Timbuktu post office and finally came upon an adobe structure with an "envelope" symbol on the door. Barb confirmed it to be a post office and I handed my postcard to a white-robed gentleman at the desk. The mail travels down river by boat to Gao, backtracks by plane to

Bamako, on to Dakar, and then to its final U.S. destination via Europe. It should take a month or two to reach Nebraska.

The four of us found a small café in which to sit, collect our thoughts, and have tea to rehydrate. As I reached for my cup, I caught a glimpse of the hands on my watch reading 10 a.m. and realized we needed to head back to the General— now! Less than an hour and a half in Timbuktu was not long enough to contemplate its history. We searched for more than twenty minutes and could not find a taxi, so with desperation we began to walk, then run, hoping to find some transport on the main road.

Finally, a crumpled blue Datsun pickup drove toward us. Someone on the General sent the driver when they noticed four of us were missing. Barb yelled to the driver, "Vite, vite, tout de suite" as we climbed in the rear bed. By now, it was almost 10:30 a.m. and well past departure time. The Datsun tore down the road toward the General.

As we approached the makeshift dock, a sick feeling gripped my stomach when I watched the black smoke puff from the riverboat's stack. The General had departed without us. The Datsun stopped where the road ended, short of the General by two hundred yards. Adrenaline pumped to my legs, reminiscent of my eighth-grade blue ribbon dash. Not only was this twice the distance of my memorable grade school achievement, but also I ran in sandals in ankle-deep sand with 110 degree heat. I ran those two hundred yards along the riverbank toward the General like my life depended upon it, screaming, "Wait, wait!" I didn't want my tombstone to read, "Susan Greisen, deserted in Timbuktu—a place lost in time."

My friends brought up the rear. Fortunately, the behemoth riverboat took time to acquire speed, and now I trailed the General by a few yards. In my peripheral vision I saw the same villagers who had greeted us with food and trinkets more than two hours earlier. From their canoes they witnessed our dilemma and were caught up in the frenzy. Speaking to each other in Fulani, two canoes now paddled alongside us as we ran on the riverbank toward the boat. After about fifteen minutes of running, in what felt like quicksand, I was now dead-even with the General, but it would not stop. I ran, flailed hands and shouted in English to the captain, "Stop, Stop!" Passengers watching from the boat's railings laughed, waved, and cheered. One hundred feet of water separated the hysterical tourists running on the riverbank and the gently moving General on the river.

My track-star ability saved me thus far, but this farm girl never learned to swim and that could be my demise. The two dugouts maneuvered between us and the General, when the villagers motioned us to climb in. Gratefully we did. The nimble canoes quickly closed the one hundred-foot gap between us and the enormous riverboat. Soon we bobbled alongside the *General A. Sumaree.*

Passengers from the lower deck reached their hands toward us. The dugout canoe swayed in tandem with the riverboat while my legs trembled from the heat, adrenaline, and my two-hundred-yard sand dash. I mustered my last ounce of energy to straddle on the wobbly canoe and then reached to the welcoming hands. Africans from the top grabbed and pulled while others from the bottom pushed and shoved. The four of us clambered safely onto the General's deck, seizing hands, railings, ropes, or anything that would support our weight. As I came over the railing, people cheered. I felt like I had won an Olympic gold medal. It was the best feeling ever.

During this entire debacle, the *General A. Sumaree* never lost its stride and I wondered if the captain left many tourists in Timbuktu. I envisioned him laughing at the helm.

Totally exhausted, we reached the top deck. Our fellow tourists warmly greeted us, including the couple who sent the rescue Datsun pickup, the loving pair I observed hugging on deck on New Year's Day. We bought them a beer while we shared our story of how we got ourselves into that predicament. Abruptly, the General stopped and we lunged forward, nearly falling off our chairs with our celebratory beer bottles scattering across the deck. We stumbled to the railing to discover the *General A. Sumaree* had hit a sandbar. After our panic, only minutes earlier, the General had run aground. The engines revved forward and backward numerous times until it jarred free from the sand's clutches...two hours later.

"Mr. Captain of the *General A. Sumaree*, I think *I* got the last laugh," I said to my fellow tourists. "Bring another round of beer."

Air Maybe

Two more days passed as the General moved ever so slowly down the Niger River weaving around scattered sandbars searching for the deepest water. A beehive of activity ensued as soon as the General stopped mid-river at two remote villages on our route to Gao. Within minutes, fifteen dugout canoes filled with villagers gathered around our riverboat. Some loaded and unloaded passengers, dried food, or live animals. Others sold trinkets, beignets, dates, and calabashes filled with fresh goat or camel milk. The General was the lifeline to these villages. What do they do when the riverboat stopped for three to four months during dry season when the direct route between Mopti and Gao was cut off?

On our final day we traveled silently for hours, with only the slapping of the river paddles trailing sounds over the desert. A hum of excitement emerged among the passengers when they noticed a change in the terrain. I moved to the railing and became breathless at the contrast of the encroaching Sahara as it met the Niger River's inner delta—the end of the General's journey. The Sahara sand dunes to the north stretched toward the blue sky as tall as ten stories with cliffs dropping straight into the river. To the south, the grass-filled Niger delta reached its fingers into the desert like a green-gloved hand caressing the sand. The *General A. Sumaree* cut through the terrain like a knife separating the parched Sahara from the lush delta, only temporarily, until the flow became a shallow estuary in a few weeks as the rainy season subsided. On the horizon, the end of our riverboat journey came into view, the small town of Gao. An hour later we disembarked and found their policemen to be aggressive and suspicious of tourists. Within seconds of pulling out my camera, three policemen grabbed Marshall, Barb, and me and escorted us into their bureau to be reprimanded. Barb translated our scolding, "No photos can be taken here and need to be destroyed." Even though we were warned on the boat to avoid taking photos in Gao, I'd never been harassed like this before. I pleaded innocent by vigorously shaking my head "No" and was spared. However, Marshall did not fare as well as they ripped the Kodak film canister from his camera. Gao did not feel like the same Mali I knew in Bamako or Mopti. Soon I became much more obedient when I spied gun-wielding soldiers wherever we walked.

One night in this remote town sufficed, and we purchased plane tickets to go our separate ways. Barb, Gerald, and Marshall planned to fly back to Bamako, while three other tourists and I awaited a plane destined for Ouagadougou, Upper Volta. I, however, planned a stopover in Niamey, Niger, to visit Steve.

Steve and I corresponded by mail since our meeting in the Virgin Islands during my Peace Corps training many months ago. The Peace Corps had hosted a couple of chaperoned parties intermixing the male and female trainees. At one party, Steve flirted with me. I informed him, right off, that I was spoken for and he said he understood. Blond like Doug, I found him intriguing, sweet, and very smart. His dad was a TV producer in L.A. One evening at our Dorothea Beach training camp the two of us sat on the beach when he turned my chin and our lips gently met. I turned away quickly as a small voice told me to do, but as the night progressed, Steve missed his transport back to his camp. My roommate Linda and I hid Steve in our room and he spent the night on the floor between our beds. The following morning, our supervisor, Ms. Picket, knocked on our door, came in, and summoned only me to a meeting before breakfast in the dining room. Just as she left, I saw Steve's feet sticking out from under my bed. Surely, I would be in big trouble now.

When I entered the dining room, Ms. Picket pointed for me to sit next to Kathy and Sheila, and with her commanding posture she towered over us and demanded, "I was told at the gathering last night there was a strong odor of marijuana at your table. I want to know who was smoking and where did you get it."

Kathy and Sheila responded in unison, "Not me!"

"Not me either," my response delayed by the shocking accusation. I was more concerned about harboring a man in my room.

Ms. Picket declared, "Marijuana is forbidden here and if I catch any of you in possession, you will be terminated immediately. Is that clear?"

"Yes," we replied.

Who did she think I was? I would turn twenty the following week and I possessed complete control of my impulses and knew right from wrong, for God's sake. I never even slept with Steve that night, even though I could have. Evidently she didn't know I was an upstanding Catholic.

Twenty months later, while I awaited my flight to Niamey, my feelings for my high school sweetheart were waning. I saw no future for us. Before departing Gowee, I removed his pearl ring from my finger. Fleeting fond memories of Steve warmed me. I was anxious and excited to see him.

I boarded an Air Mali twin-prop plane. Air Mali was often called "Air Maybe" by the local Peace Corps volunteers only because one could never be guaranteed to reach the destination. No facts could confirm this hype, so blindly and innocently I secured my seatbelt hoping for safe passage and visa forgiveness in Niamey, Niger.

The plane, full to capacity with about thirty passengers, reminded me of the mayhem of money-bus rides in Liberia. Limiting carry-on baggage did not seem to be enforced or even a regulation, for that matter. The aisle was blocked with more carry-on items and people milled about the cabin with no regard for seatbelts. Overhead bins bulged with bags of every nature, often secured with rope to contain their contents. But the steamy cabin enhanced the odors wafting from other treasures protruding from above: slabs of rock salt, bound with twine handles; tattered cardboard boxes, blood-stained from dead fish; and knotted cloth bundles securing salt-dried camel meat. I inhaled shallowly and slowly to keep my breakfast down.

About an hour into the flight, I reluctantly walked to the lavatory at the rear of the plane. Our flight attendant stood in the aisle casually chatting with a passenger. I sucked in my belly and maneuvered sideways past her until my path was blocked by a man squatting at the front of the lavatory door. A Muslim, wearing a prayer cap and a long white robe, heated a kettle of water for his afternoon tea on a gas primus stove.

Yes, this was an *open flame* on an airborne flight. I quickly calculated my three options: yell, "Fire" in French (which I did not know), tell the flight attendant there was an open flame on board, or...just ignore it. I chose the latter. I'm sure this was *not* the first cookfire the plane had ever seen. It certainly was *my* first and hopefully my last. "Air Maybe" was living up to its reputation.

Upon my exit from the lavatory, afternoon prayer replaced the teakettle. As Air Mali soared above the Sahara Desert, the man prostrated himself on his prayer rug toward Mecca in reverence to Allah. I gingerly stepped over the religious ritual, returned to my seat, and prayed like I've never prayed before. Prayer was all I had. With God and Allah listening, maybe prayer was all *we* had.

Deportation

When the wheels screeched on the tarmac, I praised the Lord for my safe arrival in Niamey. Even with one more hurdle to jump—my lack of a visa for Niger—I didn't worry because Steve would be there, and I knew the American Embassy could bail me out if needed.

I entered the customs line, warmed my smile and handed the blue-uniformed official my Peace Corps passport. This specially issued identification for the volunteers hopefully carried extra clout.

The officer's beady eyes and narrowed lips melted my fake smile in an instant and he asked me in French, "Ou est votre visa?"

I assumed what he wanted and told him in English, "I was not able to get it in advance due to the boat issue and I'd like to buy it in the airport...si vous plait." I ended with a smile.

"Ou est votre visa?" he demanded much louder than before.

I repeated myself, to no avail, and looked for someone who could speak English and asked carefully and slowly, "Speak...English?"

With a motion of his hand he sent another officer to summon assistance. Minutes later that officer came back empty-handed.

Out of nowhere two green-fatigued soldiers, each with an AK-47 slung over their shoulders, flanked me and forced me out of the customs line for further interrogation. In a meek respectful voice, I whimpered, "I'm just a Peace Corps volunteer innocently traveling to visit a friend. I won't be a threat to your country. I...I promise." When the soldiers' grip nearly squeezed the blood out of my arms, I realized they took their job seriously.

French expletives dashed back and forth between the soldiers and the customs officer. From their gestures, pointing to the plane on the tarmac, I gathered they wanted me to leave on the next flight out. They didn't know I was an experienced traveler at age twenty. I was aware that every major airport had an international zone, an extraterritorial area not subject to any country's border control policies. So, I stood there between the door I had just entered and before the customs desk—the international zone. I called it my "safe zone." There I would stay until help arrived or their defenses softened, allowing me in the country.

Contacting Steve was impossible because there was no phone communication to his village and he didn't know the exact date I would be arriving, only an estimate I had written him a month earlier. I gingerly approached the customs officer, flushed with anger, to ask in slow and special English, for him to get me help. I figured he could understand the four English words, "American...Embassy. The...Ambassador."

The two soldiers and the officer shook their heads and temporarily abandoned me in my safe zone. I helplessly retreated to the bank of chairs next to the customs desk. Almost an hour later, a tall Caucasian man in dress slacks, a white shirt and tie arrived and identified himself as Fred, a Foreign Service officer from the Embassy. I didn't get the Ambassador but Fred's presence meant I would soon be on my way to locating Steve.

After I explained the entire situation to Fred, he spoke in French with the customs officer, as I had hoped. That is what they do at the Embassies around the world, looking out for Americans. Right? However, the Nigeriens were adamant about me leaving and I made it clear to Fred I would stay in the international zone as long as needed until this blew over. After fifteen more minutes of serious debating, Fred moved toward me with his shoulders slumped, shaking his head, and said, "There is nothing I can do."

I asked, "What do you mean *nothing* you can do? Sheer will power, determination, or knowing the right people had always gotten my needs met before. Why not now?"

"Border security in Niger has heightened in the past few months and they can no longer make exceptions," Fred said solemnly. "You need to leave. I'm sorry. The customs officer stated you must re-board the plane right now that you arrived on from Mali. This plane will take you to Ouagadougou, the capital of Upper Volta."

"Please go tell them, one more time, I have no money for a ticket, and I have no visa for Upper Volta." I wasn't willing to give up hope. I remained defiant as I sat in my safe zone somehow feeling protected.

The Upper Volta flight had boarded all its passengers and announced last call in French. The officer and the two gun-slinging soldiers surrounded me again and demanded in French that I board the plane. "Allez, Allez." Go, go... like they were speaking to a dog.

Shaking my head vigorously, I pleaded, "No, no, no" I knew they understood. They were going to have to carry me.

Thirty-some locals in the airport now gathered around me, a crazy Peace Corps woman taken hostage, as if *I* were the rogue being beaten in the village. I heard their jeers and laughter directed at me. I felt no shame, only determination. I was so close to seeing Steve.

A hush overcame the airport terminal when all eyes turned toward the plane on the tarmac. A man came down the flight stairs, a French pilot in his navy blue slacks, white short-sleeved shirt with red, white, and blue service bars on his shoulders. With purpose in his step he marched twenty-five yards across the landing strip directly up to me, looked sternly in my eyes, and said in perfect English, "Get...on...the plane!"

My defenses and determination wilted like fresh-cut flowers lying on that blazing tarmac. I looked back at Fred and asked him to get a message to Steve telling him I tried my best. He nodded. One soldier flanked me on each side and they grasped my arms so tightly I could not change my mind. Like a death squad they marched me behind the pilot toward the plane.

I sniveled one more time, "I have no ticket and no visa." No one responded.

The soldiers released my arms as I came to the flight stairs. I dragged up those twenty-two steps and found myself aboard a flight to Upper Volta for which I did *not* pay, going to a country for which I did *not* have a visa. The other passengers glared at me. Why should they be so upset? I was the one negotiating my rights. Besides, I delayed their departure by only two hours. I did not speak or make eye contact with anyone on the flight as I considered what might happen next. What would the Upper Volta customs officers demand? Would I endure more scrutiny, be thrown in prison and have my nails ripped out? For a moment I wondered if this was what my parents worried about regarding my life in Africa. Probably not. Not even I could dream this up.

Two hours later we landed. I entered the customs line. I handed the official my Peace Corps passport now stamped with a *"Non Admis,"* the deportation insignia from Niger.

The customs officer asked me in French with a pleasant welcoming voice, "Voudrais vous un visa de Haute Volta?" (Would you like a visa for Upper Volta?)

With my head down, I answered, "Oui."

I didn't get interrogated or have my nails ripped out. Instead the customs officer in Upper Volta stamped my passport and directed me to purchase a visa at the immigration bureau in Ouagadougou as soon as possible.

I never returned to Niger and I never did see Steve during my remaining months in Africa.

Was I to Blame?

Upper Volta was the antithesis of Niger (I later learned drought, political tensions, and a coup d'état had created extra security alerts in Niger). The friendly Upper Voltans and accommodating local Peace Corps volunteers embraced my presence with their hospitality. Except for their French language, Mali and Upper Volta seemed nearly devoid of their colonial history. Reflected by their dress, music, and food, these landlocked countries seemed virtually pure and intact in their ethnic culture. Western dress was rare as the indigenous people from the Hausa, Fulani, and Taureg tribes wore their traditional long flowing gowns, robes, and head ties or turbans. Music from calabash harps called koras, meals of roasted camel or goat meat, and beverages of camel milk sipped from a gourd gave the impression of a culture untainted by European influence.

I moved on alone for my final week of travel. From Upper Volta I entered Ghana, an Anglophone country possessing few language challenges. By bus and taxi through the plains of this beautiful region, I traveled through a brilliant montage of unique mud and thatched huts along with magnificent baobab and strangler fig trees only God could envision in His wisdom. As I traversed south through the dry plains of Ghana, toward the ocean, my hair, skin, and lungs sucked up the coastal humidity like a sponge. The arid vegetation of the savannah gradually transformed into a lush rainforest.

I said goodbye to the warm welcome of Ghana and ended my vacation in the Francophone country of Ivory Coast. With only a few French words added to my vocabulary, I became seasoned and comfortable using body and sign language to bridge my communication gap. Traveling for a brief period in a country where I did not speak their language was of no real concern. I was familiar with these challenges.

I boarded a flatbed ferry holding about twenty people and a couple of trucks as we crossed the lagoon of Lagune Aby, the natural boundary between Ghana and Ivory Coast. The evening became serene and magical when the sun dipped below the horizon. Most people on the ferry spoke French as many were returning to their homes in Ivory Coast. For a split second I realized I was the only white person on the ferry but brushed it off as common occurrence when living in Africa.

I leaned over the railing, totally absorbed in the beauty of the glass-flat lake and birds fluttering in the wake of the ferry, when a young Ivorian man, about my age, approached and began a conversation in perfect American English. He wanted to know about my travels, where I lived and asked other typical get-to-know-you questions. He introduced himself as Taki and explained he worked for the American Embassy in Abidjan, the capital of Ivory Coast. Smartly dressed in khaki slacks and an African print button-down shirt, he possessed a caring tone with thoughtful questions and did not display a forward attitude as some of the Liberian men had. The forty-five minute boat ride passed quickly as we chatted. The generator lit up the ferry like a small Christmas tree as we motored along the lagoon in the darkness until we arrived at our destination.

The ferry revved its engine to dig the bow deep into the dirt bank, the gangplank lowered, and the people and trucks unloaded. Only smatterings of vehicle headlights, lanterns, and torches illuminated our so-called ferry terminal. Probably twenty taxi drivers hailed to the ferry passengers. "Allez avec moi," "Madame, Monsieur, Taxi." Several drivers, yelling in French, grabbed and pulled at our clothing and bags. Taki said we could take a taxi together to his mother's home, where he lived, and then decide on further plans. I told him I wanted to get to a hotel in Abidjan. He agreed to my request and in French skillfully negotiated a taxi for us. I thanked him for his kindness.

An hour and a half later the taxi dropped us at his mother's home where she and Taki's sister greeted us. He kindly introduced me in my French name as Mademoiselle Suzanne. Their large modern four-bedroom home had electricity, a stove, fridge, indoor bathroom, and even a television set, something I hadn't seen in a private home since I left the farm in Nebraska a year and a half earlier. His mother generously served us soup and rice at about 9 p.m. Having not eaten since morning, my food barely touched the plate before it vanished.

Taki and his mother insisted I spend the night, but I maintained my desire to go to a hotel as I had originally planned. Surprised at my refusal, they hailed for a taxi and Taki offered to take me to a hotel he knew in town. His offer to escort me did not seem unusual because having a command of French was more important than I imagined, especially traveling at night.

We arrived at a moderately priced hotel in a good location around 11:00 p.m. and Taki told the clerk, in French and interpreting to me in English, he planned to pay for the room as I checked in. "That is not necessary," I said, but he insisted. He and the hotel clerk seemed to know each other as they spoke in French. Their laughs and conniving tone concerned me, but I shrugged it off.

"I will carry your backpack to your room," Taki said.

"No thank you, I can manage. I thank you for all your help tonight."

"Oh, please let me carry your heavy pack."

A sudden tightness gripped my stomach, and a chill ran through to my fingers. Something did not feel right, but I had no reason to distrust him. Besides, he never once asked me for loving-business. I agreed, and up the flight of stairs we went. As I began to unlock the door to room 203, a queasiness struck me as he stood outside my room. Before I could say thank you and goodbye, Taki was *in* my room.

I was in a serious dilemma. I was not in my own house, not in my own village. And my landlord, Jacob, was not within yelling distance. My sense of fear escalated as my situation became uncertain; I was in a French-speaking country and in a hotel room with a man who was a total stranger.

"Thank you so much for your help but I am very tired and need to go to sleep," I said in the calmest voice I could muster as my knees trembled.

"Mademoiselle Suzanne, I want to do loving-business."

"No, you must leave." I got the impression by his lack of response that my *no*, meant *maybe,* as it did in Liberia.

He reached behind and closed the door. Now I was trapped. Adrenaline rushed through me. My Liberian suitors, including Dr. Mattie and the diamond commissioner, never made me feel this way. I knew how to handle them; Taki was an unknown.

He gently reached for my hand. I jerked away. Each proceeding gesture became less playful and more aggressive in nature. Soon he chased me around the room. I kept the bed between us when he jumped toward me.

"Taki, No. Get out!" I demanded. My words seemed powerless as I quivered with fear. Now other emotions started to emerge, stronger than fear—anger and disgust. I was pissed beyond measure. I stood erect and shouted at the top of my lungs, "GET OUT!" Like raising a stick to an attack dog, my rage and assertiveness caught Taki off guard and he backed down immediately, not wanting to create a spectacle in the hotel room. I risked leaving the protective bed that separated us, moved deliberately to the door, and with conviction opened it and screamed, "GET OUT!"

The whimpering attack dog moved slowly toward the door, but his sorrowful eyes seemed to express I *might* change my mind. I yelled "GET OUT," one final time.

He walked slowly past me then I quickly slammed the door behind him and locked it. My heart raced as my hands pushed firmly on the door.

Taki tapped on the locked door gently calling my name, "Mademoiselle Suzanne." He turned the doorknob to no avail.

"Get out of here. I don't want to *ever* see you again!" I yelled for him to go away several more times as he cried my name and pled his desires. How could I ever go to sleep? There was no phone in the room. The charade outside my door went on for the next thirty minutes as I remained quiet.

Finally, silence fell in the hallway. I put my ear against the door of number 203 to listen for the thug I had just kicked out. I heard nothing. Weak from exhaustion and still shaking from fear and anger, I collapsed on the bed in relief and began sobbing. Where in this situation had I gone wrong? What had I done to deserve this?

I pulled the covers back and lay fully clothed on the bed. I feared getting undressed. Deep breaths in and out between my sobs helped me to relax. "Oh Lord, please let me sleep." I flipped the switch off to the bare light bulb dangling from the ceiling. "Please let darkness help me to sleep. God, I am so sorry."

As my fists began to uncoil, a stone hit the window. I bolted upright. I cautiously peered between the slit in the tattered flowered curtains. Taki looked up at me in my second-floor window. I jumped back. The stones and calls continued. He was an unrelenting son-of-a-bitch. I yelled, "I hate Africa! I hate men! What in the hell possesses them to do things like this?"

After more minutes than I could count, silence finally fell. I peered out between the small gap in the curtains and I saw no Taki. I didn't sleep all night. I vowed I would *never* be so trusting and stupid again.

As soon as daylight came, I threw my few items into my backpack and went downstairs to check out. The clerk grinned, and I suspected he conspired in the whole affair. He said the room was *not* paid for as Taki had promised, which didn't surprise me. I slammed my francs on the counter and got out of the hotel as soon as I could get a taxi. "Peace Corps, si vous plait," as I cobbled together a command in Liberian English and French to direct the driver to the Peace Corps office in Abidjan.

Once I arrived, I fortunately ran into two volunteer friends traveling from Liberia, Jack and Betty, my East Africa travel partners. They invited me to stay in their hotel room that night after I told them of my horrendous encounter. I finally relaxed, being in a place with people I knew. Flying back to Liberia the following day filled me with peace, and I just wanted to be back safe in Gowee.

On my flight home I relived my Taki encounter. I recalled Dad's words when he said to me as an eleven-year-old, "...boys have no control over their bodies," and "I will never trust you." I wondered if he was right to think that. I should not be so trusting of boys or men who cannot control their sexual impulses. Maybe I made all the wrong decisions. On my flight home, I wondered if I *was* to blame.

PART VII

GOWEE, THE FINAL MONTHS

Give Twins a Chance

Fatima waddled in followed by her husband, Mohamad, for her first antenatal visit. Quiet and shy, she avoided eye contact with me. Fatima's delicate facial features, slender lips and nose, and tall stature were typical of her Mandingo tribe. I explained to the couple what to expect during their clinic visits. Fatima spoke Mandinka and had little command of Gio and neither spoke English, so communication trickled back and forth from me to Peter, Mohamad, and Fatima. She informed us this was her first pregnancy and it seemed uneventful thus far. Mohamad was the first man to accompany his pregnant wife to our clinic and his gentle attentiveness to her needs impressed me. I recognized him as a diamond digger in Gowee who worked long hours in the mine not far from the clinic.

After taking her blood pressure, I asked her to lie on our exam table. Her large abdomen was taut, seemingly ready to burst. Well into my second year as a volunteer, I became more proficient at my antenatal assessments, and after careful examination, I determined her gestation to be about eight months. I explained the use of the fetoscope and placed it to my ear, listening to all aspects of her beach-ball-looking belly. The fetal heart rate was most prominent over the left lower side at about 140 beats per minute. Surprisingly, I heard an echoing heartbeat at the same rate. I continued to move the scope around her abdomen and I found another loud rapid heartbeat on the upper right corner. I repeated listening several times, just to be certain and not to mistake it for the mother's. Now with the two distinct fetal heartbeats, I worked methodically to locate the head and found it floating above Fatima's pubic bone and the baby's back on her left abdomen. Moving to the top right, I palpated another back and head at the top of the uterus. I checked again and again. I asked permission for Peter to examine Fatima and they agreed. Peter listened and palpated. Not experienced in the area of antenatal exam, Peter was the best medical backup I had, and he agreed with my assessment that Fatima and Mohamad were going to have twins.

The delivery of twins was not good news in Gowee. Several unfavorable stories had circulated in the village, none of which I could validate. The most common scenario described twin births with one baby being smaller and weaker than the other. In addition, a mother's inadequate nutrition—both antenatal and postpartum—often made breast milk insufficient for nursing two babies. Rather than having each twin at risk, the weaker infant would be terminated or neglected until death. I witnessed my dad euthanize the runts of the pig litters, but for this to be done to a human being, I couldn't bear the thought. I saved my weakling pig, Daisy; I could surely save a surviving twin if we were prepared with food supplements and education.

I explained my assessment in Liberian English, so Peter could interpret in Gio, then Mohamad to translate in Mandinka for Fatima to fully understand. Clarity can be lost in translation three times over, so I carefully and methodically simplified my explanation. I inhaled deeply and stood at eye level with Fatima and Mohamad and said, "Thank you, ya, for coming to clinic today. Fatima, you have taken good good care of yourself and yur belly."

Peter and Mohamad translated.

"I have news about yur belly. I took a good good look and hear not one...but two babies. Yes, two babies." Holding up two fingers. "They will be born in one month."

Once the translation met both their ears, Fatima shook her head and her mute mouth dropped open.

She looked at Mohamad and said, "How dis doctor woman know dat? Only Allah know dis, so da Quran tell us."

Mohamad and then Peter translated to me and I sensed more fear than doubt in my credibility as a practitioner. I said, "I will make visits to yur house when da babies come, to help you and da babies to make good good food for all of you."

Mohamad's income of less than a $1.00 a day was insufficient to buy baby formula or more nutritious food for Fatima. After talking with her for a few more minutes, she seemed relieved they would receive our support. With Fatima's advanced gestational age, I asked them to return to the clinic in two weeks. They departed with a mix of fear and elation on their faces. My feelings mirrored theirs. Had I promised too much?

After a couple of weeks they returned for Fatima's second exam which proved to be on target with her delivery at any time. Her designated midwife, one I had trained earlier, was alerted. As far as I knew, prior twin deliveries were successful in Gowee, and I must trust it now.

Two weeks later, a child came to the clinic to tell me Fatima had delivered by midwife. That same evening when I arrived at their home, Mohamad and Fatima shook my hand and bowed with deep respect.

"Only Allah know if belly having two babies." Mohamad and Fatima told me repeatedly. "You da Allah woman doctor."

Fatima looked well and happy, and the babies...oh the babies. They were probably the healthiest looking twins ever born in the bush in Liberia. They appeared to be about five to six pounds each; two beautiful boys. I could not detect a visual difference in size, and a couple of days later at the clinic, their weights were confirmed at 5 pounds 4 ounces and 5 pounds 8 ounces. I didn't take credit for Fatima's healthy pregnancy because she came late to our clinic for antenatal care. My focus now was to keep both twins alive.

Making home visits to the mothers, babies, and their families were the favorite parts of my work. I made rounds in the evening when the father and schoolchildren were present, for two reasons: not only more people available to educate, but also a better chance to find someone to interpret, because the schoolchildren could speak Liberian English.

My next challenge during the following home visits to Mohamad and Fatima was to uphold my promises to maintain the mother's nutrition for adequate breast feeding for two robust boys. I discussed daily quantities of protein and greens but also gave her powdered milk for her consumption to enhance her nutrition. Protein, a rare and prized food source, such as bush meat, chicken, dried fish, ground pea, or eggs, was expensive—three to four times more costly than palm oil or rice. In any Liberian family, the men get the bulk of the protein, and the remainder goes to the women and children. Even then, the quantities men consumed were often less than one to two ounces once a day (the average American consumes three to four times this amount).

With the help of a schoolboy who spoke Liberian English and Mandinka, I stressed to Mohamad and Fatima the importance of the mother's intake of protein and greens as critical to provide enough breast milk for the babies. I discouraged bottle feeding not only due to the cost but the sanitation issues. I carefully noted their reaction and asked if they could comply with my request. "Yes, because the 'Allah woman doctor' had spoken. Younga Ti, we be good to do all you say and take good good care of Fatima and da babies," Mohamad reassured me.

Following tradition, babies are not named until about two weeks after birth. The proud parents named those remarkably chubby, healthy boys, Moussa and Sekou. At four months, I taught Fatima how to make rice porridge with powdered milk added to supplement Fatima's breast milk. I beamed like a delighted grandmother watching them grow into healthy infants when Fatima brought them to the Well-baby clinic for their series of three DPT vaccinations.

Some weeks after Fatima's delivery, while returning from an afternoon home visit, Larta, a midwife I had trained a few months earlier, motioned for me to follow her. She had assisted delivering twins to a woman who walked in from a nearby village the night before. When I entered the hut, I found the

mother, unknown to our clinic, lying on a small raised plat-
form bed with a cloth pad between her legs soaked with bright
red blood and a bucket beside her holding similar pieces of
saturated cloth. Even though I trained the midwives about
postpartum hemorrhage, I had never personally encountered
this before.

Emergency mode kicked in and my practical nurses training came to me like my final exam in school. Question 1:
What is the first thing to do when discovering postpartum
vaginal bleeding? Answer: Examine the fundus. Following
my textbook recall, I placed my hand on her abdomen to feel
for the top of her uterus. A normal fundus is firm, but her fundus was not. The textbook called it boggy. Question 2: Is the
fundus boggy? Answer: Massage it until firm. I didn't have a
clue what a boggy fundus felt like, only a firm one. Her fundus was not the latter, so I followed my memory and
externally massaged the fundus with one hand while stabiliz-
ing the lower part of the uterus with the other.

When the placenta pulls away from the uterus, it exposes
the blood vessels, rendering it like a raw wound: massaging
the uterus helps to contract the vessels of this large muscle
and slows the bleeding. I followed my practical nurses teachings to the word; my only tools in my toolbox were my brain
and my hands. Within minutes, her soft fundus began to firm
and her hemorrhaging slowed. My anxiety waned when I saw
the immediate results.

I told Larta to keep track of the number of soaked cloth
pads and to encourage fluids. I instructed her to feel the firm
fundus and if the bleeding increased she was instructed to
massage the fundus as I had shown her. If it did not lessen,
she was to summon me for the next step. But only after the
bleeding was controlled did I notice the twin baby girls, each
swaddled in a lappa, lying on a mat on the floor. Larta said the
babies were well and breast feeding without difficulty. I
walked home that afternoon hopeful Larta's new knowledge
would be passed on to other midwives, just as their wisdom
and expertise had for centuries. Teetering on the brink between life and death was a daily reality; it could be so easy to
die and at times so easy to save a life.

The following morning, I returned for a home visit. The mother was up and walking. Her vaginal bleeding was controlled and within normal postpartum limits. The baby girls were a healthy size and doing well. This mother, too, like Fatima and Mohamad, raised her healthy twins with our clinic support. I was filled with a joy reminiscent of the day when I delivered the baby pigs on the farm or saved Daisy, the runt of the litter. To save a life was the best feeling I could ever have. I only hoped these two Liberian families would encourage others to give twins a chance.

One Person at a Time

Amand walked through our clinic door cradling his six-year-old son, Saye, who was fifteen to twenty pounds underweight and unable to walk. A tattered dirty t-shirt and shorts hung on his shoeless stick-like body. The father heard rumors of the "white-woman doctor" in Gowee and carried Saye over three miles in his last desperate effort to save his critically ill son.

Now in my second year in Gowee, my reputation as a healer and an alternative or adjunct to their traditional country medicine gradually took hold as people began to see some improvements in their health, such as nutrition and treatment of minor illnesses. But I was far from being a "doctor."

When Amand brought his son to the clinic that day, I diagnosed Saye as having severe kwashiorkor, a state of protein malnutrition. Previously, I only read about this ailment in medical textbooks during my nurses training. Saye presented with the classic kwashiorkor symptoms: a bloated abdomen, puffy face, spindly arms and legs, swollen feet and hands, and brittle blond hair. Listless, without a trace of a smile, he had lost one-quarter to one-third of his normal body weight.

After gathering the medical history, I learned the critically ill boy had experienced severe diarrhea months prior, and his family chose to treat this condition with country herbs and potions through the local medicine man. These treatments may have resolved Saye's diarrhea before he was brought to our clinic. However, after suffering significant weight loss from his prolonged illness, the medicine man informed

Amand his son was witched and needed additional country medicine of herbs and rituals to clear Saye of the curse. Amand followed his guidance along with a prescribed diet of only white rice with no protein. After weeks of this regimen, the medicine man's treatment ultimately led to the boy's kwashiorkor. Gowee clinic had only existed a few years before my assignment. I discovered country medicine practices were hard to influence even when those methods were no longer effective; the locals still believed in them.

After working with Fatima, Mohamad, and their twins, I clearly understood the hierarchy of food distribution and customs among Liberian families. Children are the last to receive protein and might consume only a teaspoon of protein for an entire day. This was not sufficient for the strong healthy growth of a young child. Traditionally, an ill child often received no protein. Treated with country medicine alone and force-fed white rice, the child's stomach was filled, but lacked sufficient protein and nutrition.

Peter and I worked together to help the malnourished boy with our limited resources. Amand knew some Liberian English, but Peter translated in Gio for a deeper understanding. I taught the father the basics of nutrition and local protein-rich foods. All were available to the family. I emphasized the need for adequate protein for the women and children.

Stocked with few clinic supplies, we placed our *main* hope in the vegetable oil and powdered milk supplied by CARE. Because Saye had not received regular food in weeks, I introduced a diet easily tolerated and demonstrated how to make a nutritious rice cereal with the CARE food supplements that provided fat and protein.

Gradually, over several weeks, Saye became stronger as he resumed a normal diet. His bloated belly, puffy face, swollen feet and hands shrunk, and his limbs filled out. The blond brittle hair gradually disappeared and was replaced by jet-black growth. Slowly, but surely, the six-year-old became strong enough to walk; something he hadn't done in months. After weeks of care and monitoring, I experienced my first joy: I caught Saye's smile.

Four months passed. While preparing for our Well-baby clinic, I heard a male voice calling my Liberian name, "Younga, Younga Ti!" Amand and his son stood at my front door, a proud father with his young healthy boy. More dressed up than usual, both Amand and Saye wore plastic sandals, clean t-shirts and shorts. Coming to my home was out of the ordinary for Amand, and I couldn't imagine the purpose of his visit.

"Babua, Younga Ti."

"Aahoo," I replied.

I gestured for them to come in and sit when the father spoke softly in the few Liberian English words he knew, "Younga Ti, my two wives and five children say thank you, ya, for saving Saye. We want to give you Saye for yur own." He paused, took a deep breath, and went on, "You, can take good good care of Saye, *mo* better than me. Take, Saye, I beg you, ya."

I paused searching for words...any words. I inhaled deeply then responded in my best Liberian English, "Amand, I thank you and yur family for all good you do for Saye and bring him to clinic. I am so happy for his good good health."

"Yes. *You* save him," Amand pleaded.

I swallowed the lump rising in my throat and replied, "Amand, thank you, ya, for yur kindness. But... Saye need his family. Saye need his village and his people. Saye need *you*, his father. I could never give dat to him. I would take him back to America where *all* would be so so different. You can give Saye his family, his village, and his people. You did a *good* job. You are a good good father."

Amand's eyes fell and his shoulders slumped. I was uncertain if it indicated disappointment or relief. Displaying the traditional Liberian gesture of respect, I bowed my head and grasped my right forearm with my left as I shook Amand's hand. He bowed in return.

Then my chest swelled when my eyes met Saye's longing gaze. Did he know we were talking about him as he understood no English? My knees nearly buckled as I bent down and gave him the biggest hug. I dared not blink to contain my tears.

"Younga Ti, thank you, ya. Thank you, thank you." Amand choked on his words. "You are a good good white-woman doctor. I now take Saye back to my family." The grateful father took his son's hand, and just as they approached my front door, both turned to me and smiled, then departed.

Despite the hot humid day, I shivered from my sense of empty success. I've never been a parent, and I could only imagine what it would be like to give a child away. I believed Amand was *not* an uncaring father and sought the resources with which he was familiar. He offered me the only valued thing he had to give for saving his first-born—the most precious of the Liberian children—and that was to *give* me his son.

"The toughest job you'll ever love. Join the Peace Corps." That catchy Peace Corps commercial I saw on our TV a couple of years earlier of the young female volunteer walking through her village with a trail of happy African children seemed like a forgotten memory. When I woke up the following morning after Amand and Saye's departure, I knew I wasn't going to save even a quarter of my village or community in my two-year stay. The most I could hope to accomplish was to help just one person, one family at a time, however few that might be.

Girls Bush School

One pleasant evening I walked home from Sami's, meandering between the huts, smelling the wood burning fires, and glancing at the full moon on the horizon. "Babua," I extended my greetings in Gio to others out for a stroll. I abruptly stopped at the yelping, whining sound trailing from a nearby hut. A silhouetted man, who appeared to look like Jacob, kicked a dog who had exited the home. The four-legged animal on the ground scurried away. I hurried past the disturbance so I wouldn't be detected; the dog could be injured and come my way.

The following morning, Martha came to my house and told me Jacob discovered she slept with a Liberian dresser, Dominic, who had visited our clinic for the past month. When I saw her swollen face and bloodshot eyes, I realized the creature on the ground had been Martha. She told me Jacob not only beat her, but also took a knife and shredded her mattress.

Martha could have been Jacob's fourth wife; however, due to her infertility, she was not marriage material. In Gowee, women unable to bear children were a dispensable item—to be cast aside on a whim. An infertile woman in remote parts of Liberia is often perceived as adding little value to the family, except as a man's sexual object. More children added more labor to meet farming needs. Therefore, becoming a mistress would be Martha's lot in life, a predestined reality throughout most of Liberia. On the surface it appeared she had it all; she lived with her parents, had gifts and money from Jacob and didn't have to work as hard as his other wives. On the other hand, she was thrown out of her own home by Jacob. Martha soon recovered from her injuries and went back to him. The hierarchy of men versus women was something we accepted in this small village.

A woman's life in Gowee was more complex than I understood. I was just beginning to learn of the supernatural powers of the devils and the traditional treatments of the medicine men. I hungered to further understand their customs and culture. When I heard of the girls bush school I asked Bendu, the head midwife, if I could witness a portion of the event.

Every few years the Gio and Mano tribes conducted the bush school—a one-week initiation for preadolescent boys and another for girls, ranging from about eight to thirteen years of age. What transpired there, deep in the bush, was clandestine and known only to the elders, medicine men, and midwives who conducted the schools. The ceremonies and rituals occurred only at night in a secluded location far from the village.

Peter told me the boys bush school provided instruction about the life skills of becoming a man. One major part of the ritual included circumcision. Peter freely shared this information because he became clinically involved treating male complications including bleeding and infection. I hoped to influence safer practices such as hand washing and using clean razor blades similar to the instruction given to the midwives during their training.

However, details about the girls bush school were more difficult to obtain. I hoped with time, I could build their trust to witness and learn more about these activities, as I did when I observed my first country delivery some months earlier. Bendu told me the midwives and female elders led the girls school and I could only hope and wait for an invitation.

One particular night, unlike any other, the descent of nighttime swept like a curtain of darkness over Gowee. I sat at my dining room table to light my Aladdin's lamp when I heard someone say, "Bock, bock." Martha stood at the front door, exuberant because Bendu had summoned me to attend one of the ceremonies of the girls bush school. I quickly grabbed my torch and off we walked through the main section of Gowee heading north toward the edge of the village onto an unfamiliar path. The brush was freshly wacked with a cutlass to create the new route.

My heart pounded and my breathing labored even though we weren't running. In some respects, the country delivery I witnessed in the past had a known outcome—a baby. However, anxiety and fear consumed me as I wondered what I would find.

Upon arrival, some thirty minutes later, we stopped in front of a six-foot-high walled compound made of impenetrable woven palm fronds. The newly constructed barrier smelled sweet, like fresh cut grass. Behind the wall, a raging fire cast a huge orange glow sending sporadic sparks into the sky. Martha called for Bendu to meet us outside the compound.

Within moments she arrived and I greeted her. "Babua, Bendu."

"Aahoo," she replied. "Iswoudou, Younga Ti," she thanked me for coming and asked me to wait while she conferred with the elders inside, before granting me permission to enter.

From behind the walled barrier, chanting, singing, and drumming pulsated in the humid smoke-laden air. The combination of darkness, floating embers, and rhythmic music filled my senses. Soon I became mesmerized and entranced. I sat on a log outside the wall for the long five-minute wait until Bendu returned. Her face told me what I didn't want to hear; my entry was denied by the elders and other midwives. I did not press, only thanked her and we departed. Somehow, I was relieved. Maybe they knew I would interfere just as I had done so innocently at the country delivery.

During our walk back to the village, Martha said, "I go to dis school five year ago."

With the close relationship we had developed, I inquired with some ease, "I know you are sworn to secrecy, but Martha, can you tell me, what da bush school was like for you?"

She flashed her toothy smile and explained, "Miss Sue, you are my good good friend. I can tell you da young girls learn how to be wives. One of many wives. They learn how to be da servant to da husband. The girls learn of loving-business and dat to be given when the man want it. Then later dat week, they cut da girls."

"What do you mean, cut da girls?" I squeaked the question through my constricted vocal cords.

"Da head midwives cut a piece of skin above where da baby come out," Martha said.

My stomach seized. My mind reeled. Did she mean the *clitoris*?

"You alright?" as Martha grabbed my arm when I tripped and stumbled on a root in the path.

"Yes, I fine-o. Why, I mean...why...da midwives do dis to da girls?"

"Dis believed if da skin is gone-o, it will keep da girls from looking for other men because dis area give woman pleasure. Da cut will keep them faithful to der husband." Martha moved her hand to muffle her giggle, "Not all midwives do such a good job-o; I still like loving-business." Her laughing tone became somber as she went on, "Sometime der be problem-o with infection and bleeding. Only country medicine or da midwives can make da cure cause no others can help in dis secret bush school."

After observing the poor sanitation practices in my first country delivery, I expected the surgical complications could be dire. If country medicine or midwifery treatment failed, massive scarring, infections leading to infertility or even death would ensue. As a nurse, I was aware of these outcomes from any untreated infections in the pelvic area. I couldn't bear the thought of the pain they endured without anesthesia. My mind raced. Could this be the reason for Martha's infertility? Her botched surgery may have afforded her continued sexual enjoyment, and possibly why Jacob found Martha sleeping with another man.

These young girls had little option but to follow their pre destined path. Women who made different choices, like Martha, suffered the consequences when she was beaten by Jacob, even though he took her back. Few chose another path, like Rita who roamed from town to town seeking her many lovers, or the woman stoned in front of my house by the villagers for committing adultery. I shook my head. Is bush school the price to pay for being a girl: suffering painful surgery, being denied choice and sexual pleasure, and risking infection and infertility? Oh dear Lord, what...a price...to pay.

As Martha escorted me back to my house, I thanked her for taking me and being such a good friend. When she departed, I slid the bolt on the door, lit my kerosene lantern and lay fully clothed on my bed. My voice echoed off the wall of my bedroom, "I can't believe this. This can't be true." In my stillness I wondered, could this be called *female circumcision*? Even though I never had an orgasm, I was still appalled by the practice. I could not believe the girls were being mutilated by their respected female elders and midwives who also promoted the practice. I raised my eyes to watch the lantern shadows flicker on the ceiling and asked aloud to my higher power, "God, in your name, what compels people to do this?"

I waited for a long, long time...I got no answer.

Five days later Martha summoned me again as the twenty-five girls, led by the midwives and female elders, paraded through the village. The midwives chanted in Gio as the girls followed them through the center of Gowee. My attention was drawn to the girls' beautifully marked white face-paint that accented their forehead and eyes along with perfectly corn-rowed hair. New lappas adorned their virgin mutilated bodies with careful attention to expose their plump non-sagging breasts. All those adornments announced: here was the new bride material for any man ready with a handsome dowry to add a wife to his family.

Everyone in the village stopped their activities to follow the parade. When the girls reached the clan chief's house, they were motioned to sit on the ground in a semicircle. At least a hundred villagers now crowded around them: men, women, and children. A young man placed a bench inside the circle for the two honored head midwives. Chief Manuel exited his house wearing his ceremonial embroidered robe and cap and gifted a large basin of unhusked rice placed to the left of the midwives.

While one midwife spoke in Gio to the crowd, I looked intently to find the young girls who frequented my house. There they were: Matu, age eleven; Nora, age eight; and Yah, age ten. With my arms weighted in despair, I raised my camera to take their photos and document history in the making. Only then did I see the pain reflected on their sober aching faces. Did they know their lives would never be the same again? Most of the girls were not yet teenagers and some may not have experienced their first menstrual cycle.

At age eleven my life changed forever when my dad told me I bore the burden and responsibility to push men away to protect my virginity, just as I had done to Doug, Taki in the Abidjan Hotel, Dr. Mattie in Gowee, and the numerous suitors who came to my house for loving-business. However, the girls who sat in front of me carried a different obligation and duty: to *welcome* their man at any time from that day forward.

I felt helpless and insignificant. This experience was so painful, I shut it out from my mind. During the remainder of my stay in Gowee, I never brought the topic up again to anyone, not even Martha.

Unspoken Words

Before leaving the farm, the term "queer" was only mentioned in a whisper and generally frowned upon by the locals. Since arriving in Liberia, I learned that same-sex practices were likewise not accepted there. Heterosexuality, however, was ubiquitous. I received loving-business requests nearly every day and observed Jacob practicing polygamy with three wives and a mistress. But I was naïve when it came to understanding same-sex relationships.

My good friend Tom, from Zapa, displayed some understated manners. He avoided the general male aggressive or assertive behaviors I was accustomed to. He was sensitive, intuitive, and cared less about impressing women, though he sometimes brought a date to our parties. We could talk for hours and I truly enjoyed his company. He was a best friend and I valued our platonic relationship. I suspected something unusual about his sexuality, but I didn't care. Besides, Tom had saved my life months earlier when I nearly died from Shigella dysentery.

When weekends came, I liked venturing out from my village to visit friends. One Saturday, Tom invited me to spend the night at his village, a full day by taxi from Gowee. After enjoying the evening with his Lebanese friends feasting on a delicious dinner of hummus, baba ganoush, and lamb kabobs, we strolled back to Tom's home where his houseboy was finishing his chores. Even though he had a spare bedroom at his disposal, Tom made a point of saying, "Alonso, no need to make up the guest bedroom, Miss Sue will be sleeping in my bed."

Tom's statement certainly placed me in a predicament. Much like my farm community back home, Liberian villages were the "Peyton Place" of Africa: everyone knew everyone's business. I was already the talk of my small village because no one had witnessed a man spending the night in my bedroom since Doug left months before. But my Catholic indoctrination held strong, as God was *my* witness.

Before Alonso departed, we retreated to Tom's bedroom and closed the door. In my night clothes—with an uncanny calmness—I lay beside him, without fear, worries, or expectations. He reached over to turn out the kerosene lantern and we went to sleep.

The following morning, the sun leaked through the closed shutters and the cock's crow rang in our ears. Like two roommates sharing the same bed, we arose. My subconscious told me we may have *both* benefited from our night's pretense. Before we were awakened, Alonso, most likely, had spread the rumors throughout the village that "Miss Sue slept with a man and Tom has a new girlfriend."

With early morning still in our eyes, we drank our Nescafé, ate our jellied baguette, and never spoke another word about what it all meant. No need. We both knew. The villagers would draw their own conclusions.

I Lost a Brother

I counted on Sami in so many ways, but most of all for his unconditional friendship. Despite our differences, he was always there for me, whether providing needed supplies, socialization, transportation, or a listening ear. Sami was my rock. We supported each other in our failures and reveled in our few successes. But most of all, he *never once* asked me for loving-business. For that alone, I placed him in the highest regard.

Nada, his mistress, pregnant with Sami's second baby, came to the Antenatal clinic one Thursday morning for her checkup. At barely seven months, she appeared to be having early contractions. Sami had not been informed of her symptoms. But after explaining the risks of an early labor, I encouraged Nada to tell Sami and have him take her to Sanniquellie Hospital for further evaluation. Within an hour the three of us rushed to the hospital.

The doctor admitted her and prescribed bedrest. However, Nada's contractions continued, and it was determined the baby was breech. Unable to manage her care in Sanniquellie, the doctor recommended transport to the LAMCO Hospital. Nervous and scared, Sami drove white-knuckled down the dusty road while I comforted Nada, moaning through painful contractions in the front seat of his Chevy pickup. Once admitted, the doctor encouraged us to return home and they would try to calm the contractions. And so we did.

Sami spent the following day in LAMCO, returning in the evening to Gowee to inform me that Nada had delivered a baby girl. Sami and Nada decided to name her Susie, the endearing name Sami had given me. We were all relieved Nada and Susie were doing well. The next day Sami and I returned to LAMCO.

Before we entered Nada's room, the nurse pulled us aside and said, "Sami, last night your baby did not live. We have not told Nada as she is very tired and we want her to rest."

I opposed shielding this information from Nada, but I kept silent. Sami collapsed on a chair outside her room holding his head in his hands. Gently resting my hand on his shoulder, I said. "She will be OK, Sami." We cried in disbelief. After a few moments we composed ourselves and entered Nada's room. She saw our reddened eyes and immediately asked, "Why dey not let me see baby Susie?" We bowed our heads. "Is she dead?"

Sami said, "Yes."

We came to her side as tears flowed and Nada wailed.

Susie was dead. Two people that I cared about grieved their loss. I supported them as much as I could, while burying my own personal sorrow. I couldn't think about myself, not when they needed me.

Sami changed after Susie's death. He stopped pigeon hunting on Sundays and became sullen and depressed. Six months later he divulged to me his business was failing due to unpaid credit from the small Mandingo merchants. At the same time President Tolbert continued to pressure foreigners to divest from their businesses. Sami told me of family letters begging for his return to the war zone of Lebanon, and his Lebanese friends in Monrovia recommended he depart for his home. I didn't want him to leave, and he had mixed feelings about going.

While I was on business in Monrovia, Sami received official word from the Liberian government that he and other foreign merchants must vacate the country. He was forced to leave his mistress and daughter in Gowee. Before I could return, he closed his doors and went back to Lebanon. I never got to say goodbye.

Heartbroken, I too felt abandoned in some way. Sami's store was barricaded shut. Who would be there for me? Where would the villagers and the midwives get their supplies? How would the Mandingos stock their small market tables? The entire village grieved, especially Nada and Eleham.

Shortly after his departure, Sami wrote three endearing letters asking about me, Nada, and Eleham. He sent money to help support them. I should not have been surprised when I read that his parents arranged a marriage to a fine Lebanese woman named Ciham. He bragged about his ten-pound weight gain and asked me to visit his new wife and family. The political unrest in Lebanon continued, but he assured me it would improve. His words overflowed with longing, yet fulfillment. My heart swelled when I read his signature, "Your best friend, your brother, Sami." Yes, he was a best friend and a brother to me. I missed him so much. After those three letters from Sami, I lost contact with him. A bittersweet ending for such a giving, loving man who was looking for family and a home. I hoped he found it.

Difficult Choices

Returning directly to Nebraska after my Peace Corps assignment was a distant possibility. A year had passed since Doug's visit to Liberia and our relationship was all but over. I wanted to delay my return home and my RN training for now and instead pursue other overseas work more related to clinical nursing, rather than health education.

The Peace Corps office in Tonga—an island country in the South Pacific Ocean—was requesting a nurse to supervise their national tuberculosis and typhoid vaccination campaign. The description of Tonga appeared seductive. It was known as the Crown Jewel of the Pacific. This archipelago in the South Pacific has over 170 islands, thirty-six of which are inhabited. Located south of Samoa and roughly between Hawaii and New Zealand, the Polynesian islands of Tonga became a British protectorate in 1875, the only South Pacific island group to avoid colonization. With a population of about 90,000, the three main island groups originated from volcanoes and barrier reefs. What a contrast from the tropical rainforest of Liberia.

Restlessness and anxiety kept me awake at night thinking about leaving a place that had become my home for the past two years. Yet, I knew my goals for the health of the Zor Clan would be limited by our resources. Besides, Sami—my rock—was gone. Rainbow, my soul sister, was dead, and my

African family was on the decline with Rita rarely visiting Gowee. I was ready to take another step, ready to move on, but I certainly was not ready for Nebraska. My parents were not surprised to learn of my plans via aerogram and had probably given up hope that I would ever comply with their wishes to marry a good Catholic boy and be a farmer's wife.

One late afternoon in January 1973, I walked into a typical Peace Corps party in Sanniquellie. Kwi PCVs in their finest African prints each held a cold Club Beer, and the smell of palm butter and cooked rice filled the room. African highlife music blasted from a boom box on the kitchen counter and several people swayed to the rhythm in one corner of the crowded room. As I pushed my way between the twenty-five people crammed shoulder to shoulder in the small house, someone yelled, "Gowee Sue." I exchanged hugs and greetings with my friends.

Unexpectedly, a magnetic energy came upon me. I scanned the room to find the most gorgeous man I had ever seen in the opposite corner, his eyes focused directly on me. I suddenly felt chilled and flushed while my limbs became weak and stiff. My feeling of awe resembled the time I laid eyes upon that majestic Maasai warrior who boarded our bus in Kenya. Ironically, his features resembled that of my high school sweetheart: tall at about 6'4", thin, muscular, with a gentle appearance. There was a *big* difference however—his skin was dark, chocolate brown. He wasn't African; he was American.

The hum of the partygoers seemed to fall silent. Our eyes fixated upon each other while I stood motionless in the far corner of the room. He approached me slowly, parting the crowd. "Hello, my name is Michael. I just arrived six weeks ago and am stationed in Saklopea as a teacher. And you?"

Lack of verbal expression was not my character flaw, yet I seemed unable to make a complete sentence. "Susan, I mean, Gowee Sue…the volunteers call me."

After a few minutes I became more comfortable. We talked about our lives in Liberia and life back home. In between my semiconscious state, I heard the words, Ohio…

basketball... Master's program... Texas A&M... agriculture, but the remainder seemed fuzzy. What I did remember was that he *wanted* to be in Liberia. He *wanted* to help teach children. From our first meeting, I became Susan, a name he thought was beautiful. My given name was never my favorite, but now, for some reason...I loved it too.

I soon realized Michael was someone very special. He understood everything I wanted a friend to understand. We talked about our adjustments to Liberia, our background, as well as our interests. He played basketball in high school and college and I shared my interest in sports. Over the following weeks we developed a relationship, as much as one could call it in Liberia, because no one "dated" as we commonly knew in the U.S. His utter handsomeness and commanding height filled me with excitement, wonder, nervousness, fear, and longing. His manner attracted me the most; he was gentle, kind, and loving. Because we lived two taxis away—a half-day's travel from each other—Michael and I met just a few more times in my remaining months in Liberia. Through word-of-mouth communication, we were joyful to reunite at Peace Corps gatherings and parties when we could.

When he first kissed me, I was clear and said, "Don't take advantage of me." And he never did. I was falling in love.

After living in a black culture for nearly two years, I rarely noticed the color of his skin. I saw only the wonderful man he was. Despite my colorblindness, he *was* black. When I saw his skin through my parents' eyes, I knew for a fact this relationship was *never* going to work for my family. Being in love with a black man would put me on a suicide mission with my parents. My relationship with Michael could never be.

In my final month of my two-year assignment, extending another year in Liberia became an option for me. With Michael now in my life, I considered it only briefly. I never shared my parents' prejudice with him because I saw no reason. I must end our improbable relationship. So with that, I chose Tonga. Michael seemed understanding of my choice and had a keen sense of my determination and strong will. He never demeaned me for my goals or desires and I respected him for that. Michael and I said our goodbyes. As impossible as it seemed to communicate from West Africa to the South Pacific, we vowed to write to each other as often as we could.

In the days prior to my departure, the people in Gowee told me they didn't want me to go. My heart broke when I learned my Peace Corps position would not be filled and the clinic would go on without me. I couldn't help but wonder who would keep Peter in line. Would the fridge still be there to hold the DPT vaccines? Would the clinic still receive the CARE oil, milk, and flour? Who would make the home visits to remind the mothers to come to the clinic for their antenatal and baby care? Would Peter continue the health education lessons? I blocked out the answers.

Sentimental gifts and gestures poured in from the villagers. One man hand-carved a small eight-inch stool with etched designs for my mom and dad. Others gave me cloth and hand-carved gourds for me and my family. These were gifts from families who earned 50¢ a day at best. They wished me well, asking me to come back.

For two years the villagers of Gowee became my African family, especially Martha, Rita, and Clara, including Sami— the family who loved and accepted me the way I was. Our lives bonded when I ate rice with them by hand from one common bowl and when I held the baton of the tall devil. By the full moon I danced with my people to the sound of the talking drum. I carried a baby on my back while I walked through my village. Martha and Rita plaited my hair so I looked like them. I nearly died, at least once, from a tropical disease. One infant boy in the village was named after my dad. Sami's daughter was named in my honor, but she died before I could hold her. In those special moments, I became one of them. There was no other place I would rather have been than Gowee.

For the times my diary held the words "I hate Africa, I hate Liberia, I hate African Men," those words seemed alien to me now. My deepest pain also held my deepest love; of course, Africa will always be my first love.

Despite abandoning Michael, a wonderful man, a new adventure beckoned. On May 15, 1973, I packed my luggage. Almost all of my Nebraska possessions that filled my green duffle bag two years before were now gone. The rubber boots, rain hat, jacket, and umbrella were never used. No polyester tops and knit skirts—all gone. Not one of those items returned with me except for my diaries and my cameras from the Virgin Islands. Inside the tattered diaries my words co-mingled with palm-oiled-fingerprints, red laterite dust, and tears. More importantly, the pages were filled with treasured memories of my two years in Africa. My SLR and movie cameras captured the cherished images of my African experience that my written words failed to document. I carefully packed the duffle bag now with precious handmade clothing, artifacts, jewelry, and special handcrafted gifts for my family and friends.

When the money-bus arrived at my house, several people gathered around: Martha, Jacob, Clara, many of the people who became my family away from home. We hugged and cried. Like one of the locals, I took my seat on a rear bench in the bed of the money-bus. As it pulled away, I looked though the tailgate, taking one last view as each landmark passed by my vision like a movie played in reverse: the glimpse of my house; the clinic; the path through Gowee; the main road; Sami's store, now boarded up; the Go Tree; and then the bridge over the Yar River with the women and children washing their clothes. My emotions and memories were etched in my being as tears parted the dust clinging to my cheeks. Even with my heart overflowing with affection and admiration for Gowee, I sensed I would never return. I cried harder with a heaviness in my heart as I gazed from the rear of the money-bus and watched my village fade into the dust.

PART VIII

BACK TO THE FARM

The Power of Shame

Mom raised her eyebrows and shook her head when she spotted me exiting my Frontier flight in Kanton in May 1973. She had not seen me for two years. My previous chin-length hair with bangs was now transformed into a long straight mane flowing down my back, parted in the middle. I wore my handmade African-print bellbottoms. My Catholic medal from high school, still around my neck, was obscured by a beaded choker from Kenya. An elephant hair bracelet from Tanzania and hand-pounded silver bangles from Senegal adorned each arm. Rings from a variety of countries laced five of my fingers and silver-filigreed earrings from Ethiopia completed my ensemble. Once carefully applied makeup made way for a bronzed, tanned natural look. I hadn't plucked or highlighted my eyebrows once in two years. I stood before her as a mature twenty-one-year-old African fashion plate. Mom's tepid smile was my only welcome greeting. Hugs were foreign in our family—so I didn't get one. She helped load my bags in the car and moaned, "Did you bring home the kitchen sink?" Then off to the farm we drove.

Randy greeted me at the front door and gave me a big hug. "My, how you've grown," I remarked. Now thirteen and nearly my height, he wanted to know all about Africa. Bob, now married, lived just a few miles away and was working in Kanton. I couldn't wait see to them and their two-year-old daughter, Jennifer, and four-month-old, Stephanie. Within minutes Dad came in from the barn without any welcoming fanfare. Instead, a palpable tension filled the room. Soon the criticism began to flow. Mom asked, "What's that you are wearing? My, what is all this funny-looking jewelry?" Not so much as a glad-to-see-you greeting. Her interrogation continued into the evening. She pestered me with more questions, "What happened to your hair? It looks a mess. God, you've gained weight. Why are you going back to the Peace Corps again? Didn't you have enough?" Dad was silent. Disapproval and harsh judgments filled my homecoming. I fumbled with my responses but quickly realized I had changed and grown in those two years, and clearly they had not.

I hadn't driven a car since I left two years earlier, but I needed to get out of the house and asked for the keys to the yellow Mazda. I drove six miles down the country roads to Bob and Joan's house. I held their two children for the first time. Jennifer was dressed in the Liberian shirt I sent her after her birth and Stephanie wore the boots I had knitted in Liberia. They welcomed me with open arms and smiles all around, and gladly accepted my special African gifts. Joan said, "Look at this." Proudly she held up my postcard they received from Timbuktu—only about two months after I mailed it. We laughed, but it became crystal clear how remote Africa really was. They planned a welcome home party for me and I needed that more than they knew.

I joined Joan, now pregnant with their third child, on a shopping run to Kanton. I momentarily froze staring at the grocery shelves: five brands of catsup and mustard; eight varieties and textures of toilet paper; soap in every shape, color, and smell one desired; packaged bread products of every kind: muffins, buns, sliced, brown or white. Though the Peace Corps warned us of reverse culture shock upon reentry to the U.S., I was surprised by my disgust at Western abundance and America's obsession with choice. Did we really need five or eight varieties of anything? With relief, I'd be leaving for Tonga in a few weeks.

In the following days, to calm the strain with my parents, I shared my African photos, slides, and movies. Some photos portrayed my house in Gowee, the villagers, my travels, and Peace Corps friends. I joked about the Christmas photo of the four Peace Corps guys and girls with whom I roomed in a hotel in Bamako, Mali, where two friends and I slept on the floor. My heart sank when my experiences and stories were met with criticism, snide racial comments, or indifference. Only a few days into my visit, I realized the chasm between our values and beliefs had only widened, and their acceptance of me and my mission in Africa was not to be.

On Sunday our family attended Mass at St. Anthony's. After service, many church members talked of Nixon's announcement of ending of the Vietnam War. A few noticed my arrival and greeted me. Only one person asked me about my work or my life in Liberia. Some young women wore hair long down their backs, but only I had a hippie-type-look, letting mine go natural without sleeping in curlers or teasing it to the perfect pouf. I wore no eye makeup, and my handmade clothing and jewelry from Africa certainly caught a few stares. I stammered a few times answering in simple Liberian English, but quickly corrected that mistake. Several women my age were now married, carrying a baby or two. My two-year absence seemed more like a lifetime.

After church, Randy went to a cousin's house for the day. I grabbed the opportunity to break the tension between me and my parents and walked into the kitchen with my green duffle bag slung over my shoulder. Carefully and methodically I unpacked the numerous gifts wrapped in one large piece of African tie-dyed cloth. I gently placed each article on the kitchen counter and said, "Mom and Dad, these are gifts from me and the people in my village. Dad, here is a hand-crafted stool from Samuel in Zorgowee and this is a set of hand-carved mahogany bookends from Kenya." Even though Dad didn't read anything but the newspaper, I hoped he admired the beautifully carved wood. As if the items were contaminated, my parents refrained from reaching toward the gifts. They frowned and their eyes filled with scorn.

I continued, "For you, Mom, here is a silver teapot from Ethiopia. This is a necklace and earring set from Kenya. Here is handmade tie-dyed cloth from Liberia." I explained the origin and significance of numerous other gifts I carefully placed on the counter. I received no thank you, no comments, and no response at all.

After my fifteen-minute presentation, I looked up to find their eyes cast to the floor and hands by their sides. Their grave, silent reaction could not have been more ominous than had I announced I was pregnant. But I *wasn't* and could not imagine what warranted this mute response for these thoughtful and precious gifts. Didn't Dad remember that out of deep respect a baby in Gowee was named after him? But I dared not bring it up. When I could no longer stand the silence, I returned to my upstairs bedroom. Nausea gripped my throat.

I put my angst aside as I prepared to meet Doug later that day. While we spoke over the phone daily since my return, I deferred our meeting for a few days, using family as the excuse until I gathered enough nerve to tell him officially that our relationship was over. I planned to return the pearl ring I wore faithfully up until my last couple of months in Liberia. I placed the ring back on my finger and drove to Kanton where he rented a room. The cloudy cool spring day left me chilled as I knocked on his door.

Doug was as handsome as I remembered. His thick blond hair was shorter now. His blue eyes were still captivating. Our awkward embrace at the front door set the stage for our impending conversation. We sat on the couch, our bodies not touching. I fumbled with small talk about what I had done during my first few days home. No need to share the anxiety of my homecoming, as I had more dread to deal with right then. He glanced at my left hand and in amongst two other African rings, he spotted my promise ring where he placed it two years earlier.

Without eye contact, I inhaled deeply and said, "Doug, I have thought long and hard about the two of us since your visit to Liberia. I was honored you came that distance to see me. Your visit, however, made it very clear to me I have changed. I'm not sure if I want to be married right now, but I *am* sure I want to go to Tonga for my next assignment and later go back to school to become a registered nurse." I choked out the faint words, "I think it best we go our separate ways."

Doug watched me remove the pearl ring from my hand as I placed it on the coffee table in front of us. His face turned ashen white. I watched his lips tighten and could see the pain reflected in his reddened eyes. I burst into tears and we hesitantly moved toward each other, embraced, and wept. We spoke no words of love. We said our goodbyes and agreed to not see each other again to avoid further pain.

I walked down his porch stairs with an emptiness I never knew existed. Now my life, love, and future seemed uncertain and scary. I didn't want to go home but had no other place of refuge. My friends wouldn't understand. Bob, Joan, and Randy were as confused about my choices as my parents. After two more hours parked on a country road crying about a love lost, I blew my nose one final time and dabbed my red eyes in the mirror. I had no makeup to hide my trauma. I started the ignition and drove toward the farmhouse—up the long driveway over the spillway, past the granary where Daisy had slept each night, and next to the hill where I learned how to ride my bike. I pulled into the garage from where we hauled in our beloved black-and-white TV sixteen years earlier. Only Mom was home. I told her I ended my relationship with Doug. Mom slapped her hands on her apron, shook her head and said, "He's a nice boy. Why did you do that to him?"

Mom never fully approved of Doug because he wasn't Catholic. Now, for some strange reason, he became a *nice boy*. I'm damned if I do and damned if I don't. I retreated to my room and avoided my parents as much as possible.

The following day I came downstairs for breakfast and discovered all the African gifts I presented to my parents the day before in a haphazard pile on the kitchen counter. Scattered among them were a few of the photos I had shared. Mom and Dad arose from the table. My apprehension intensified. The three of us gathered around the African treasures like a funeral wake.

"*Who* are these people in the photos?" The photos of me mixed with guys, with gals, and some with both. "Are you dating any of these guys? Is that why you broke up with Doug?" Dad demanded.

I muttered a faint, "No."

Dad pressured me even more. "What about *this* guy, the *black* guy? There are lots of photos of him and you together!"

"He...he was a good friend, that's all." I could not meet his eyes and stared at the floor.

"Besides, we don't approve of you sleeping in hotel rooms with mixed company. We raised you better than that! Do you think you're a whore?"

I purposely avoided my dad's rage and ultimate disapproval my entire life. I never forgot the time Dad kicked my twelve-year-old brother, Bob, across the kitchen floor when he flunked the sixth grade. Now, my day of reckoning had come. Dad's face reddened and lips tightened. He clenched his hand and raised it above his head. Like the force of a sledgehammer, he slammed his fist on the kitchen counter closest to me. The African gifts leapt in the air, and the power of his blow shook the counter, traveling down to the floor and back up my body.

"If anyone finds out about you and that nigger we will have to *sell* the farm. You will not only bring *us* shame, but shame to our whole damned community. We don't want any of these gifts those God-damned niggers made. Take them all back!"

Fear, rage, and brokenness permeated the room. Dad now stood taller in his rage. I wanted to be invisible. Mom withdrew a few feet from the counter. I never expected her to defend me from Dad's fury. This was the same retreat she made when Dad kicked my brother Bob. I glanced at her face mixed with emotions and sensed fear. I hoped she was never victim to Dad's hand. Yet there was a faint gleam in her eyes sending me a message that I was getting what I deserved.

I fumbled hurriedly to gather the precious gifts. Treasures I had specially chosen and carefully packed now lay in a heap on the counter like worthless trinkets. I unfolded a piece of tie-dyed cloth, laid all the gifts in the center, and gathered the corners. In my haste, Mom's Kenyan earrings and necklace dropped to the floor. She curtly picked them up and threw them in the pile. I scrambled up the stairs to my room, placed my bundle on the floor, and lay face down on my bed, bawling. After two hours, my tears no longer flowed and gut-wrenching moans arose from my stomach. My sobbing was like the wails the Liberians made over the loss of a loved one—a deep guttural cry. In between my sighs I heard an incoherent mumble traveling up the stairway from Dad's continued rage and Mom's lowered voice.

My parents' deep-seated beliefs, values, and misunderstandings were more rigid than I ever imagined. The faint thread connecting me to them was now severed. I closed my heart off from my mom and dad at that moment. If I ever wondered about returning to Nebraska one day, that hope was gone. Now an outcast in my own home, I no longer belonged.

No further discussions about anything of significance occurred between me and my parents for the remaining weeks. My brokenness was scattered across the farmstead during my humiliating six-week home leave. I struggled to pick up the pieces. My stomach was so knotted, I hardly ate. My bedroom became my refuge. I visited my brother's family and friends as much as possible. Finally, I packed my bags again and left behind the farm, my family, my high school sweetheart, Liberia, and a new boyfriend, all for a new country and my new Peace Corps assignment in the Kingdom of Tonga.

PART IX

TONGA

An Island Paradise

Fragile and overrun with emotion after my departure from Nebraska, my coping abilities were at a tipping point. I used work as my salvation. In the summer of 1973, I began my one-year assignment as a Peace Corps nurse educator in Tonga. My new role gave me purpose and a focus. The differences from my previous Peace Corps assignment were significant. Rather than living far from the major city as I had in Liberia, I was assigned to the capital of Nuku'alofa on the island of Tongatapu. More than half of the country's population—about 45,000—resided there, quite a contrast from Gowee of only 1,000 villagers.

My three-bedroom mud and stick house in my remote village in Liberia seemed posh compared to my new digs in Tonga. I chuckled when my Peace Corps Director drove me to my new home: a one-room thatched house with its exterior damaged from the roaming neighborhood pigs. My house in Gowee had no indoor utilities, but came with a propane stove, oven, a kerosene fridge, and a bed. My house in Tonga provided indoor utilities with a toilet, electricity, and running water, but no refrigerator or stove (only a primus burner). I slept on the cement floor with a woven mat, cushioned with folded layers of tapa cloth—the pounded local bark made into fabric. Despite my modest Tongan lodging, the ease of living on these islands was remarkable. It registered "five stars" as I *never* encountered snakes, cockroaches, spiders, malaria, runny belly, or any sickness for that matter. Best of all, *no one* ever asked me for loving-business. I was in paradise!

Each volunteer enjoyed the customary gesture of being assigned a Tongan mother and father. Tuneo and Fano became my new family and invited me to special events throughout the year. This custom gave me the loving and accepting parental figures I longed for. I now added another prename to my repertoire; I was called Susana in Tonga.

The disparities between the health and cultures of Liberia and Tonga were substantial. Poor nutrition and sanitation, a plethora of illnesses, witchcraft, and bare-breasted women were my experiences in Gowee. Tonga, on the other hand, was noted for a healthy population, despite people's obesity. Being gay was readily accepted in this island nation. Living under the missionary influence of the Church of Jesus Christ of Latter-day Saints (LDS) that permeated the islands, women were required to have as little skin exposed as possible. I wore clothing from my neck to my wrists and ankles. No more minidresses.

Despite the general good health of the population, I trained the district nurses in administering tuberculosis and typhoid vaccinations throughout the country. I reported directly to an Infection Control Physician who taught me everything I needed to know about my role in disease prevention. The Tongan government provided equipment, vaccines, and transport to complete our work, with great outcomes. My mission to be successful in a nursing role was fulfilled.

While I committed my soul to the Tongan people and found great ease in living and working in such a wonderful environment, my longing for Michael deepened. Our weekly letters, traversing one continent and two oceans, constantly crossed in the mail. He carefully packaged his personal voice tapes and recorded love songs of Al Green that I listened to daily on my battery-powered tape recorder. It wasn't until landing in Tonga and receiving Michael's sweet letters and voice messages that I realized how much I missed and loved him. Michael was no longer a mere Maasai warrior fantasy or apparition, but a caring person who loved me emphatically and unconditionally.

In the spring, Michael returned from his Peace Corps assignment in Liberia and rented a studio apartment in Berkeley, California. Through our letters and tapes our mutual love and commitment deepened. Unlike the letters between my high school sweetheart and me, I envisioned a life with common interests and goals. Michael and I had a love I had never known. We planned to move in together in Berkeley upon my completion of service later that year. My loving relationship with Michael had a future.

PART X

REENTRY TO THE U.S.

Returning to My Love

Shortly after my 22nd birthday in 1974, I bid farewell to my Tongan family and Peace Corps colleagues and boarded the Qantas flight. Before I returned to Nebraska, I planned a brief layover in Berkeley to reunite with Michael.

Through my letters, I informed him of my plane information and arrival time. In the midst of my travel, mechanical difficulties led to an extended and complicated layover in Hawaii with a plane change. In a final airport scramble, my connecting Qantas aircraft departed Hawaii four hours later than initially planned. I was unable to inform Michael about any of these modifications and, having crossed the International Dateline shortly after departing from Tonga, I could no longer distinguish day or time. Totally disoriented, I just wanted to be in Michael's welcoming arms. The overbooked flight, fortunately, bumped me into first class where I was seated next to Frank, an accountant from Oakland. Our plane landed in San Francisco at 10:05 p.m., hours past my originally scheduled arrival, at a different gate, with a different flight number. Clinging to my green duffle bag, I walked off the jetway trembling from expectation and weak from the twenty-eight-hour journey. I looked frantically for Michael in the arrival area. He was not there. I waited until I was the only passenger remaining. Disillusioned and dejected, I explained my dilemma to the gate attendant who offered to page Michael. Again, more minutes passed and no response. I called Michael's home from a public phone; no answer, no answering machine.

Weary and brokenhearted, I lugged my carry-ons to the baggage claim area to await my checked bags. With my head in my hands, I debated what to do: take a taxi to his apartment or stay in the airport until he answered his phone. Could I have communicated the arrival date incorrectly because of crossing the International Dateline? For only a moment I wondered if he could have changed his mind about me.

My first-class seatmate from Oakland, Frank, walked by. He asked, "Susan, what happened?"

"My boyfriend didn't meet me with all the flight confusion and he's not answering his home phone," my voice cracked.

"Well, heck, I have my car here. I can take you to his place. I'm heading to Oakland. You said he lives in Berkeley, right?"

Within minutes we traversed the Bay Bridge in his compact blue Toyota. The bay reflected the San Francisco skyline like glistening Christmas trees—all new to my Nebraskan, African, and Tongan point of view. This would be my new home.

Soon, we arrived in Berkeley and drove up University Avenue. With Michael's address in hand, Frank pulled alongside a six-story white stucco apartment building with red-tile accents. "Yes, this is the address," I said. I appreciated Frank's kindness so much more, as midnight approached and drizzle and darkness filled the chilled night. We walked up to the entry with a bank of apartment-numbered buzzers and an intercom speaker. I pushed button number six. No one replied even after several more attempts.

Frank said, "OK, let's ring the manager and see what we can do." I temporarily lost all my problem-solving skills. Besides, this city experience was all new to me. High-rise apartments with intercoms—I'd never heard of them before. Within moments, a kind female voice spoke through the speaker. After I explained the situation to Josephine, the manager, she opened her door and offered me the option to wait there until Michael returned. Completely overwhelmed by the graciousness of complete strangers, I turned to thank Frank for his kindness and gave him a friendly hug as he departed.

Well past midnight, Josephine, in her robe and slippers, welcomed me into her home. She told me how excited Michael had been over the past weeks waiting for my arrival. Noting the concern on my face she assured me he'd be home soon. Josephine offered me a bite to eat and said a warm shower would make me feel better. Then she astutely left a message on Michael's door to find me in her apartment.

Not five minutes out of the shower, Josephine's buzzer rang and there he was, my long awaited love—Michael. We rushed to each other's arms. Our embrace lasted for minutes. Neither of us wanted to let go.

Burying Anger and Blame

Exploring intimate love with such a wonderful man was everything I'd hoped for. Michael and I talked nonstop for days about our past and what our future would hold. Our romantic, two-week interlude temporarily ended with my trip back to Nebraska. An earlier letter to my parents explaining my plans to move to Berkeley and attend school in the area received only a condescending reply. I dreaded my return to the farm.

When my plane landed in Kanton, I never anticipated a warm welcome. Possibly, because I'd never received one before. The chill from Dad and Mom continued during my entire visit—no smiles, and no positive enquiries about Tonga. I presented them with some token gifts, having learned my painful lesson from my home leave a year earlier. No need to make an emotional investment this time around. Ironically, my parents didn't return my Tongan gifts. Tongans are not black.

"So, what is so special about Berkeley that you can't find here?" Mom blurted in my first real conversation with them.

"I'm going to nursing school in San Francisco and they have indicated they will accept some of my prior practical nursing course work." It was true few schools accepted out-of-state credits. I certainly did not tell my parents the real reason for choosing Berkeley: to live with Michael.

My short two-week stay at the farm was merely filled with packing my prized childhood possessions and visiting family and friends. My other family members saved my homecoming from being a total disaster when they welcomed me. Joy filled my heart when I played with Bob and Joan's three children including their newest child, Michelle, now two months old. Bob's family and Randy, now fourteen, were what families should be about.

I counted the hours before my departure, and on that day— Dad said a brief goodbye as he headed out to the cornfield that morning. No hug, no well wishes. Mom drove me to the airport in Kanton and as I reached into my purse for my plane ticket, she saw my packet of birth control pills that I had gotten from the Peace Corps doctor in Tonga.

"What the hell are you doing with those?" she demanded.

"Well, I need these. I'm going to live with Michael."

"Is he the black man in those photos?"

"Yes."

"We knew it! We knew there was something going on with you two when we saw those photos of you together last year. You're hopeless. You will rot in hell for this and just in case you don't know, interracial children are plagued. Don't bother to write us because we want nothing more to do with you."

I turned and boarded the plane. There was a finality to her words. I would never be understood. I was rejected and disowned by my parents: a price I paid for my right to choose and my right to be. I sat in my seat and discreet tears rolled down my checks. I never once looked out the window to see my mom or the sight of Nebraska.

I had not shared all the gruesome details about my parents with Michael before. This information now seemed crucial as we became a couple. Sympathetic and supportive, he listened intently to my family stories and eased my transition into our shared life together.

My parents' rejection of me and my choices grew into anger and blame. I buried my despair by continuing to fulfill my requirements for nursing school. I completed my prerequisites at a local community college while I supported myself by working as a hospital LPN. San Francisco State University accepted me into its BSN program the following year. With the help of grants, scholarships, and loans I was able to focus on the rigorous school schedule and graduated three years later with magna cum laude honors in 1978. I had realized my dream to become an RN. I had Ruth to thank for that.

My parents refused to attend my graduation because I "lived in sin," but my brother, Bob, his wife, and their three daughters came out from Nebraska to celebrate my achievement along with Michael and local friends. Randy could not attend but did stop over to visit us before my graduation on his way to South Korea for his Army deployment. Their support meant everything to me.

Loss on Both Accounts

My anger toward my parents grew in response to their increasing need to control me. Over the next five years, I never spoke to my parents, but received an occasional letter from Mom telling me what a horrible daughter I was. Only through my brothers did I learn our parents retired from the farm in 1979 and now lived in Florida. They replaced the truck camper with a motorhome and planned to travel throughout the U.S.

On Christmas Eve morning of 1979, I awoke with plans to wrap my holiday gifts. Opening the window shades, I noticed a strange Winnebago parked at the curb. Mom and Dad were sitting in the cab. A cold fear ran through my veins. I rushed to Michael to tell him the news, who up until that time had only heard my secondhand stories. Michael's soft eyes and warm arms embraced me. "It will be all right," he said calmly. "This won't be the first time I've received disapproval because of the color of my skin."

I searched deep for a meaningful reply and said, "Yes, but this is also happening to me and to the man I love. And above all, they are not just any prejudice wielding people, they are my parents."

Still holding me tightly, Michael's eyes cast downward. It was then we both knew this would be new territory for both of us.

We waited to see if they would come to our apartment. I paced from room to room, wrapped gifts, and washed the dishes. Finally, when I could wait no longer, I gathered my courage to walk out by myself around noon and knocked on the motorhome door. The door swung open, and Mom's penetrating glare clearly defined their mission as punishment rather than courtesy.

"Hello, what a surprise," I said nervously.

"Well, we stopped to see what the hell you are *really* up to."

I ignored her statement and welcomed them to our apartment to visit and meet Michael. Mom looked toward Dad, sitting on the motorhome couch. He yelled, "We don't want to enter your sinful home!"

I remained calm, understanding that living with a black man and cohabiting out of wedlock had never met with their approval. "Well, would you like to go out for something to eat with us this evening?" I asked, maintaining an optimistic tone.

For reasons I didn't understand, they reluctantly agreed. We set a time of 7:00 p.m. I returned to our apartment and Mom slammed the Winnebago door. We waited for seven more hours. Those were hours of trepidation for me. I folded clothes for distraction, baked Christmas cookies, and tried not to speculate about why the hell they had come. Michael and I were calm, but nervous, not knowing what they might do.

At 7:00 p.m. we came out, and I knocked on their door. I introduced them to Michael for the first time. Mom and Dad never made eye contact with either of us. The awkward and unpleasant experience left me with the impression I was living with a convicted felon. Michael was cordial and offered a handshake, which they refused. They agreed to come in my car to the restaurant. I can't remember much of what we talked about during the meal, except that they traveled the western states with the Winnebago all the way from Florida. Michael and I seemed to make most of the insignificant small talk. Dad remained nearly silent.

After our tense short meal, at their request, Mom and Dad wanted us to attend Christmas Eve Mass with them. Michael and I glanced at each other and nodded in agreement. If this meant something to my parents, we would go. Michael was of no particular faith and I was no longer a practicing Catholic. The shame and guilt living with me daily diminished my religious zeal. Just as I knew God would not judge the people in Gowee for their lifestyle, deep in my heart I knew He would not judge me for mine. I was not going to hell because I loved and lived with this wonderful black man.

Even though my Catholic devotion had waned, I did what was familiar to me; I prayed during the Christmas Eve Mass. I asked God for strength and understanding. After the service, we drove back to our neighborhood and my parents returned to their Winnebago. Michael and I spent a sleepless night while I ruminated for hours wondering if they would physically pull me away from him.

Christmas morning, a knock at our front door awakened me. In my robe, I met my mom, visibly shaken. "We are leaving!" she said in a strained, angry voice. "You are causing your father to nearly have a heart attack. I hope you are happy now!" She abruptly returned to the motorhome and they departed.

What had we done for them to drive 3,000 miles to be rejected outright—was it Michael's skin color or my fall from the Catholic doctrine? They resolutely played the Catholic guilt card during their surprise visit by suggesting we attend Mass. Absurd as it may sound, my deep-seated Catholic values kept me tethered to my parents by a thin thread. "Honor thy Father and thy Mother" was a commandment I tried to live by my whole life. I longed for their love and acceptance. But I wanted what I received from Michael—love and acceptance without conditions. As a result of their punishing visit, the chasm of estrangement between me and my parents only deepened. We severed contact. The holidays of 1979 were a dark time for me. If their mission was to ruin our Christmas, they did it brilliantly. I hoped I had ruined theirs too.

In the years following my parents' Winnebago debacle, my relationship with Michael became fraught with disagreements.

I found myself depressed, lethargic, and angry. The refuge of comfort I once sought in his arms began to wane while my frivolous complaints began to mount. He left the toilet lid up, the toothpaste cap off, and never could see the dust balls in the corner of the rooms. My relentless nagging later focused on some of my bigger concerns. He no longer followed his agricultural education and aspirations. Instead he worked in photography sales at a photo shop in San Francisco. Earning only minimum wage plus commission, Michael spent money he didn't have. He bought a sporty used TR7, fulfilling one of his dreams. Much of this seemed irresponsible and absurd and I let him know exactly what I thought. He tried relentlessly to mend our relationship and professed his love and acceptance of me just the way I was. We grew apart and broke up more than once. Most often I'd find him at my front door or on the other end of the phone. In my mind, Michael was wrong for me in every way I knew possible. He was not good enough for me, I said to myself as my parents' voices rang in my ears. After seven years together—resorting to what I knew best—I pushed Michael away and ended our relationship for good.

As my first intimate partner, Michael taught me about the meaning of unconditional love. Unfortunately, I was unable to reciprocate and learned this concept too late to save our relationship. His devotion and love were too perfect, undeserving, and unfamiliar. My only first-hand observation of a long-term relationship was that of my parents—one filled with criticism, conditional love, and domination. Confused and scared, I did not want a relationship that resembled theirs. Pushing Michael away was all I knew.

Even though our breakup met my parents' wishes, my estrangement from them did not end. We continued to be alienated, off and on, for many more years though I visited them a handful of times.

I had lost on both accounts.

PART XI

HEALING

Reconciliation

When Dad and Mom retired in 1979, they auctioned off the farm equipment and moved to Florida. They rented out the farmhouse and land for the next ten years. Mom, who never liked the farm, was elated to be back in Florida. Dad, on the other hand, gradually lost interest in doing hobby-type activeities. On November 22, 1989, they sold the 160-acre farm to the highest bidder. That ended an era of farming for our Greisen family.

On my last visit to the farm, after it had been sold, I drove through our community. Not only did I find District 20, my one-room grade school, shuttered, but also Morgan High had closed. These small schools that held my fond childhood memories had locked their doors to consolidate for school district rezoning.

As I approached the farm, driving over the rolling hills past the familiar homesteads, I crested the third hill from the neighbor's corner, slowing to make the turn into our long half-mile driveway. I drove right past it, slammed on the brakes, and put the car in reverse. My grip on the steering wheel loosened and my hands dropped to my lap when I saw the farm. The once well-defined tracks of our driveway were covered with overgrown weeds. A leaning broken post was the skeletal remains of our mailbox, the one that had held my

Peace Corps application. Life for me began on that driveway and my memories lay in its path: the red pickup that delivered our first television set, the bike I rode to school, and the tractors I drove while working the fields.

I lifted my gaze, beyond the remnants of a driveway, to the bank of trees I played in each summer—they were no longer there. My playhouse, gone. Not one farm building remained. Eight-foot cornstalks towered over the exact location where our farmhouse once stood. Everything was leveled. The gray misty sky reflected my sadness when my eyes blurred with moisture as I squinted to imagine where our house once stood. Only one thing familiar remained: Mark's fence line bordering the north side of our property—the same fence Dad followed during the blizzard to save our neighbor boy. All the rest was gone.

The ever-present Nebraska wind rippled the weeds, grass, and cornstalks over the land as if no one had ever lived there. Not one person could ever love this land as Dad did for forty-five years. He possessed an unbridled passion for farming. It pulsated in his blood every waking hour and possibly in his dreams. Just as I enjoyed the pleasure of caressing the lace on my Sunday dress, Dad combed the cornfields after supper, touching their leaves at shoulder height. I often walked with him, pulling the stray sunflowers and Russian thistles, as he admired his crops. Each of us pulled a shaft of brome grass from its stem to suck and chew on its sweetness. My walks in the cornfield with Dad began my understanding of true love and passion—to do what you love.

Over the years, Dad witnessed the farm's demise as renters allowed overgrown weeds and buildings to rot. It tore at his soul and spirit. According to my brothers, after our parents' move to Florida, Dad's fun-loving spark could no longer be aroused. During that time, my parents sold their home in Florida and moved to a retirement community in Mesa, Arizona.

During the years of estrangement from my parents, Bob informed me Dad and Mom had divorced and remarried. After two short years, my parents divorced their new spouses as well. The driving force, according to my brother, seemed to be the doctrine of the Catholic religion. Their new marriages were not acknowledged by the church and their access to the religious services was limited. As a result, my parents annulled their second marriages and remarried in a civil ceremony. Their tense relationship that existed prior to their initial divorce only escalated after their remarriage. They seemed to prefer to be unhappy together—how they had lived much of their married life.

Through Bob, I learned of Dad's Alzheimer's diagnosis in 1993. In May, two years later, I was shocked to receive two messages from Dad on my answering machine. He had never called me before. After more than two decades of estrangement and rejection from my parents, a premonition gave me courage. His reaching out to me was all I needed. He had something to tell me. I made efforts to return his call but Mom intercepted and grilled me about my lifestyle, told me I was a horrible daughter, and that speaking to Dad would only upset him. Out of desperation I flew to their home in Arizona and called from the hotel to attempt a visit. Mom reluctantly agreed. I braced for the drama. Bob had told me Mom was recently diagnosed with depression and was on medication. None of us should have been surprised by this information. Her lifelong distaste for the farm, lack of support for her issues, and coping with Dad's cognitive decline were certainly a recipe for depression.

With their Mesa mailing address in hand, I drove up to the arid, treeless, gated retirement community of doublewide trailers just outside Superstition Mountain. My knees weakened as I stepped out of the rental car and knocked on the screen door. Mom answered with a scowl on her face. Ten feet behind her stood a submissive gaunt-looking man wearing a one-piece tan jumpsuit—my dad. His prominent nose, large ears, and wrinkled face, from years in the Nebraska sun, were recognizable, but his comb-over concealing his bald spot was gone. He appeared much older than his seventy-six years. As soon as our eyes met, he began to weep—something I had never witnessed before. Sadness overwhelmed me and tears, heavy with years of grief, flowed from my eyes.

In a high-pitched voice he choked out the words, "I know who you are, but I don't remember your name."

236 · SUSAN E. GREISEN

"I'm your daughter, Susan."

"I know...but I can't remember a damned thing."

Without hesitation I walked up to him and wrapped my arms around his thin frame. Slowly he lifted one arm to envelop my shoulder. For mere seconds, we stood in an unprecedented embrace.

Mom stood silently fifteen feet from us with a clenched jaw and angry eyes. She shook her head as our unusual father/daughter affection only seemed to elevate her disgust. I always wondered if she was jealous of the rare moments of approval Dad had given me during my childhood. Yet under her veil of anger I sensed pain and possibly jealousy. She, too, may have rarely received hints of approval or acceptance from him. I may have been unwelcomed competition for Dad's unyielding love.

Uncomfortable with our outpouring of emotion, I began to engage in simple conversation. We talked about trivia and caught up on some of the lost years. He struggled to follow our conversation and spoke incoherent thoughts. The longing in his eyes and his effort to communicate with me after so many years of being estranged and disowned told me, perhaps, he wished our bond had been different—more loving and caring. When his attention waned and I tired of Mom's criticism I left. I returned twice during my two-day stay before flying back to my home in Seattle.

Three weeks later, in June 1995, Alzheimer's took a firm grip on his brain. Dad tragically took his own life.

If anyone knew my dad, it was a logical thing for him to do. The runts of the litter or even our aged domestic dogs, Spotty, Silver, Yogi, and Tiny, met their deaths prematurely. When our farm animals suffered in misery from old age or illness, had little chance of survival or low quality of life with no hope of repair, they met the end of a gun. That too, was how Dad met his end.

Our family gathered in Arizona for a memorial service a few days later and I spoke these words:

...No floods, hail, or tornadoes could ever make Dad feel like abandoning the farm. He was always committed to the work he loved. Our dad had Alzheimer's and as his disease

progressed, his mind was a living hell. The only reprieve he had from this caged mind was to reminisce about the farm. It was his piece of heaven and paradise. Our dad is now in eternal paradise. He is in heaven. We love you Dad.

Dad never once told me, "Do what you love." More than anything, he wanted one or all of us children to follow the path *he* loved. Unaware, he inadvertently instilled in his children the most wonderful gift, to find and follow their passion. And each of us did. Bob, a natural born artist, acquired his talent from Mom's side of the family and became a successful commercial illustrator. Randy followed Dad's footsteps and excelled in the Army as a career officer serving our country. I became an accomplished nurse in a variety of fields helping those in need.

Mom struggled off and on with depression in the years following Dad's death. She continued to live in Arizona for a short time, but eventually lived near Bob's home in California. Despite our tense relationship, I began visiting her annually. After years of cursing the farm and all it had to offer, since my earliest memory, surprisingly, Mom began to reminisce of her life there as if it were her long-lost love. As she declined mentally and physically, Bob and his family moved her to a retirement home. At age eighty, her rough edges seemed to soften; as her rudeness and criticism diminished, a sense of humor emerged. One day while visiting, I took a bold move and told her for the first time that I loved her. I didn't expect a reply and never got one.

Neither of my parents were able to share their acknowledgement of my career accomplishments. However, at age eighty-five and in her early months of dementia, Mom made a surprising comment. One day, coming down to the lobby of her retirement home, my mom, brother, and I walked past six residents sitting in wheelchairs and she enthusiastically said, "This is my daughter Susan, a nurse, who joined the Peace Corps in Africa." My chest swelled with pride, as I had never heard this praise before. My shoulders slumped when she went on to say with a sarcastic tone, "Can you believe she left me behind to take care of all those Muslims?"

Mom's condition continued to decline and she was moved to an adult family home for total care. During one of my visits, in what I hoped was a lucid moment, she said something remarkable. My mom—who once told me at age seventeen that becoming a nurse would be the worst profession, who criticized my hair, my dress, my cooking, and my choices—cupped my face in her hands and said, "You are so beautiful. I love you and I am so proud you are a nurse."

At age sixty-one, I never thought I'd hear those words. Prior to that day, Mom never told me she loved me or approved of my choices. Possibly she harbored those thoughts all along. Perhaps she felt safe expressing them only when she neared the end of her life and had nothing to lose. If my qualities and accomplishments were competition for something she never had, that meant little to her now. Her approval and love were the hopes I had been clinging to all along.

At age eighty-nine, Mom entered the hospice program. During her slow demise, I reflected on her life going back to her difficult childhood—the loss of her parents at a young age and being raised by a domineering and unpleasant grandmother. While I sat at her bedside in her final days, I caressed her hand in mine and told her, "You are so beautiful, I love you, and I am proud you are my mother."

Mom passed away peacefully and silently in July 2014.

Forgiveness is Freedom

We Greisens are fearless, determined, defiant, and smart. The qualities of my parents echo through me daily. I often see Dad in some passing gesture when I pull a stray weed from my garden or chew on the shaft of grass to taste its sweetness. I see Mom when I highlight my eyebrows or cook delicious Italian pasta. And yet for all my adult life I managed to live as far away from Dad and Mom as physically possible. I was unsuccessful in distancing myself from them emotionally. My adult mind knew I needed space for self-preservation. But my inner child longed for their unconditional love and acceptance, not a love I had come to know—one often filled with pain and rejection. I came to believe that as their daughter, despite my many achievements, I was never good enough. After struggling for years to cope with shame, guilt, anger, and blame, I realized that being consumed with these emotions was far more taxing than embracing acceptance and forgiveness. With counseling and the passage of time, I began to rebuild my self-worth.

While writing this book, I was surprised to discover that my healing process started in Gowee with the Zor Clan. I was a young volunteer with little knowledge, few resources and armed only with determination. The villagers, who saw me as their "white-woman doctor," took a leap of faith to trust, love, and accept me without conditions or judgement. Believing in myself began in Liberia. I set out on my Peace Corps mission to "help save the people in Africa." Actually, they helped save me.

Dad and Mom were products of their strict childhoods. They loved me the way they were loved—the only way they knew how—without physical or verbal expressions of affection. Their upbringing defined their character, strong and defiant. My parents did their best with their awareness, values, and principles. Just as Amand nearly lost his son by following his cultural beliefs, my parents lost me by living within their strict rules and Catholic doctrine.

There were many things Dad and Mom didn't understand, such as the value of an education or my unique qualities and sensibilities. Unbeknownst to them, my talents were the makings of an excellent nurse. Mom's relentless denigration of my character may not only have portrayed her feelings about me but also served as the messenger of Dad's edicts. Was this like the midwives in Gowee when they carried out the commands of their male dominated culture by performing female circumcision and maintaining a social order?

My parents held a narrow view of the world, often filled with fear of the unknown. Africa was one such place. They never knew anyone who had become a nurse or heard of someone traveling abroad except in war. Their dream for me was to live a safe, familiar, and predictable life. They believed their responsibility was to shield me from the unknown. Reminiscent of the elephants guiding and protecting a newborn in the African savannah, my parents' role was to protect and guide the only daughter they had.

When Dad and Mom each reached out to me in their final days, those brief moments meant I wasn't as bad as I was led to believe. I was good enough to earn their love and acceptance in the end. That was all I needed, and in fact, all I ever wanted.

Finally, after years of counseling, I stopped being a victim and reclaimed the power I had willingly given them. I began to trust my decisions, inner strengths, and create my destiny filled with its own set of failures, but also its rewards and accomplishments. My parents' persistent rejection and their refusal to acknowledge my worth and independence, formed and reinforced the foundations of my character. Over time, I understood it was not what I allowed them to take from me, but what they gave to me—resilience, determination, and passion.

Both my parents are now gone. Before they left this earth, I grasped my last chance to make peace, and sincerely forgave Dad and Mom silently in my heart. My heavy burden of sadness, anger, and resentment has lifted. I can, wholeheartedly and lovingly, dedicate this book to them. Forgiveness is freedom.

The Pink Flamingos Found Me

I never saw the sun the first two weeks I moved to Seattle in 1983. I wondered when I would feel its warmth again. Moreover, I had already suffered one job rejection when I joined a wonderful Health Maintenance Organization (HMO). The interviewer told me, "We hire for attitude and train for skills." I became a home health nurse, visiting and caring for patients in their homes. I worked for that HMO organization for twenty-five years in six different nursing roles, receiving a variety of awards for my service. Like my commitment to Peace Corps, I was fully dedicated to their philosophy. I worked for people who believed in me and I believed in them.

My home health experiences were, in many ways, like my home visits in Gowee. Entering a patient's home was very personal. As a nurse I easily grasped the culture, support system, general health, and nutrition from the environment and its inhabitants. I was a quick study and brought valuable expertise to the job.

One patient remains very special to me. Desiree, a sweet, thin woman in her 80s, lived alone in a small bungalow on the top of Capitol Hill. Her chronic and debilitating heart disease left her homebound. My weekly visits helped to monitor her condition and treatment plan. Even though her heart disease left her frail, her silver gray hair was perfectly coifed and she always wore a smart print dress with matching jewelry for my visits. A spark lingered in her character as she became animated when she spoke about her husband who passed away several years earlier. They had no children but lived a good life. During my first home visit, Desiree ambulated carefully with her walker toward the couch and gestured for me to sit on the hassock.

"Desiree, I'd like to start by taking your blood pressure."

"If it's over 200, I'll have to sell."

We laughed when Desiree explained how she often dabbled in the stock market. Reaching for the blood pressure cuff in my bag, I looked up, shocked to find hanging on the wall a familiar childhood image. I beheld the mirrored framed print of the four pink flamingos wading in the serene lake, flanked by palm trees, lush green vegetation, and a peaceful blue sky.

"Are you OK?" Desiree asked.

"Sure," I said. "It is just...well...just that picture behind you...it is so beautiful."

"Oh yes, isn't it a lovely print? I acquired it back in the '50s, I believe. The original was painted by Turner and this print and many like it became the rage back then when Art Deco was very popular," she said as nostalgia reflected in her eyes. "Why are you so struck by this print?"

"Well, I never thought...I would...ever see it again."

"What do you mean?"

"Well, when I was eight years old in Nebraska, I used to see this same print at a restaurant we frequented. It was one of the images that guided my quest to Africa where I lived and worked."

Desiree asked me more about my work in Africa. She was impressed and regretted she never made it to that continent. She, too, loved the pink flamingo print, something we had in common.

In preparation for my fifth visit to her home, I made the usual phone call to prearrange my arrival time. But there was no answer after several attempts. After a call to her doctor's office, the nurse told me Desiree passed away at home from a heart attack the day before. She asked if I would call Desiree's sister who had something for me to pick up at her house.

The following day I drove to the top of Capitol Hill and rang the doorbell of the two-story historic home across from Volunteer Park. A genteel gray-haired woman, resembling Desiree, answered the door and introduced herself as Mabel. We spoke briefly of Desiree and I was thankful her passing seemed peaceful and painless.

Mabel said, "Wait here, I have something for you."

She walked to a back room and returned holding something large in her hands and said, "Desiree spoke of you often and how much you meant to her. She knew how special this was to you and wanted you to have it."

I took the two- by three-foot pink flamingo print in my trembling hands as my eyes welled. "Look on the back," Mabel said. Taped there was a handwritten note: *To Susan Greisen, I want a dear nurse to have this picture and may she love it as I have. Desiree.*

For over thirty years this treasured print has hung in my various homes. While writing my final chapter of this book, I walked into my bedroom to gaze at the image. When I was a little girl, those four mirrored strips within the frame hanging high on the wall reflected various portions of Louie's restaurant, and only one of me. Now as I stood directly in front of the print, I saw my image in *all* four mirrors—my complete loving self. Symbolically, my being and spirit surrounded and embraced the four pink flamingos. I smiled to think my quest for them was *never* about some hand-painted pink feathered birds. Instead, my journey was about looking for forgiveness and unconditional love, not from others, but from within myself—what I had been searching for all along.

EPILOGUE

Little did I know that after I departed Liberia in 1973, tragedy upon tragedy would hit this small country like recurring aftershocks.

The first major blow began a cascade of events that turned the country inside out. Samuel Doe of the Krahn tribe led a coup d'état in 1980 to overthrow and kill President William R. Tolbert. Thirteen members of Tolbert's cabinet were executed by a firing squad at a beach near Monrovia. The international community was in shock as the covers of *Time* and *LIFE* magazines displayed the carnage.

The coup did not result in peace. An election, widely held to be fraudulent, resulted in Samuel Doe becoming President of Liberia. Conflicts soon developed between the Doe-led government and the Gio and Mano tribes who inhabited my village of Gowee and the surrounding areas.

In December 1989, a rebel group led by Charles Taylor invaded Liberia from neighboring Ivory Coast and captured Butuo, a border post in Nimba County, near Gowee. Taylor recruited many Gio and Mano tribesmen who felt oppressed by the Doe government. In May 1990, the U.S. Government ordered the evacuation of all Peace Corps volunteers. In September of that year, President Doe was captured, tortured, and executed by a rebel group that had broken away from Taylor. Unfortunately, the death of Doe did not end the war. Taylor carried the war to Monrovia and throughout the country, ravaging villages and engaging in widespread killing and raping of innocent civilians. He captured children and recruited them as soldiers.

The civil war continued off and on for seven years, plunging the country and people into mere survival mode. With the intervention of the international community, the war was stopped, and elections were held. Charles Taylor was voted in as president in 1997. Many people thought the election was unfair since voters believed Taylor would resume the war if not elected.

In 1999 a second civil war began between Taylor and new emerging Liberian factions in the north and south. The diamond trade in the north helped financially support Taylor's war efforts for the next four years. His brutality to any opposition, including women and children, eventually led to his exile in Nigeria. He was arrested in 2006 for his involvement in war crimes during the Sierra Leone Civil War. In 2012, Taylor was charged and convicted of war crimes by the International Criminal Court in The Hague and remains imprisoned.

Between 1989 and 2003 more than 250,000 Liberians died and a million more were displaced in refugee camps in neighboring countries. More than 38,000 children are estimated to have taken part as soldiers in the conflict. Entire villages were emptied, including Gowee, as people fled for safety. I have since lost contact with all who lived there. The diamond trade funded the civil wars. The excavation of these precious gems which once paid the villagers in Gowee 50¢ a day to feed an entire family, later produced diamonds that fueled the war. It was a brutal time for such a loving and caring people.

After decades of revolving one-party elections, coup d'états, or wartime dominance, the democratically held election in 2005 chose Ellen Johnson Sirleaf as Africa's first female head of state. Peace had finally arrived after twenty-five years of war and strife, and Liberia has rebounded slowly. By 2013, over 155,000 Liberians returned home after years of violence.

Another assault on Liberia was the HIV/AIDS epidemic. In 1986, just a few years before the first civil war, the first AIDS patient was diagnosed in Liberia. With civil wars raging in the '90s, the HIV/AIDS health programs and data were destroyed, hindering efforts to attack the disease. The most accurate WHO information collected in 2016 noted 1.6 percent of Liberia's population reported having HIV/AIDS and 2,800 deaths annually. This is one of the lowest percentages in Africa, but likely the country's weakened health infrastructure underreported this disease.

Tragedy hit Liberia again in 2014, when the country experienced one of the worst health disasters documented by the WHO. Ebola ravaged the country, eventually killing over 4,800 people before the epidemic finally ended in May 2015, over a year after it began. With Liberia's weak infrastructure and the transmission of Ebola misunderstood, witchcraft and superstition caused mortality to rise to epidemic levels. Most non-medical international professionals and Peace Corps volunteers, who had returned after the civil wars in 2010, were again evacuated.

In 2017, George Weah, a former soccer star, was elected as the new President of Liberia with 61.5 percent of the vote. It was the first peaceful democratic transfer of power in Liberia in more than seven decades. President Weah's promise to four million Liberians was to eradicate corruption and bolster the weak economy. As of 2019, the Peace Corps has a growing program focusing mainly on education. Yet, the number of volunteers in Liberia today is small compared to the almost 350 volunteers during my assignment.

Monrovia's infrastructure is still in recovery after years of war. Today, only 20 percent of the people in Monrovia have access to electricity. Ebola is in check but the country has a high crime rate and many health concerns. In 2018, President Weah made constitutional changes to allow people of non-Negro descent to be citizens and allow foreigners to own land. This was a far cry from my experience during President Tolbert's rule.

I lived in Liberia during a time when it seemed to move toward prosperity. There was a sense of security and peace. I could travel safely and live alone in my village as the only white person in a remote portion of the country. There were health concerns, little education, and prevalent poverty, but rarely did I worry about my individual safety.

The same could be said for many of the thirteen countries I visited while in Africa in the early '70s. During my travels, tensions were building in Uganda, Ethiopia, and Niger. But at the time of this publishing, due to extremist activities, kidnapping, and tribal war, the U.S. State Department currently has travel advisories and precautions for Americans visiting nine of the countries I traveled: Sierra Leone, Ivory Coast, Mali, Niger, Burkina Faso (Upper Volta), Kenya, Tanzania, Uganda, and Ethiopia. Africa is a continent still finding its footing after centuries of colonialism.

Both of my beloved homes—Liberia and the farm in Nebraska—have changed dramatically. Neither will ever be the same.

Just prior to publication, I came across Sami's heartfelt letters he wrote forty-five years earlier after he was expelled from Liberia. After losing contact with him, I wrote to the address, hoping I could locate him or his family in Lebanon. I found his family, but unfortunately Sami had passed away twenty-one years earlier of a heart attack. His wife is still alive with three daughters and two sons. All the children have Arabic names except the first-born child, a girl. They named her Susan and call her Susie, the endearing name Sami gave me in Liberia. The eldest son calls me "family" and they all have invited me to visit.

As I have searched for remaining connections to my past, the pink flamingos served as an important metaphor, one that hasn't ended with my self-discoveries or finding my namesake. I believe each of us has our own pink flamingos to search for and find. More importantly, what meaning will we discover when they are found?

As a little child I had wanted to become a nun. My Catholic faith provided guidance and foundation for my life. In following my true calling—to be a nurse—I also found a purpose broader than one religion can embrace: to be of service to others. On the wall in my home I treasure my framed plaque from the Peace Corps. *"The Beyond War Award honors you, Susan Greisen, for your efforts through the Peace Corps to build a world beyond war."* The words, "beyond war," fill my heart with a daily reminder that my role was more than just helping a few people. In my fifty years as a nurse, I worked to make the world a better place, and in doing so, touched the lives of many patients, colleagues, and students. I lived up to the words of Thomas Paine, *"The world is my country, all mankind is my brethren, and to do good is my religion."*

ACKNOWLEDGMENTS

I have deep gratitude to the Peace Corps for my experience as a volunteer that broadened my view of the world and enriched my personal and professional life.

I am forever indebted to Ruth and Harold Jacobson, the couple I met in Liberia. Upon returning from the Peace Corps, I asked them to be my surrogate mother and father, filling the hole in my heart from my estranged parents. They whole-heartedly agreed. In addition, I also adopted Ruth's ninety-three-year-old mother, Signe Hanson, as my grandmother— the loving grandparent I never had. Through them I learned how to reciprocate unconditional love and acceptance. Ruth inspired me to tell my story, when, in her 90s, she published two memoirs about their life in Liberia. Ruth, Harold, and Signe have all since passed, but their love and memories are eternal. Over the years I became a surrogate mother to a young student nurse that I mentored, Kat Alex. When she created her own family, I became a surrogate grandmother to her newborn son, Lucas. I'm honored to carry on this tradition.

I thank every individual portrayed in my book as I traveled on my personal journey, including my parents who prepared me for a life of tough love and hard knocks, and my brothers, Randy and Bob Greisen and his family, for their ongoing love and support. The villagers in Gowee and the Zor Clan were instrumental in beginning my healing. Martha, Rita, Clara, and Sami became my African family; without them my stay in my small remote village, and the valuable lessons I learned may not have been possible. I am grateful to Michael who laid the foundation of my most valuable lesson—intimate unconditional love.

When I met Betty Friedan over forty-five years ago, I was clueless about her message regarding women in society. Oddly enough, she never left my memory. I recently read her 1963 book, *The Feminine Mystique,* and discovered her message, in essence, told my story. As a woman, in my early adult life, I struggled to break the stereotypic image of my feminine role. I am grateful to Betty for giving my voice a meaning and my actions a reason.

When the going was tough, two individuals remained steadfast and a beacon of light: my therapists, Lenore Bayuk and Anne Spreng. Their guidance and skill set me on a healing path for which I am forever grateful.

It may take a village to raise a child, but it takes a family and a community to publish a book. Without the support of the vibrant writing community in Bellingham, Washington, I could have never written my memoir. Village Books, a local independent bookstore, provided open mic readings, writing groups, and anthology publications. Village Books, Whatcom Community College, and the Chuckanut Writers Conference, along with other writing classes, were critical to my development as an author. Support and networking through my membership in Whatcom Writers and Publishers and the Red Wheelbarrow Writers were key. I send gratitude to multiple individuals for their unwavering support, some of whom became my cheerleaders and beta readers in my seven-year book project—Bob and Joan Greisen, Cathryn Booth-LaForce, Norm and Diane Couturier, Cindy Burman Woods, Rod Haynes, Richard Pearce-Moses, Carolyn Young, and Glo Harrison. I am grateful to Herb Messer who cried with me as I read him every chapter and his daughter, Chelsea Messer, for her message to maintain a common thread throughout the book. I also thank Kat and David Alex, Judith Yarrow, Vikki Renneckar, Dodee Weihe, Ken LaForce, Liz Wade, Gina Saettone, Leslie Strong, Sherri Wenrick, Kathy Foster, Nancy Button, Kathy Pendras, Jean Waight, Daria Kurkjy, Candace Wellman, Shar Figenshaw,

Peter Arneil, Lyn and Jim Gray, Stephanie Vickers, Donna Robinson, Paul Hanson, and Cami Ostman for their critique, advice, and support.

I thank my talented and thorough developmental editor, Laura Kalpakian, who took my scattered building blocks of documented memory, multiple pages of unnecessary rumination, and held my hand while she encouraged me to dig deeper. Laura skillfully guided me to restructure my message into this memoir.

I am grateful for finding my "book doctor," Andrew Shattuck McBride, my copy/line editor. He fixed the ills of my memoir and made it shine.

My publisher, Jes Stone at Penchant Press International used her expertise to hone my manuscript into a beautiful book I am proud to share.

Thanks to Andrea Gabriel, Thomas Post, and Lisa Dailey for their skills in building my website.

The actual publishing of my book hinged on one individual who has known me the longest. My brother, Bob, validated my truthful account of our family history and my own experience. He told me without solicitation, "Release it to the world." Because of his unwavering acceptance, you hold my memoir in your hands.

Photo by Radley Muller Photography

Susan E. Greisen, raised on a remote farm in Nebraska, defied all odds to seek adventure and a broader understanding of life. Her work as a nurse with the Peace Corps and CARE took her to remote parts of the world. She has journeyed to over forty countries on six continents and is a published poet and author. Her travel photographs have been published online by the *BBC News*. Susan lives in Bellingham, Washington, where she enjoys life with a vibrant and supportive writing community.

You can find photographs, home movies, and maps from the stories depicted in this memoir at www.susangreisen.com. Additional resources including books, videos, movies, organizations, and discussion questions are also available on her website. Contact Susan regarding her availability for speaking engagements or attending your book club, either in person or via video chat.

CPSIA information can be obtained
at www.ICGtesting.com
Printed in the USA
BVHW032238070122
625602BV00006BA/195

9 780999 804841